MARIJUANA LEGALIZATION

WHAT EVERYONE NEEDS TO KNOW®

MARIJUANA LEGALIZATION

WHAT EVERYONE NEEDS TO KNOW®

Second Edition

JONATHAN P. CAULKINS, BEAU KILMER, AND MARK A. R. KLEIMAN

OXFORD
UNIVERSITY PRESS

OXFORD
UNIVERSITY PRESS

Published in the United States of America by Oxford University Press
198 Madison Avenue, New York, NY 10016, United States of America.

© Oxford University Press 2016

First Edition published in 2012

Second Edition published in 2016

Library of Congress Cataloging-in-Publication Data
Names: Caulkins, Jonathan P. (Jonathan Paul), 1965–author. | Kilmer, Beau, author. |
Kleiman, Mark A. R., author.
Title: Marijuana legalization : what everyone needs to know /
Jonathan P. Caulkins, Beau Kilmer, Mark A. R. Kleiman.
Description: Second edition. | New York, NY : Oxford University Press, 2016.
Identifiers: LCCN 2015043342 (print) | LCCN 2015047763 (ebook) |
ISBN 978-0-19-026241-9 (hardcover : alk. paper) |
ISBN 978-0-19-026240-2 (pbk. : alk. paper) |
ISBN 978-0-19-026242-6 (Updf) | ISBN 978-0-19-026243-3 (Epub)
Subjects: LCSH: Marijuana—United States. | Marijuana—Law and
legislation—United States. | Drug legalization—United States.
Classification: LCC HV5822.M3 M2935 2016 (print) | LCC HV5822.M3 (ebook) |
DDC 362.29/50973—dc23
LC record available at http://lccn.loc.gov/2015043342

1 3 5 7 9 8 6 4 2
Printed by RRD-Harrisonburg, USA

*We dedicate this book to the public servants
wrestling with the difficult job
of implementing new marijuana laws
and trying to make them work for everyone.
Whether or not those laws prove to be good for the country in the end,
we all benefit from the honest and diligent efforts
of these underpaid and often unappreciated officials.*

CONTENTS

4 What Is Known About the Nonmedical Benefits of Using Marijuana?   67

8 How Is Legalization of Marijuana Different from Legalization of Other Drugs?   121

11 Between Marijuana Prohibition and Commercial Legalization: Is There Any Middle Ground? 169

PART III THE CRAZY QUILT OF CONFLICTING POLICIES TODAY

12 Where Are We, and How Did We Get Here? 189

13 What's Really Happening in Medical-Marijuana States?   199

14 What Is Happening in Colorado and Washington?   216

15 What Is Happening in Alaska, Oregon, Jamaica, and Uruguay?   231

16 What Happens When Marijuana Laws Clash?   239

ACKNOWLEDGMENTS

Partial support for this work was provided by a Harold and Colene Brown Faculty Fellowship from the Pardee RAND Graduate School. The views expressed imply no endorsement by any funder.

This book inherited much from our earlier Oxford University Press books *Drug Policy: What Everyone Needs to Know* and *Marijuana Legalization: What Everyone Needs to Know*, co-authored with Angela Hawken. Although other commitments prevented Angela from fully participating in the current effort, we benefited greatly from the insights and hard work she contributed to those earlier books and from her comments on this version.

We received many useful comments on this volume and other assistance from friends and colleagues including Alberto Aziani, James Anderson, Martin Bouchard, Shawn Bushway, Marjorie Carlson, John Coleman, Maria Cuellar, Steve Davenport, Tom Decorte, Michael Farrell, Erin Flanagan, Richard Hahn, Laura Griner Hill, Kevin Haggerty, Wayne Hall, Caitlin Hughes, Marian Jarlenski, Sam Kamin, Magdalena Kulesza, Jonathan Kulick, Miles Light, Erin Kilmer Neel, Pat Oglesby, Rosalie Liccardo Pacula, Mafalda Pardal, Bryce Pardo, Melissa Piccard, Rosario Queirolo, Peter Reuter, Mark Ristich, Alison Ritter, Steve Rolles, Sue Rusche, Eric Sevigny, Joe Vesely, Chris Wilkins, and a federal prisoner who prefers not to be named. We thank Jeyashree Ramamoorthy for managing the production process. Of course none of them bears any responsibility for our views.

We are deeply indebted to Angela Chnapko for her editorial guidance—and patience.

For additional information about the book and the authors, please visit http://www.marijuanalegalization.info.

MARIJUANA LEGALIZATION

WHAT EVERYONE NEEDS TO KNOW®

INTRODUCTION

Should marijuana be legalized?

If you picked up this book in search of a clear yes or no answer, consider putting it back on the shelf. We won't tell you how you should vote. We instead want to help you reach your own informed conclusion and appreciate that the issues are more nuanced than advocates on either side of the debate will usually acknowledge.

The consequences of legalization are unpredictable: no one can say for sure how much more marijuana might be used after legalization, how much of that additional consumption would involve teenagers or people with serious drug problems, or whether heavy drinking, tobacco smoking, and other substance-abuse problems would increase or decrease as a result. That isn't to say that we have to decide entirely in the dark: a vast amount is known about the use of marijuana, about the use of other psychoactive chemicals, and that store of knowledge contains some valuable hints about likely futures. But the uncertainties remain.

Even people who agree in their predictions might still disagree about the desirability of legalization, because they value the projected outcomes differently.

And even if we had perfect foresight and agreed entirely about values, the question "Should marijuana be legalized?" would still not be answerable, because "legalization" doesn't describe a specific alternative. Allowing home-growing is one form of legalization; so is a completely free market that allows joints to be sold like corn-flakes. There's no reason to expect someone who likes (or dislikes) one form of legalization to like (or dislike) all the others.

Moreover, the alternative to "legalization" is "prohibition," but that, too, comes in a variety of flavors and colors. There is tremendous variation in the intensity of marijuana enforcement and sanctions for violations, even within the United States.

So the smart response to "Are you for marijuana legalization?" would be a pair of questions: "What kind of legalization?" and "Compared to what kind of prohibition?"

That does not keep most Americans from answering the pollsters' question "Do you favor legalizing marijuana use?" Four years ago, when we wrote the first edition of this book, public opinion was just about evenly split, representing a remarkable upsurge in support for legalization over the previous twenty years. Opinion has continued to shift in a pro-legalization direction: supporters now usually outnumber opponents by more than ten percentage points.

In the interim, four states have replaced their prohibition policies with commercial legalization, giving us for the first time actual evidence about some of the early consequences of letting companies supply marijuana to any adult. Also, in 2013 Uruguay embarked on a very different approach, with co-ops, home-growing, and government-controlled distribution, but not the commercialization. Jamaica is setting up an odd hybrid model, medical on the surface but aggressively commercial underneath.

Marijuana remains forbidden by federal law and by international treaties (as well as laws in the other forty-six states). But there is continued demand for change.

The goal of this book is not to persuade you to support or oppose legalization; as chapter 18 shows, the three of us—colleagues and friends, in general agreement about the facts and with very similar world-views in many ways—differ on what ought to be done. Our goal instead is to provide the raw material needed for you to develop informed opinions by presenting the issues fairly and sweeping away the myths and fallacies common to these discussions.

We have been studying marijuana and marijuana policy for a combined total of nearly seventy years, but what we know is only a fraction of what is known, let alone the vast amount that remains unknown. A thorough understanding would draw on ideas from agronomy, anthropology, botany, chemistry, cognitive science, economics, history, international relations, law, management, medicine, neurobiology, operations analysis, pharmacology, philosophy, policy analysis, political science, psychology, public administration, sociology, and statistics.

In the face of all this complexity, we have done our best. The rest is up to you.

PART I
MARIJUANA AND PROHIBITION

1

WHAT IS MARIJUANA?

What does "marijuana" mean?

"Marijuana" is the common (and legal) American term for the dried flowers and leaves of the plant *Cannabis sativa*, and for the plant itself. The flowers contain concentrated amounts of psychoactive (mood-altering) chemicals known as cannabinoids (produced only by this plant), terpenoids, and flavonoids; the leaves that have become the symbol of marijuana contain lesser quantities of the same chemicals. The amounts and mixtures of these molecules vary with the genetics of the plant, growing practices, and the timing of the harvest.

Most of the rest of the world (and most of the scientific literature) refers to marijuana as "herbal cannabis" and hashish—which is made by extracting the cannabinoid-rich trichomes—as "cannabis resin," with "cannabis" being a catchall term that includes both products.

What is marijuana legalization?

Marijuana is the most commonly used illegal drug in the world; various forms have been used for thousands of years for their medicinal, social, and aesthetic effects, in addition to the industrial use of other parts of the cannabis plant for food, fuel, and fiber.

International treaties and the laws of most countries forbid growing, selling, and possessing marijuana. That makes lawbreakers out of the more than 125 million people who have used the drug in the past year, and also those who supply them. It creates illicit markets with a total value in the tens of billions of dollars per year—in the ballpark of $40 billion per year in the United States alone. Some of that illicit activity leads to violence and to the corruption of public officials. Millions of users are arrested for possessing the drug, and smaller but substantial numbers go to prison for growing and selling it.

The legalization question concerns whether to change the laws to make it legal to produce, sell, and possess (nonindustrial) marijuana, and, if so, what rules should apply.

Legalization would replace illicit market production and distribution with an aboveboard industry. There could still be rules and regulations, just as there are rules and regulations governing production and distribution of alcohol, or for that matter of automobiles and avocados. But the bulk of the trade would be conducted by farmers and merchants and retail clerks, not by criminals.

There are many ways to liberalize marijuana policy short of legalization. Use could be tolerated but production and sale still forbidden, or possession of small amounts could be treated as a civil violation rather than as a crime; that's the policy confusingly called "decriminalization." Use and sale of small quantities could be tolerated while production and wholesale distribution remained forbidden; that's the current policy in the Netherlands.

There are also many options for legal supply without jumping to a commercial market along the lines of alcohol. Production, sale, and use could be permitted only for certain specific medical purposes. Or the whole activity could be restricted to noncommercial channels, with users growing their own or forming cooperatives.

Even commercial legalization could include more or fewer restrictions on sale and use. Alcohol can only be sold to adults and by licensed sellers, while caffeine—in the form of coffee or cola drinks—is sold without restriction. Thinking about marijuana legalization, then, involves an exercise in policy design. Repealing current laws is simple in concept; what's complex is figuring out what might replace those laws.

Legalization of most currently banned drugs has little political support. Marijuana is different. Public opinion polls typically find that more than half of all Americans support legalizing the drug, and four states have already created legal for-profit marijuana industries (Colorado and Washington in 2012; Alaska and Oregon in 2014). Other states are considering marijuana legalization, including California. Change in federal law, too, seems much closer now than it did just a few years ago.

How does it feel to get high?

The sensation of being under the influence of marijuana varies with the type and quantity consumed, the person and his or her experience and purpose in using, and the social circumstances ("drug, set, and setting").

Science has little to say about the feelings generated by marijuana intoxication or about how those feelings compare with the feelings generated by other drugs. The marijuana experience is complex. Most drugs taken for other-than-medical use can be classified as either central-nervous-system (CNS) stimulants (such as caffeine, cocaine, amphetamines, and MDMA) or CNS depressants (such as alcohol and the opiate pain relievers, including morphine, oxycodone, and heroin), but marijuana is neither. While most psychoactive drugs used for pleasure influence the systems pertaining to one or more of three neurotransmitters—dopamine, serotonin, or GABA—the chemicals in cannabis react with two other systems (CB1 and CB2). And—again unlike most recreational drugs—marijuana contains a large variety of psychoactive molecules, not just one. This complicates efforts to define a dose or the marijuana equivalent of a "standard drink" (roughly half an ounce of pure alcohol, whether as a can of beer, a glass of wine, or a shot of spirits).

The effects of those actions and interactions are multiple and oddly assorted: focusing attention on sensory experience, impairing short-term memory and the "executive function" in ways that interfere with absorbing complex information and managing divided attention, suppressing nausea, enhancing appetite for some foods, and making users more receptive to humor and more attentive to music. The effects are not always pleasant; users can experience intense anxiety and panic attacks (see chapters 3, 4, and 5).

What are the active ingredients in marijuana?

Until recently, most discussion about the effects of marijuana focused on a single chemical: delta-9-tetrahydrocannabinol, better known as THC. THC is the main psychoactive ingredient in marijuana, and the one most responsible for its intoxicating effects.

The THC in the living plant occurs mostly in a nonpsychoactive form called THC-A, which is converted to THC by drying and heating. Once in the body, THC is further converted into scores of metabolites, some of which are also themselves psychoactive. Many common tests for "marijuana" in the human body actually measure these metabolites. As to the plant material, the percentage of THC (including THC-A) by weight is a good measure of intoxicating potency.

The effects of the other cannabinoids are less well understood than those of THC. As far as is now known, none of them produces a "high" in the absence of THC, but they interact with THC to alter its impact in a variety of ways: enhancing or attenuating it, speeding up or slowing down its onset, and influencing how long the effect lasts.

One compound drawing increasing attention from both scientists and medical-marijuana providers is cannabidiol (CBD). CBD is not intoxicating—CBD alone doesn't produce a high—but there is evidence it can blunt the anxiety sometimes produced by high doses of THC, and it may also have independent anti-anxiety, antipsychotic, and antiseizure actions that might make it therapeutically useful. It seems likely that marijuana with a lower ratio of THC to CBD may pose less risk of overintoxication and dependency than the high-THC, low-CBD strains now typical of expensive marijuana, but the science remains unresolved.

Most marijuana users—even those who know what CBD is—cannot detect its presence or absence in the material they use, and even in stores in states where marijuana commerce is legal, the labels in the stores or dispensaries do not always accurately convey the product's chemical content. Accurate testing and labeling might help consumers use the material more safely.

Growing knowledge about the roles of THC and CBD—replacing earlier views that THC alone mattered—suggests that more surprises may be in store as scientists learn about the roles of other compounds in marijuana. Research in this area remains in its infancy, and to date scientists have paid relatively little attention to subjective experience, as opposed to measurable impairment.

What are the varieties of the cannabis plant?

The myriad strains of cannabis fall into three broad groups: sativa, indica, and the lesser-known ruderalis. Each type can be crossed with the others to produce hybrids. Many users report sharp differences between sativa and indica, not just in appearance (sativa plants tend to be taller, with thinner leaves, and slower to bear fruit), but also in psychopharmacological effect. Indeed, on average, sativas tend to have a higher THC to CBD ratio compared with indicas; sativas are commonly thought to yield an energetic high, while the effect of indica strains is sometimes referred to as "couchlock."

What are the varieties of marijuana products?

Regardless of genetics, the stalks and stems have almost no psychoactive content; the leaves have some, the flowers ("buds" or "flowering tops") still more, and the tiny hair-like trichomes on the flowers the most of all. Consequently, marijuana that contains large proportions of stems and leaves is less valuable than marijuana consisting mostly of the flowering tops.

Cannabis plants are either males producing pollen or females capturing pollen and producing seed. Female plants produce a sticky resin that traps grains of pollen from the air; that resin contains high concentrations of psychoactive molecules. Marijuana growers have learned that unpollinated females keep producing more and more resin, thus increasing the cannabinoid content of the product. Flowers that are never pollinated never produce seed; therefore the high-potency marijuana produced by keeping females unpollinated is seedless and is called "sinsemilla," from the Spanish *sin semilla* (without seed). Sinsemilla typically runs between 10 percent and 20 percent THC, or about three times the level of the "commercial-grade" marijuana that comes from pollinated plants and in some cases contains leaves as well as flowers. Thus—the effects of selective breeding and other advanced growing techniques aside—the change from the marijuana most common in the 1960s and early 1970s (the leaves of pollinated plants) to the sinsemilla flowers most common in today's commercial stores and medical outlets represents a very sharp increase in potency.

Hashish, made by pressing together the resinous trichomes, can exceed 40 percent THC. Hashish is produced mostly in Asia and North Africa and is therefore more widely used in Europe than in the United States. It has a special mystique connected with its use by Baudelaire and other nineteenth-century French bohemians. Some users claim it has qualitatively different effects from even very potent herbal marijuana, perhaps due either to the sheer concentration of THC or to the higher CBD content of the North African hashish usually used in Europe.

The product called "hash oil" is a chemical extract of marijuana. It has nothing in common with hashish save the name and its high potency. Rare until recently, hash oil is now sold in many medical-marijuana dispensaries and state-legal stores in the United States, and has a growing market share. Hash oil is referred to by many other names, including liquid cannabis and butane hash oil (BHO). "Wax," "shatter," and "budder" refer to various semi-solid forms of the same material. It has gained notoriety for the explosions that sometimes result from amateur extraction using butane as a solvent.

"Ditchweed" is at the other end of the potency spectrum. As the name implies, it is typified by wild weeds growing on the sides of roads. The average THC content of ditchweed is below 1 percent, giving it little value as an intoxicant.

What is industrial hemp?

Industrial hemp is marijuana's sober cousin. The oil and seeds of the cannabis plant can be used as nonintoxicating food for animals and people; the fiber can make rope, paper, and cloth, and the whole plant can be burned for fuel. Cannabis grown for such purposes is called industrial hemp.

Hemp has been cultivated for thousands of years and on almost every continent. Both the cordage and the sails of sailing ships consisted largely of hemp; the word canvas derives from cannabis. A "hempen necktie" meant a hangman's noose. Inexpensive cloth made of hemp was associated with the poor: in *A Midsummer Night's Dream* Puck refers to Nick Bottom the weaver and his fellow rustics as "hempen homespuns."

In colonial times and up through the late nineteenth century, the United States produced significant quantities of industrial hemp. The industry subsequently declined as Manila hemp (made from abacà rather than cannabis), nylon, cotton, and other substitutes were found to be cheaper or better. However, it enjoyed a brief resurgence during World War II, when the United States lost access to Manila hemp from the Philippines and needed cannabis hemp for rope.

Industrial hemp is produced in roughly thirty countries, with China and Canada accounting for most of the production. Growing it has been prohibited in the United States for decades, but the importation of raw and refined hemp products is permitted. The passage of the federal Agricultural Act of 2014 allowed universities and state departments of agriculture to grow industrial hemp for research where that activity is not forbidden by state law.

What are the alternatives to smoking?

Traditionally, most marijuana was consumed in cigarettes ("joints"), water pipes ("bongs"), or hollowed-out cigars ("blunts"). Outside the United States marijuana is often mixed with loose tobacco. All of those are forms of smoking; the plant material is burned to produce heat, vaporizing the active chemicals for the user to inhale.

Cannabinoids can also be vaporized using an external source of heat. "Vaping" marijuana is increasingly common and is analogous to consuming nicotine in e-cigarettes. (The "smoking" of crack cocaine or opium also involves vaporization rather than combustion.) There are devices on the market to vaporize herbal marijuana, as well as concentrates such as hash oil. Semisolid concentrates ("shatter" or "wax") can be flash-vaporized by "dabbing" them onto a very hot piece of metal, such as a nail that has been heated with a blowtorch. Dabbing allows rapid intake of many more active molecules than smoking or conventional vaporization.

Marijuana can also be ingested in edibles (brownies, cookies, etc.) and beverages (e.g., teas and elixirs). "Green dragon" is made by infusing liquor with marijuana extracts; the limited evidence available suggests that combining alcohol and marijuana may have more-than-additive effects. Edibles and potables have proliferated in legal medical and commercial outlets.

The route of administration affects the speed of onset and the nature and duration of the high: smoking and vaporization hit harder and faster, but edibles and beverages are more prone to result in accidental overconsumption. Craft-scale production of ingestibles may not spread the cannabis evenly; two brownies from the same batch may vary widely in their intoxicating powers. More fundamentally, the longer and less predictable delay between taking the drug and feeling its effects (minutes to hours for ingestion vs. seconds-to-minutes for smoking or vaporization) challenges attempts at "titration": taking a little, waiting to feel the effects, and then deciding whether to take more. Those who don't wait for the full effects to develop before increasing the dose may end up ruing their impatience. While laboratory evidence suggests that even experienced smokers aren't as skilled as they think they are in regulating dosage, attempts to "titrate" oral doses have an even greater risk of ending unhappily when an inexperienced user mistakes the initial effect of a dose for its full effect.

There are myriad other forms of marijuana consumption. Users responding to an internet survey administered just before Washington State's legal marijuana regulations took effect also mentioned using topical lotions and soaps, capsules, tinctures, and suppositories, as well as eating or juicing leaves. Topical administration is reportedly helpful for joint pain but does not produce a direct psychological effect; the tetrahydrocannabolic acid (THC-A) molecule that occurs in the plant is not psychoactive until it has been chemically transformed (decarboxylated) into THC by heat or drying.

Has marijuana been getting more potent?

Yes, by quite a bit, though like everything else about marijuana, the extent of this change has sometimes been exaggerated in the debate.

The concentration of cannabinoids, and in particular THC, is much higher in cannabis products today than it was in the 1960s, when marijuana first found a mass market in the United States. Increased potency results from four factors: the change in the market from selling leaves to selling flowers (in Washington State, leaves are not even included in the legal definition of "usable marijuana"); the shift away from pollinated plants to sinsemilla; advanced growing techniques, including a carefully controlled environment with regard to lighting, fertilizer, and soil; and selective breeding. Much less is known about changes in the levels of other cannabinoids, but CBD content seems to have fallen as THC content has risen.

These patterns show up in laboratory assays of seized marijuana. As recently as 2000, more than 90 percent of cannabis samples seized by law enforcement were classified as basic "marijuana"—primarily commercial-grade material imported from Mexico—as opposed to higher-potency products such as sinsemilla or hashish; the average potency of those seizures was below 5 percent. The potency of that basic marijuana has increased (from roughly 4 percent to 6 percent), but, much more importantly, sinsemilla now accounts for half or more of the seizures. Seized sinsemilla samples average about 12–14 percent THC; the average THC level claimed for flower sold in Colorado is closer to 17 percent. A noteworthy trend is the growing share of sinsemilla and the falling share of commercial-grade material. The United Kingdom and the Netherlands report similar trends.

Overall, the claim made in drug-prevention programs that "this is not your grandfather's marijuana"—with its implication that baby boomers who recall using the drug safely should not be complacent about its use by their grandchildren—has a solid basis. Counting the extracts, today's material is perhaps five times as potent, on average, as the material the baby boomers started smoking in the 1960s. Even then, there were niche markets in sinsemilla and hashish, but the volumes involved were tiny. Dabbing is an entirely new phenomenon; no one knows how common it is.

Is higher potency bad?

While there's not much dispute that potency has increased, there is dispute over how much it matters. How much more dangerous those high-potency products and the associated consumption practices turn out to be—in terms of both acute bad reactions and long-term bad habits—is as much a behavioral question as a purely pharmacological one. No one yet knows the answer.

In purely commercial terms, higher-potency marijuana is more valuable because a user needs less of it to attain any desired high. A user trying to minimize cost per hour of intoxication should be willing to pay about twice as much for marijuana that is twice as potent, and there does seem to be a price gradient based on potency, though other factors also influence price. But if more potent pot just meant that users smoked half as much, the main result would be a beneficial one: less throat irritation, and perhaps less lung damage, from smoking.

But there are three reasons to worry that more potent pot tends to lead to higher highs and a greater incidence of bad effects such as panic attacks.

First, marijuana users, especially those without experience, may have no reliable way of judging the potency of the material they consume. A user who smokes a joint weighing a half gram will clearly get higher if that joint is 15 percent THC than if it is 5 percent THC. Even users who don't smoke a fixed amount of material but try to titrate—smoking enough to get the desired effect and then stopping—may find it more difficult with higher-potency marijuana simply because each individual puff contains such a large dose of intoxicant.

Second, the intensity of the subjective high is determined by the rate of change of the blood concentration of the drug as well as by the maximum level attained. Smoking or vaping high-potency pot—and, in the extreme case, dabbing—compresses the time over which cannabinoids enter the brain, thus generating a more intense intoxication for any given amount of chemical.

Third, a high ratio of the anxiety-inducing THC to the anxiety-relieving CBD, which is typical of high-potency material, may put the user at greater risk of negative side effects.

So there's reason to think not only that pot has gotten more potent but that more potent pot—especially if it also has high ratios of THC to CBD—could be more dangerous.

The changing age-pattern of use constitutes a separate source of concern. The college students who experimented with marijuana in the 1960s were about four years older than the typical person who begins using marijuana today, and earlier ages of initiation are associated with much greater likelihood of dependence and other problems.

How long does intoxication last?

The duration of the high depends on the potency of the drug, how much is used, how and in what environment it is used, and the user's history of marijuana use.

When marijuana is consumed in joints, typically less than half of the THC is inhaled and absorbed by the lungs; the rest is burned up in the smoking process, lost to the atmosphere as sidestream smoke, or exhaled without being absorbed. The THC enters the bloodstream and begins to reach the brain within seconds; effects are typically perceived within a minute or two and peak after several minutes more.

The intoxicating effects do not end abruptly. THC is eliminated from blood plasma in minutes, but the THC and its active metabolites are distributed to the brain and other body tissues and continue to produce pharmacological effects. Hence, unlike the case of alcohol, there is no strong correlation between plasma concentrations and impairment. Many physiological and behavioral effects return to baseline three to five hours after use, but a recent Dutch study showed that smoked marijuana continued to increase anxiety and reduce the sense of "feeling stimulated" for at least eight hours.

As for ingesting marijuana orally (e.g., eating marijuana-infused baked goods), the fraction of THC and its metabolites that end up in the user's bloodstream varies with what else is in the user's digestive system; the bioavailability of the active agents is much greater if marijuana products are consumed on an empty stomach. Compared to smoking, the effects of eating take longer to be felt, typically half an hour to two hours after ingestion. Both variable bioavailability and delayed onset undermine efforts to adjust the dosage level to get to some target high. That leads some users to continue eating more in the belief that the original dose wasn't strong enough, sometimes producing unintentional overdose and hours of intense psychological distress. The effects of orally ingested marijuana also tend to last longer than smoked marijuana. While a smoker who feels too high can stop smoking with the assurance of not getting much higher and being nearly back to baseline within a couple of hours, a marijuana eater who starts to feel anxious still has to deal with whatever chemicals remain in the gut on their way to the bloodstream.

How long after use can marijuana be detected?

Employers and criminal-justice agencies use chemical tests— primarily urine tests—to detect the use of banned drugs. For heavy users, marijuana remains detectable longer than most other psychoactive substances.

The body's fatty tissues store both some of the THC itself and some of its metabolic by-products. Over time, the fat cells re-release those chemicals into the bloodstream, though generally too slowly to have much intoxicating effect. Thus marijuana can be detectable in a user's system well after the high has abated, and there is no simple relationship between the amount of THC metabolite detectable in a user's urine and time since consumption. How long the chemical traces remain in the body depends on many factors, most notably the user's metabolic rate and the amount and frequency of marijuana use.

This makes marijuana testing imprecise. Most users will have detectable levels of THC in their urine within about thirty minutes of use. First-timers and infrequent users could expect to test positive for only a few days. Frequent users will typically have a much longer "detection window," because THC metabolites accumulate more quickly than they can be eliminated. As a result, a frequent user could test positive weeks after he or she stops using. (This can have the perverse result of encouraging people subject to drug testing—at school, in the workplace, or in the criminal justice system—to switch from marijuana to more dangerous drugs that have shorter "detection windows," including methamphetamine, opiates, and alcohol, or to drugs not tested for, such as synthetic cannabinoids.)

Hair testing extends the detection window to months, and does so for many illicit drugs, not just for marijuana. But hair testing—more complicated, more expensive, and slower to produce a result—is much less common than urine testing.

Blood tests are also used to confirm impaired driving, though not usually to detect it. The typical sequence of events begins when impairment is detected by observing poor driving. A breathalyzer test for alcohol is administered. If the breathalyzer is positive, then the investigation generally stops there. If it is negative, the driver might be taken to a medical facility to obtain a blood sample that can be tested for THC. But since THC in blood does not map closely to impairment, that approach can lead to convictions for "driving under the influence" even when the driver was quite sober at the time of the traffic stop.

Is medical-marijuana the same as illegal marijuana?

Yes and no. It's the same plant, and it has the same chemicals in it; the molecules don't know whether they're legal or illegal, or why they're being used. In principle, medical users are taking a drug recommended by a physician to help some ailment, rather than trying to get intoxicated; in practice, that distinction tends to blur, especially in states such as California, Colorado, Oregon, and Washington where the limits on medical-marijuana recommendation-writing are vague and poorly enforced. Some medical-marijuana dispensaries, but not all, are more careful about what they sell than the typical illegal dealer: they test the material for pesticides, fungus, and mold, and sometimes label it for its levels of the various active agents. High-potency marijuana and concentrates seem to account for a larger share of dispensary sales than they do of strictly illegal sales.

There are also conventional, government-approved pharmaceuticals derived from the cannabis plant. Synthetic THC in capsule form is an approved drug sold under the trade name Marinol. Sativex is roughly a 50/50 mixture of THC and CBD extracted from cannabis plants, prepared as a spray to be taken under the tongue, and sold legally as a medicine in about two dozen countries (but not yet in the United States) (see chapters 5 and 13).

What is synthetic marijuana (Spice or K2)?

"Spice" and "K2" are names of products that contain plant material mixed with synthetic chemicals whose effects are similar to those of the cannabinoids in marijuana. Some, such as HU-210, are much more potent than THC itself—as reflected in the name "K2," which refers to the world's second-highest mountain. But their principal appeal lies in legal and chemical loopholes (now partially closed). The health effects of various chemicals sold under those names are unknown; some of them are probably more harmful than the cannabinoids in marijuana, and the risks are accentuated because users have no way of knowing what chemicals, in what quantities, make up a given package of "spice." The US Controlled Substances Act, and similar legislation elsewhere, originally outlawed only the products of a specific plant (cannabis). It proved possible to invent and synthesize chemicals that do not appear in the plant, but which influence the same receptors; these "designer drugs" thereby skirted the law. In 2011, the Drug Enforcement Administration started adding some of these synthetic chemicals to the list of prohibited drugs, thus closing that legal loophole with respect to those specific chemicals. The US law automatically extends to other chemicals which are similar in structure and effect; some other countries' parallel provisions are more narrowly drawn, and synthetic cannabinoids and designer drugs more generally continue to pose a greater challenge there.

There is another loophole that remains partly open even in the United States: synthetic marijuana is not detected by many standard drug tests. While laboratories now offer tests that do detect the synthetics, many employers and criminal-justice agencies don't use them yet. Moreover, the synthetics present a moving target: a test that catches the metabolites of one of them might miss those of another. Thus some users are likely to continue to prefer the synthetics, despite the greater health risks they bring.

Additional Reading

DuPont, Robert L., and Carl S. Selavka. "Testing to Identify Recent Drug Use."
Iversen, Leslie L. *The Science of Marijuana*.
Pollan, Michael. *The Botany of Desire*.
Rosenthal, Ed, and David Downs. *Beyond Buds: Marijuana Extracts*.

2

WHO USES MARIJUANA?

How many people use marijuana?

Marijuana is the world's most widely used illicit substance. Around the world, between 125 million and 225 million people use marijuana in the course of a year; that's 3–4 percent of the population aged 15 to 64. The amphetamine-type stimulants and the opiates come next, each with about a fifth as many users as marijuana.

The prevalence of marijuana use in the United States is several times the global average, though less out of line with other Western democracies. The 33 million Americans who report use in the past year far outnumber the users of all the other illicit substances combined. For the general population, cigarette smoking is about twice as common as marijuana smoking, and drinking about six times as common.

Not all of those 33 million people think of themselves as "marijuana users," any more than everyone who has sung in the past year is a "singer." It is conventional to equate "current use" with use in the past month; 20 million Americans say they've used marijuana in the past month (compared to 136 million for alcohol). About 7 million of those 20 million report using marijuana daily or near daily, and more than 4 million meet the clinical criteria for marijuana abuse or dependence.

These figures include adolescents, and marijuana use is common among high-school students; 45 percent of twelfth graders report having tried the drug at least once, and 6 percent report using daily, versus 47 percent who report having been drunk and 2 percent who report using alcohol daily. The typical age at first use of marijuana is 15 or 16. This is similar to the typical age of first alcohol use, but younger than the initiation ages for other illicit drugs. Marijuana use peaks among 18- to 20-year-olds; their past-month rate (21 percent) is three times the US average.

The actual numbers are probably even higher, because some respondents are reluctant to admit their use. (Others exaggerate, but that seems to be less frequent.) Some studies suggest that roughly 20 percent of current marijuana users deny their use in these surveys, and there are hints that the figure might be even higher.

How has marijuana use changed over time?

Marijuana did not achieve mass-market status in the United States until the mid-to-late 1960s, but historically it is among the oldest of the psychoactives. (Industrial use is even older; archeological evidence of hemp cord dates back some ten thousand years, before the Neolithic Revolution.) The first recorded medicinal application was in China around 2700 BC. Early writings tell us that the Chinese were aware of marijuana's psychoactive properties, but these were considered secondary to its value in healing the body. Marijuana use in India was not primarily medical; there are records of religious use going back to 2000 BC. Herbal cannabis (the Arabic word for which, confusingly, is *hashish*) was known to the Arab world by the tenth century AD: the "hashish eater" is a target of ridicule in some of the stories in the *Arabian Nights*. The Qur'an forbids alcohol (specifically, wine) but makes no mention of marijuana, though many Islamic scholars now consider it forbidden.

Westerners were late adopters, with little interest in marijuana's intoxicating effects until the early nineteenth century, even though cannabis had long been used in the West as a medicine and fiber. Psychoactive use was introduced to western Europe by Napoleon's soldiers, who became acquainted with it while in Egypt. Napoleon tried to ban marijuana consumption, but the ban was ineffective, and returning soldiers introduced the drug to Europe.

Cannabis was grown in the American colonies alongside tobacco, but for industrial use rather than as an intoxicating product; hemp paper was in common use. (However, the widely circulated claim that the original versions of the Declaration of Independence and the Constitution were written on hemp paper turns out to be false: both were written on parchment.)

By the late nineteenth century, marijuana was a common ingredient in medicines, but widespread use as an intoxicant in the United States began only in the early 1900s, when it was introduced by Mexican immigrants. It also became associated with the predominantly African American jazz culture. That meant that anti-marijuana crusaders, including Harry J. Anslinger of the Treasury Department's Prohibition Bureau, could draw on two deep wells of prejudice. By 1931, twenty-nine states had criminalized marijuana. The federal government encouraged all states to enact laws to control marijuana use through the Uniform State Narcotic Act of 1932; the Marihuana Tax Act of 1937 imposed a prohibitive $100 an ounce tax (the equivalent of $1,650 per ounce in 2015). This effectively made possession of marijuana as an intoxicant illegal. (It could still be prescribed as a medicine.) It was finally formally outlawed under federal law by the Boggs Act of 1952.

Government portrayals of the drug grossly exaggerated its negative effects. However, it is not accurate to treat the 1936 movie *Reefer Madness* as a sample of official anti-marijuana propaganda; the movie was not made by the government and was rarely shown before the marijuana-legalization group NORML resurrected it for its fundraising events in the 1970s.

Marijuana was part of the Beat culture of the 1950s, but use remained uncommon until the 1960s, when it spread rapidly across college campuses along with the "hippie" counterculture and opposition to the Vietnam War. The first US survey of marijuana use was a Gallup poll of college students in 1967; five percent of respondents reported having used marijuana at some point in their lives. Within two years, the college student lifetime-prevalence rate had jumped to 22 percent, and by 1971 it reached 51 percent.

How have marijuana policies changed in the past half century?

In 1970, President Nixon signed the Comprehensive Drug Abuse Prevention and Control Act, which included the Controlled Substances Act (CSA). The CSA is often wrongly characterized as having launched the "War on Drugs." In reality, it merely consolidated and rationalized existing policies, and made them consistent with the Single Convention on Narcotic Drugs (1961), then the main international treaty on the subject. The CSA actually eliminated some mandatory minimum sentences and expanded support for drug treatment and research.

The 1970 act also authorized creation of a National Commission on Marihuana and Drug Abuse, and President Nixon appointed former Pennsylvania governor Raymond Shafer to head the group, which became known as the Shafer Commission. Its report, issued in 1972 under the title *Marihuana: A Signal of Misunderstanding*, concluded:

> Neither the marihuana user nor the drug itself can be said to constitute a danger to public safety. Therefore, the Commission recommends ... possession of marihuana for personal use no longer be an offense, ... [and] casual distribution of small amounts of marihuana for no remuneration, or insignificant remuneration no longer be an offense.

While the Shafer Report drew an immediate and vehement denunciation from President Nixon, its publication reflected an ongoing shift in elite opinion. In 1969, Stanford law professor John Kaplan published *Marijuana: The New Prohibition*, questioning the wisdom of keeping such a relatively benign drug illegal; that was followed in 1971 by Harvard psychiatry professor Lester Grinspoon's *Marihuana Reconsidered*. Those books helped generate a growing academic consensus that a punitive approach to marijuana was misguided.

That point of view began to have effects on policy. By the end of the 1970s, a number of states had either fully decriminalized marijuana possession or reduced penalties. President Jimmy Carter said, in a message to Congress, "Penalties against drug use should not be more damaging to an individual than the use of the drug itself. Nowhere is this more clear than in the laws against the possession of marijuana in private for personal use." To some, it seemed that marijuana might be on the way to joining alcohol as a second socially sanctioned intoxicant.

But the increase in marijuana prevalence troubled many people. By 1979 more than 10 percent of high-school seniors reported daily or near-daily use. That finding (and encouragement from the Drug Enforcement Administration) helped fuel the antidrug "parents'

movement," which in turn helped bring an end to the era of liberalization. Perhaps the watershed event was the replacement of Carter
drug policy adviser Peter Bourne, an advocate of marijuana decriminalization, if not outright legalization, with the more conservative
Lee Dogoloff. Bourne was forced to resign because of reports about
his own drug use and his illegally prescribing sedatives to a White
House colleague. Ironically, the source of the news story was one of
the leaders of NORML, then the main marijuana-legalization advocacy group, angry that Bourne was not pressing for decriminalization strongly enough.

The 1980s saw increasing levels of antidrug rhetoric. First Lady
Nancy Reagan launched her "Just Say No" campaign, and officials
perceived as "soft" on marijuana were forced out of their jobs. When
marijuana use among high-school seniors dropped throughout the
1980s, this was heralded as vindication of the hardline stance. The
decline continued until marijuana use hit its trough around 1992;
since then it has experienced two decades of more or less steady
growth. Overall prevalence and the prevalence of daily and near-
daily use now surpass their earlier peaks. However, in the face
of these rising trends, daily and near-daily use by high-school
seniors—now at 6 percent— remains well below its 1979 level.

How much marijuana do users consume?

A typical joint used in the United States contains just under half a
gram of marijuana, and a single intake of smoke, or "hit," consumes
about 1/20th of a gram. A joint of commercial-grade marijuana
might get an occasional user high for hours; one-third as much
premium-priced sinsemilla produces similar effects. Those who use
daily or near daily appear to consume an average of about one-and-
a-half grams per day; tolerance leads frequent users to need more of
the drug to get to a given level of intoxication.

Many people who have used marijuana within the last year
haven't used much of it. One-quarter report using on five or fewer
days during that year, and half report that the last time they acquired
marijuana they got it for free (e.g., by sharing someone else's supply)
rather than for money. How much marijuana is consumed within
a state, region, or nation depends less on the total the number of
people who use than on how many of them are heavy users.

The total quantity consumed was estimated to be in the range of 4,200–8,400 metric tons in 2010, and consumption has likely risen significantly since then. (A metric ton is 1000 kilograms, or about 2,200 pounds.) The midpoint of that range—6,300 metric tons—is enough for 0.9 grams per day (about two joints) each and every day for all 20 million current (meaning past-month) users. Most use much less; some use much more.

Traditionally, the bulk of marijuana appears to have been commercial-grade—grown outdoors and with THC content averages of less than 5 percent. As recently as 2000, only a very small proportion of marijuana seizures were of the higher-potency sinsemilla variety. By 2008, higher-potency forms had gained a significant share of the market, perhaps disproportionately so among the connoisseurs who dominate online discussions about marijuana, but surveys of the general population and arrestees showed that most users were still reporting paying prices that could only be consistent with commercial-quality product.

Between 2008 and the time of this writing (fall of 2015), domestically grown high-potency sinsemilla has continued to gain market share from imported Mexican commercial-grade; high-potency material dominates open retail sales in states that allow it (including both "medical dispensaries" and licensed commercial outlets in Washington and Colorado).

Can marijuana use lead to dependence or addiction?

Yes, but even among frequent marijuana users only a minority suffers from a substance use disorder.

The term "addiction" fell out of favor some years ago, in part because "dependence" was seen as less stigmatizing. The new preferred term in the fifth edition of the American Psychiatric Association's *Diagnostic and Statistical Manual of Mental Disorders* (DSM-V) is "substance use disorder," abbreviated SUD. Unfortunately, the latest national data still reflect the fourth edition (DSM-IV) notions of "abuse" and "dependence," where dependence is the more severe condition.

To simplify, the DSM-IV definition of drug abuse refers to continued use in the face of adverse consequences. Dependence is defined as such current use meeting three or more of the following conditions:

1. Tolerance (needing more to get same effect)
2. Withdrawal (a characteristic set of symptoms caused by cessation)
3. Using more than intended
4. A persistent desire or unsuccessful attempts to cut down on use
5. Spending considerable time obtaining, using, or recovering from the effects of the substance
6. Interference with important work, social, or other activities
7. Continued use despite knowledge of adverse consequences

Survey responses suggest that many more marijuana users meet criteria 4 and/or 5 than the others.

The self-report data suggest that 2.8 million Americans met clinical criteria for marijuana dependence in 2013, and another 1.3 million met the criteria for abuse, for a total of 4.1 million meeting the criteria for abuse or dependence. (That's 1.6 percent of the population aged 12 and older.) Estimates from Europe and Australia also find rates of marijuana abuse and dependence in the general population between 1 percent and 2 percent.

Regular marijuana use does not necessarily indicate dependence. Only about one-quarter of those who are estimated to have used on more than half the days in the last year self-report symptoms that suggest a diagnosis of abuse or dependence. The corresponding figure for cocaine is well over 50 percent. Someone who uses cocaine every other day or more often is probably cocaine-dependent; someone who uses marijuana every other day or more often is probably not marijuana-dependent. In this regard marijuana resembles alcohol more than it does the "hard" drugs.

On the other hand, 44 percent of those frequent marijuana users meet the clinical criteria for substance abuse or dependence on some drug besides tobacco; they might, for example, be alcoholics or dependent on methamphetamine. One can question whether a poly-drug user who has lost control of the use of some other drug is really fully in control of his or her high-frequency marijuana consumption.

How common is marijuana use in the United States?

Some years ago the Australian household survey on drug use changed the wording of its questions. One version of the survey asked "Have you ever tried ___?" about various substances. The other version asked "Have you ever used ___?" The first version documented much larger numbers, presumably because many respondents thought "Sure I've *tried* the drug a few times, but I've never actually *used* it"—that is, they didn't identify themselves as "drug users."

In truth, many people in the United States who have some experience with marijuana might be better described as *experimenters*; 40–50 percent of those who have ever tried marijuana report a lifetime total of fewer than twelve days of use. That group contributes only negligibly to market demand and to personal or social problems with the drug.

The tobacco research community often only counts someone as an ever-smoker if that person has smoked on at least one hundred occasions. We think a similar criterion (perhaps with a lower number) should be adopted for marijuana, but both pro- and anti-legalization advocates seem to prefer trumpeting the larger number that 44 percent of Americans age 12 and older have tried marijuana rather than the less exciting claim that 20 percent have ever been marijuana users in any meaningful sense of the term.

In terms of current use, about 8 percent of the population 12 and older reports consuming marijuana within the last thirty days. The rate varies little across racial and ethnic groups: slightly higher for African-Americans (9.0 percent) and slightly lower for Hispanics (6.3 percent). The only groups whose use is far from the national average are those of Asian ancestry on the low side (2.4 percent) and those of Native American/Alaskan/Hawaiian/Pacific Islander ancestry on the high side (12 percent).

Regional variations are less sharp than stereotypes might suggest: those living in the West (9.8 percent) and Northeast (8.6 percent) were only modestly more likely to be past-month users than those in the Midwest (7.5 percent) and South (6.7 percent). Figure 2.1 shows how these regional differences have evolved over time by pairs of years (combining adjacent years gives more precise estimates). Prevalence has grown everywhere since 2007, but especially in the West; this is noteworthy in that this period corresponds to the time when medical-marijuana became more commercialized along the Pacific Coast and in Colorado (see chapter 14 for more about state-specific use rates).

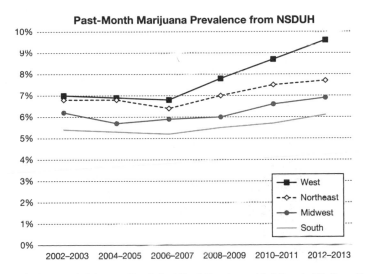

Figure 2.1 Regional Variation over Time in Past-Month Prevalence of Self-Reported Marijuana Use National Survey on Drug Use and Health

What are typical patterns of marijuana use?

The current marijuana market can be divided into user segments based on degree of abuse or dependence and frequency of use:

- Segment 1: Meet diagnostic criteria for marijuana abuse or dependence
- Segment 2: Meet diagnostic criteria for abuse or dependence on some other substance (besides tobacco), but not on marijuana
- Segment 3: No abuse or dependence, but report using marijuana on more than twenty days in past month (i.e., daily or near-daily)
- Segment 4: No abuse or dependence, and used marijuana on twenty or fewer days in the past month

As figure 2.2 shows, each of those segments accounts for 20–40 percent of the total market, depending on the measure of market size. Indeed, no matter whether one counts people or days of use, one segment has about 40 percent and the other three each have about 20 percent of the total; however, which segment is biggest depends on the

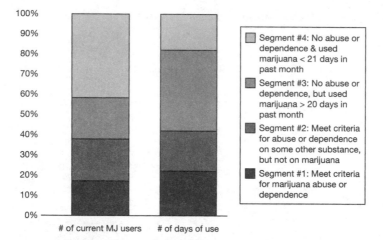

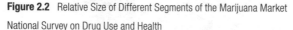

Figure 2.2   Relative Size of Different Segments of the Marijuana Market
National Survey on Drug Use and Health

measure. In terms of number of users, the largest segment is 4 (people who consume on less than twenty days a month and have no problem with abuse or dependence); 20 percent of current users fall each into segments 1, 2, and 3. In terms of days of use, the largest segment is 3 (frequent users who report no problems with abuse or dependence).

What proportion of marijuana use is "problematic" depends on the observer's notions as to what constitutes problem use. Many people view segments 1 and 2 as problematic because they involve use by people with a diagnosable substance use disorder. The last segment is usually seen as nonproblematic, at least for adult users. (Three-quarters of the people in segment 4 are 21 and older.) The third segment (frequent use with no abuse or dependence) is a contested middle ground: some worry about daily or near-daily use even if the user reports no problems, while others celebrate that some people can get so much enjoyment with so few (self-reported) adverse effects.

A stricter definition of nonproblem use would change the picture. If one defines nonproblem users as (1) adults—meaning 21 and over—with (2) no substance abuse or dependence issues who (3) use only on weekends (operationalized as using fewer than ten times per month), then nonproblem users account for just 4.7 percent of reported use days, and presumably an even smaller share of the amount of THC consumed, since frequent users also tend to consume considerably more per day of use.

To what extent do heavy users dominate consumption?

Relatively few people who try marijuana become heavy users, but those heavy users consume most of the marijuana.

In any given year, the 30 percent of past-year users who consumed on ten or fewer days in the past year account for less than 1 percent of consumption, intoxication, and industry revenues. Conversely, the relatively small number of very frequent users account for a disproportionate share of those totals.

Household survey data suggest that about 7 million Americans aged 12 and over use marijuana on a daily or near-daily basis; they are therefore one-fifth of past-year users but account for 80 percent of the quantity of marijuana consumed. This usage pattern is very similar to that of alcohol; people who average two or more drinks per day account for 80 percent of the alcohol consumed. The even smaller group who use every single day consume a disproportionate share of this 80 percent. Daily users not only use more frequently, they also tend to use larger doses.

Figure 2.3 shows the frequency of marijuana use among those who reported using marijuana within the past year.

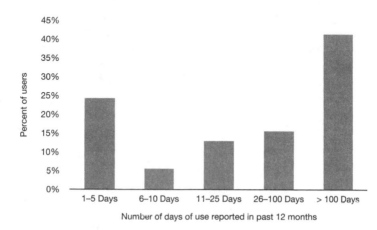

Figure 2.3 shows the frequency of marijuana use among those who reported using marijuana within the past year.

Figure 2.3 Frequency of Use among Americans Aged 12 and Over Who Used in the Past Year

National Survey on Drug Use and Health, 2013

Has heavy use become more common?

Yes, and startlingly so.

Figure 2.4 shows that the number of Americans self-reporting daily or near-daily marijuana use—defined as use on more than twenty days in the past month—grew enormously from its nadir of fewer than nine hundred thousand in 1992 to almost seven million in 2013. Survey methods have changed some over time, but not enough to account for so large a change. A different survey recorded an increase from 0.9 percent to 3.7 percent—a factor of four—in the proportion of high-school students reporting daily use over this same period.

With respect to "current use"—defined as any use within the last month—alcohol is seven times as common as marijuana (136 million vs. 20 million past-month users). However, with respect to daily or near-daily use, alcohol is only about twice as common as marijuana (13.6 million vs. 6.9 million such users).

Back in 1992 only 11 percent of past-month marijuana users consumed daily or near-daily, about the same as the 10 percent rate among current alcohol users. In 2013, the proportion of current users who consumed daily remained at 10 percent for alcohol, but had

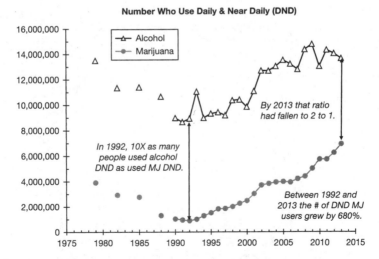

Figure 2.4 Number of Americans Aged 12 and Over Who Report Using Alcohol or Marijuana More than Twenty Times in the Past Month

National Household Surveys various years

increased to 36 percent for marijuana. The corresponding proportion for cigarettes is 66 percent: most people who smoke cigarettes do so on a daily basis. So in some sense, over the last twenty-five years the typical pattern of marijuana consumption went from mirroring alcohol to being halfway between alcohol and cigarettes.

In one important way—reflecting custom at least as much as pharmacology—marijuana use differs sharply from alcohol use. Most people who drink, on most occasions, have a drink or two and stop there. They don't start out intending to get drunk, and they don't in fact get drunk. Of course the alcohol influences their mood and behavior, but not very profoundly. That's the most common pattern of alcohol use. Getting drunk—technically, binge drinking, defined as five or more drinks on the same occasion for a male and four or more for a female—is treated as a different activity than simply using alcohol. It is far less common, though not rare in absolute terms. By contrast, a larger proportion of people who smoke marijuana—other than some very heavy users who need the drug just to feel normal and some people using it for medical purposes—intend to get stoned. So—if we put aside the qualitative difference between the marijuana experience and the alcohol experience—normal marijuana use in the United States likely resembles binge drinking more closely than it does mere drinking.

That's not an inherent characteristic of the drug. It's perfectly possible to have one hit of marijuana, just as it's possible to have one drink of alcohol, to relax and enhance social experiences. But that is not how most of the marijuana gets consumed in the United States today.

Americans now report more days of marijuana use in the past month than they do days of binge drinking (282 million consumer-days per month vs. 263 million). That is, Americans might now be getting stoned about as often as they get drunk. There's no precision in that measurement, but it's an interesting threshold to have crossed while the drug remains illegal at the federal level and in most states.

How much do users spend on marijuana?

A lot—tens of billions of dollars per year—but it's hard to say just how much.

Estimating spending seems straightforward: multiply consumption by price. Unfortunately, it's not that easy. Survey respondents are so bad at answering questions about total spending that survey designers have started to ask only about the most recent purchase rather than about spending over a longer period. Further, quantity discounts from buying in bulk complicate these calculations. An ounce of marijuana doesn't cost nearly as much as twenty-eight grams sold one at a time, and only about half of survey respondents describe their most recent purchase as being five grams or less.

The standard reference on this question is a series of reports called *What America's Users Spend on Illegal Drugs*, prepared for the Office of National Drug Control Policy. Two of us were on the team that produced the most recent estimate, for 2010, of $30–$60 billion in annual marijuana spending. That is roughly double the estimate for 2000.

Back in the early 2000s, cocaine was by far the largest market. All market estimates are imprecise, and best understood as ranges, but the single best estimate for cocaine in 2000 was $55 billion, with heroin and marijuana essentially tied for second at $22–$23 billon each. By 2010, marijuana was estimated to be the largest market (best estimate $41 billion), with cocaine and heroin essentially tied for second at $27–$28 billion each. That is, cocaine spending plummeted while marijuana shot up, and the two drugs switched places in the rankings. (However, the trends are largely unrelated; most of today's heavy marijuana users do not have a past history of heavy cocaine use.)

It's not clear whether the dollar size of the market has grown or shrunk since 2010; marijuana use has increased, but on the other hand prices per unit of THC have fallen due to a combination of decreases in per-gram (or per-ounce) prices and increasing average potency. Those trends, long established, have accelerated since 2010. Despite the emergence of legal markets, illicit production and sale still probably captures more than 90 percent of the sales revenue.

At an individual level, even allowing for the fact that heavy users tend to buy in bulk and receive volume discounts, a heavy marijuana habit is now a major expense. Paying a typical dispensary price of ten dollars per gram for 1.5 grams a day would add up to over five thousand dollars per year. Even if a heavy user wound up paying only half that price, that's still over two hundred dollars a month. Given the concentration of heavy use among people with limited education—more than half of all marijuana is used by people with no more than a high-school diploma—the financial burden can be considerable.

Additional Reading

Kilmer, Beau, Susan S. Everingham, Jonathan P. Caulkins, et al. *What America's Users Spend on Illegal Drugs, 2000–2010.*

National Commission on Marihuana and Drug Abuse. *Marihuana: A Signal of Misunderstanding.*

Substance Abuse and Mental Health Administration. *Behavioral Health Trends in the United States: Results from the 2014 National Survey on Drug Use and Health.*

3

WHAT ARE THE RISKS
OF USING MARIJUANA?

Why is it difficult to measure the consequences of marijuana use?

Marijuana use carries risks. Some are well established; some are probably real; some turn out to be mostly imaginary. Measuring the extent of marijuana-related damage to users, their families, their neighbors, and the wider public poses a research challenge.

There is no scientific consensus on many of these questions, so both sides of the legalization debate can and do refer to published studies that support their arguments and claim that the other side is "ignoring the science." That's true in the sense that both sides tend to ignore inconvenient conclusions, and sometimes promote convenient conclusions based on flimsy studies. A more productive approach is to acknowledge the uncertainties, remain openminded, and avoid surrounding oneself only with people who are like-minded on these matters.

One reason for the lack of consensus is that marijuana is a category of products, not a standardized good. Some field studies are based on people who used lower-potency commercial-grade marijuana; others address populations that had access to more potent sinsemilla; very few study dabbing. Until recently, even laboratory studies that carefully controlled the exposure to THC rarely recorded, let alone controlled, exposure to CBD or other cannabinoids that can alter the effects of THC. The lack of standardization may explain some of the inconsistencies in findings and also makes comparisons across studies difficult. Likewise, some studies look for effects from any exposure to marijuana, however infrequent, while others focus on frequent or dependent use. Some of the earlier studies were conducted when the median age at first use was 19; not all of those results generalize to populations that start using earlier. Half of current daily and near-daily users report that they started to use at age 14 or even earlier.

There are also issues surrounding the type of study being conducted. Was the research conducted with humans, on lab rats, or in petri dishes? This, of course, is not specific to research on marijuana. Many newsworthy findings that come from research with animals never pan out with humans. Daniel G. Hackam and Donald A. Redelmeier of the University of Toronto report in the *Journal of the American Medical Association* that only about one-third of highly cited animal research in leading journals was replicated in randomized trials involving humans. And even effects detected in human experiments are not always replicated in studies with other humans. Stanford's John Ioannidis found that of forty-five highly cited medical studies where the authors claimed an intervention was effective, "7 (16 percent) were contradicted by subsequent studies, 7 others (16 percent) had found effects that were stronger than those of subsequent studies, 20 (44 percent) were replicated, and 11 (24 percent) remained largely unchallenged."

Another reason for discordant findings is that not all marijuana users are alike. Some speculate that sexual dimorphism in the endocannabinoid system may produce different outcomes in males and females. Others argue that marijuana can cause mental health problems—but only in those with a preexisting vulnerability.

It is also difficult to determine whether marijuana use is the actual cause of the many negative consequences with which it is correlated. For example, marijuana use is more common among people who drop out of high school, commit property crime, or use cocaine than among those who graduate, do not commit crimes, and do not use cocaine. Thus marijuana is correlated with those outcomes. Does this mean that marijuana *caused* the outcomes? Not necessarily. Marijuana use is also more common among young males than older females, but it does not reverse aging or alter gender.

Consider, for example, the association between marijuana and mental health problems (discussed further below). While some argue that marijuana use aggravates mental health problems, others note that users may be using marijuana to self-medicate an already-existing illness. Both causal pathways may play a role for different people, or even for the same person at different times.

However, the mere fact that correlation does not imply causality of course does not mean there is no causal effect. A common error is to leap from an inability to prove a causal connection to certainty that no such connection exists. But no news about causal attribution is usually simply no news, not good news. Determining which relationships are causal is always difficult and sometimes impossible. The rules that protect the human subjects of scientific research properly forbid some of the controlled experiments that might allow scientists to make clear causal attributions: you wouldn't want researchers to offer pot to a randomly selected half of the students in an eighth-grade class just to see if those offered pot are then more likely to miss classes or to drop out of school.

How do researchers study the consequences of marijuana use?

There are a variety of approaches to learning about the effects of marijuana. Acute effects can be studied in the lab by injecting volunteers with THC or asking them to inhale marijuana smoke and then observing their reactions and performance (e.g., in cognitive tasks or on driving simulators) or using various scanning technologies to image their brain activity.

Studies in animals (e.g., mice, rats, or monkeys) can explore the effects of larger doses on longer-run physiological responses in a controlled manner. For example, brain imaging studies with humans can document *associations* between frequency of marijuana use and variations in brain structure, particularly in the medial temporal, frontal, and cerebellar brain regions. However, controlled trials assessing the effects of early-life cannabis use on brain maturation or the effects of prenatal exposure to THC can only be performed on animals.

Longer-term effects on humans can be studied outside the laboratory in two ways: (1) in a cross section, by comparing users and nonusers at a single point in time, and (2) longitudinally, by following individuals—often students or patients—for several years and assessing whether those who use marijuana are more likely to experience certain outcomes (e.g., getting arrested for a property crime or being diagnosed with cancer). When researchers do find a correlation between marijuana and a particular outcome, they first look to see whether the marijuana use actually preceded the outcome of interest. If so, the researchers then try to control for other factors that could be driving the relationship. For example, one possible explanation for why kids who commit property crimes are more likely to use marijuana is that weak parental supervision can contribute to both behaviors. Researchers try to correct for such factors statistically, but each of those corrections is subject to error. Of course, even with the same parenting, some kids are more inclined than others to take risks, and thus more prone to both drug use and theft. No matter how many of these "common cause" or "third-factor" explanations are ruled out, there are always more that might be relevant, and researchers can only address so many questions in one study. Thus no single result can really nail down causation. However, if multiple studies from multiple countries covering different cohorts consistently tell the same story, it becomes harder to doubt a causal relationship.

As a general rule, longitudinal studies are stronger than cross-sectional studies, but they are much more expensive to conduct. Much of the longitudinal research on marijuana is based on just two cohorts born in New Zealand in the 1970s: the Christchurch Health and Development Study (1,265 children born in 1977) and the Dunedin Multidisciplinary Health and Development Study (1,037 children born in 1972–1973). The impact of the experiences and life choices of these two cohorts on marijuana policy debates around the world can hardly be overstated. Studies exclusively focused on pot smoking in these two groups have been cited more than five thousand times in academic publications. (To help put this in perspective, less than half of all articles are cited within five years of publication. For academic articles published in 2000, Thomson Reuters calculated the average number of citations over the next ten years was about twenty, or about two citations per year.)

Some researchers study outcomes in the aggregate, rather than at the individual level, by examining whether those outcomes are more likely in jurisdictions where marijuana use is more common than in otherwise similar jurisdictions where marijuana use is less common; but again, the arrow of causation could point in either direction (or both). Statisticians and economists have developed strategies to "identify" what causes what, and they are always searching for "natural experiments" involving factors that directly influence marijuana consumption but not the other outcome of interest.

Even when different studies yield opposing results, that doesn't mean we need to throw up our hands and conclude that the answer is simply unknown or unknowable. Some studies are simply better than others (e.g., due to superior research designs, larger sample sizes, longer time frames, use of stronger statistical techniques), and the answers from the better studies should carry more weight. Careful reviews of the research will take the quality of these studies into account. It's harder to correct for the possible biases of researchers, funding agencies, and journal editors and the way those biases change over time. It's fair to say that a study that might find something beneficial about marijuana use is easier to fund and publish today than it would have been in the late 1980s. The attitudes of reporters and editors have also changed, which probably means that "pro-marijuana" findings are more likely to receive wide publicity now than they would have been in the past.

What is the likelihood of becoming dependent on marijuana?

This question is hard to answer for all the usual reasons, and because of some recent technical/bureaucratic changes: in particular, the change from the old criteria for the diagnoses of "abuse" and "dependency" in DSM-IV to the new criteria for "substance use disorder" in DSM-V (see chapter 2).

Based on answers to the 2013 US household survey, one in eight current (i.e., past-month) marijuana users met the clinical criteria for marijuana dependence at some time in the previous year, and one in five met the criteria for either abuse or dependence. But that is based on users' self-reported problems, and denial is a hallmark of addiction. Furthermore, household surveys may undersample populations with greater rates of problem use. So the true rates may well be higher.

Asking "What share of current users have a drug problem?" isn't the same as asking "What's the risk of developing a drug problem at some point for someone who starts using marijuana?" Epidemiological studies by James Anthony and colleagues found that about 9 percent of those who had ever tried marijuana wound up being clinically dependent on marijuana at some point in their lives, with males being at much greater risk than females. The comparable "capture rates" for alcohol and cocaine were 15 percent and 16 percent, respectively.

But that study was done on a cross section of the US population in 1990–1992. Some respondents first used marijuana as adults, simply because marijuana was not widely available when they were teens. (Marijuana did not become popular or widely available until the late 1960s and 1970s.) Initiating after young adulthood is now quite rare; in recent years over 90 percent of new users were 24 or younger. That study found a higher risk of becoming dependent among those who first tried marijuana before the age of 25: 15 percent, not 9 percent.

The larger figure is also consistent with evidence from three major longitudinal studies, two conducted in New Zealand and the other in Australia. The New Zealand studies followed entire cohorts of children born in a city in a particular year and found that 9–10 percent of the cohort met the criteria for marijuana dependence at age 21. Adjusting for those who never tried marijuana at all, the probability of dependence at age 21 among those who did try it was above 13 percent. The Australian study tracked nearly two thousand youth into early adulthood and found that 20 percent of those who had tried marijuana as adolescents exhibited dependence at age 24.

Although the Anthony et al. study is still perhaps the best of its kind, it has been twenty-five years since those data were collected. A study by Wilson Compton and colleagues at the National Institute on Drug Abuse found that the risk of marijuana dependence increased throughout the 1990s in the United States, especially for young black men and women and young Hispanic men. Since they did not find evidence of an increase in the frequency or quantity of marijuana used, they speculate that the increase in THC potency may be responsible for the increase in dependence. The combined effects of starting earlier in life and using stronger material may have increased the risk of becoming dependent.

It is important to remember that only about half of the people who ever try marijuana go on to use it more than a dozen times in their lives. So a rate of 15 percent among all those who ever try might better be thought of as an average of about 30 percent among those who use on an ongoing basis and 0 percent among those who merely experiment with marijuana a few times.

How bad is marijuana dependency compared to dependency on other drugs?

No one wants to experience dependence, or have a family member, friend, or colleague struggle with addiction, regardless of the substance. The uncertainty and suffering associated with dependence—as well as the health and financial risks—impose important costs on users and those around them.

Clinicians use essentially the same checklist of problems to assess substance use disorders for all drugs. But not all abuse and dependency is created equal. Marijuana dependence does not, on average, impose as much suffering as alcohol or heroin dependence. For example, heavy marijuana users can experience withdrawal, but the physical discomfort generally pales in comparison to that experienced by those dependent on heroin or alcohol. Withdrawal from alcohol can even be fatal if it is not properly supervised; there is no such risk with marijuana withdrawal.

Robin Room and his colleagues found that marijuana posed less addictive risk than tobacco, alcohol, cocaine, stimulants, or heroin, not only in terms of likelihood of dependence but also the degree of dependence, which they characterize as "weak." Their judgment is widely shared among experts. This finding does not deny that there are people who struggle to control their consumption or that marijuana dependence imposes a burden upon some users and their families; it just suggests that marijuana dependence is generally less severe than dependence on some other substances.

How many users enter treatment for marijuana?

In 2013, marijuana was listed as the primary substance of abuse in more than 280,000 drug treatment admissions in the United States. This figure quintupled from 1992 to 2009 and then decreased by about 20 percent from 2009 to 2013. The recent drop might be explained by a change in the perceived harmfulness of marijuana, leading to fewer referrals from parents, or a reduction in arrests, resulting in fewer criminal-justice referrals. The large increases of the 1990s and 2000s were not unique to the United States; Europe and Australia also experienced more than a doubling in treatment admissions for marijuana and hashish.

Most of those receiving marijuana treatment are adolescents and young adults, with more than half (57 percent) of admissions involving those below the age of 25. By contrast, almost half (49.5 percent) of those entering treatment for crack cocaine were 45 or older. This 280,000 figure does not count those who only attend twelve-step programs (such as Marijuana Anonymous) or other self-help groups. Since no one takes attendance at such meetings, there are no precise estimates of how many people take this road to recovery.

Some users enter treatment on their own because they need help; some are nudged by their family, friends, counselors, or employers; and others are ordered by their parents or the court to enter treatment. In fact, roughly half of those entering treatment for marijuana in the United States are referred by the criminal justice system. While some of these individuals would have eventually entered treatment anyhow, many are only there because the court ordered it, leaving it unclear how sick they really were; an arrest is not a diagnosis.

Does marijuana treatment work?

The intensity and the cost of treatment programs varies dramatically. Outpatient programs can cost less than a thousand dollars, while some residential programs cost tens of thousands of dollars per episode. In the United States, about 85 percent of marijuana treatment is provided by outpatient rather than residential programs.

Roughly half of those who enter marijuana treatment complete their programs (more for residential, less for outpatient). That may sound unsatisfactory, but it is actually better than the corresponding rates for some other substances. Still, not even those who complete the programs are necessarily abstinent, or even temperate in their use, during or after treatment.

Most of the rigorous research on drug treatment has focused on substances other than marijuana; however, there are a growing number of randomized controlled trials specific to treating marijuana users. University of Connecticut psychologist Tom Babor and colleagues with the Marijuana Treatment Project Research Group found that adults randomly assigned to two sessions of motivational enhancement therapy (MET) had fewer days of marijuana use four months later than those who received no treatment. They also found that those assigned to the more intense treatment intervention (nine sessions of multicomponent therapy that included MET, cognitive-behavioral therapy, and case management) had lower rates of marijuana use twelve months following treatment termination than those receiving the less-intensive treatment. Note, though, that this work describes success in terms of "fewer days" and "lower rates," not zero use. Even excellent treatment programs do not usually produce abstinence. Nor does everyone improve; group rates of use decline because some reduce their use, not because everyone does.

Not all studies produce such clear results. A study by Michael Dennis, a psychologist at Chestnut Health Systems, and colleagues randomly assigned marijuana treatment seekers into five different interventions. A decrease in use was detected for all five groups, but the authors found "only limited evidence that simply increasing the dosage of [marijuana] treatment had a differential effect on substance use and associated problems." The study did not include a no-treatment control condition, so it could not assess whether any intervention was better than none at all.

A review by Alan Budney of the University of Arkansas Psychiatry Department and colleagues suggests that incorporating contingency management (which provides small rewards for those who test clean for marijuana) into traditional interventions shows promise for reducing marijuana use. However, Budney and colleagues note that many community-based providers remain ambivalent about using contingency management (CM) because some are uncomfortable with providing incentives for abstinence; CM also requires resources that many treatment centers do not have.

For cocaine and heroin, studies show that even modestly successful treatment programs more than pay their way in reduced crime and other social costs. Since marijuana dependency creates fewer social burdens, and since marijuana treatment outcomes haven't been studied as closely, we do not yet have anything like a social benefit-cost analysis for the marijuana treatment effort.

For example, Todd Olmstead and colleagues examined the cost-effectiveness of both drug counseling and motivational/skill-building therapy, in both cases with and without contingency management. They conclude that you get what you pay for. The more intensive interventions produced longer durations of confirmed abstinence, but whether the extra benefit was worth the greater cost depends on how valuable it is to reduce marijuana use.

Can users experience a fatal overdose from marijuana?

A large enough dose of heroin will be fatal, even for someone who was healthy beforehand. Alcohol, cocaine, and prescription opioids also kill thousands of people a year through acute toxic effects. Marijuana does not.

The only real question is whether it is more accurate to think of the number of people who die from the marijuana-equivalent of an overdose as being literally zero or some number that is very small but still greater than zero.

Robert Gable of the psychology department at Claremont Graduate University estimated the "safety ratio" for various drugs (parallel to what is called, for drugs used medically rather than recreationally, the "therapeutic index"). Gable defines the safety ratio as the ratio of the median fatal dose (LD50, the amount that will be fatal 50 percent of the time) to the customary recreational dose. Higher ratios mean greater safety. The ratios for heroin, alcohol, methamphetamine, and cocaine range from about six to fifteen. A factor of six may sound like a pretty good margin, but not every person—or even every day or dose—follows the averages; doses smaller than LD50 can nonetheless prove fatal, especially in combination with other drugs. There is no known fatal dose of marijuana; Gable estimates that if there is such a dose, it must be at least one thousand times the amount typically consumed.

Gable's 2004 review only identified two deaths reported in the world medical literature that could possibly be attributable to a marijuana overdose, and University of Toronto pharmacologist Harold Kalant commented that these two deaths "probably involved individual risk factors without which the marijuana alone would not have been fatal." A more recent paper by University Hospital Düsseldorf doctor Benno Hartung and colleagues described two deaths that could plausibly be attributed to "acute cardiovascular complications evoked by smoking cannabis," but this too has been called into question. There is a similar case-report literature concerning marijuana and ischemic stroke. Whether marijuana can trigger cardiovascular or cerebrovascular events that lead to death is an open question. What is not up for debate is the fact that these events are extremely rare.

Still, marijuana does pose acute risks. For example, there can be interactions with other drugs. Notably, marijuana's capacity to prevent vomiting, which makes it appealing to some people undergoing chemotherapy, becomes a danger for those overindulging in alcohol, because vomiting is one of the body's defenses against poisoning.

There have also been two disturbing reports from Colorado about individuals who have consumed large amounts of THC via edibles and then died by jumping off a balcony or committing suicide. In the former case, the autopsy found marijuana intoxication as a chief contributing factor, and a publication of the Centers for Disease Control and Prevention noted, "This was the first reported death in Colorado linked to marijuana consumption without evidence of polysubstance use since the state approved recreational use of marijuana." Another gruesome and well-publicized event involved a woman who called 911 to report that her husband was hallucinating after consuming marijuana edibles and prescription drugs. He then, allegedly, shot her. It's unknown whether this murder would have occurred in the absence of edibles. Still, these events are very rare compared to similar events involving alcohol.

Can users experience a nonfatal overdose from using too much marijuana?

Yes.

A significant number of people end up in hospital emergency departments (EDs) every year for reasons related to their marijuana use. The Drug Abuse Warning Network (DAWN) estimates how many people were "treated in the ED for a condition that was induced by or related to recent drug use. . . . Unrelated drugs that are simply 'on board' are not recorded." In 2011, DAWN recorded more instances (or "mentions," to use DAWN's technical term) of marijuana (about 455,000 per year) than any other illegal drug save cocaine (505,000). The marijuana figure was much larger than the number for heroin (260,000) and far larger than MDMA (25,000). Nevertheless, marijuana is much more widely used, so the rate of ED mentions among users is lower for marijuana than for cocaine or heroin. (The number of mentions for synthetic marijuana increased from 11,500 in 2010 to 28,500 in 2011.)

With household survey respondents reporting 242 million days of use in the past month in 2011, that works out to just one ED mention for every 6,400 days of marijuana use. It also means that marijuana

ED mentions are roughly as common as possession arrests (about three ED mentions for every four possession arrests). For a long time researchers tended to assume the marijuana mentions all stemmed from drug interactions or just piggybacked on some other substance (e.g., a heroin overdose in someone who also happened to have used marijuana recently). That is probably the right interpretation of many of the marijuana mentions. Nevertheless, for about 150,000 drug-related ED visits, marijuana is the only drug mentioned.

Few of those marijuana emergency department episodes translate into hospital stays; the vast majority of patients are treated and released without being admitted. When looking at all of the hospital discharges in California in 2012, University of Pittsburgh professor Christina Mair and colleagues noted that there were only 294 inpatient discharges where marijuana abuse or dependence was the primary reason for hospitalization; however, when the analysis was extended to examine secondary diagnoses, marijuana was mentioned in more than 68,000 of the discharges.

Does marijuana use cause emphysema and other respiratory problems?

Inhaling smoke on a regular basis is not good for one's lungs, regardless of whether the smoke came from the leaves of marijuana, tobacco, or, for that matter, maple trees.

Marijuana smoke contains many of the same irritants as tobacco smoke, and in a systematic review of the evidence on long-term marijuana smoking, Veterans Affairs epidemiologist Jeanette Tetrault and colleagues reported an association with increases in respiratory symptoms (e.g., cough, phlegm, and wheeze). However, they did not find a consistent association with pulmonary functioning. Studies examining the latter were more likely to account for tobacco smoking, but the authors argue that most of these studies used inferior measures of tobacco exposure.

The preponderance of research on the health consequences of marijuana focuses on smoked marijuana, but smoking is only one way to take the drug (see chapter 2). In addition to eating marijuana-infused foods or using cannabinoid-infused lotions, consumers can also use vaporizers that heat marijuana to a point where cannabinoids evaporate, but below the point of combustion. This avoids creating some of the most dangerous components of marijuana smoke. One possible effect of marijuana legalization might be to make vaping relatively more common and smoking relatively less common. That might reduce the average rate of respiratory damage from marijuana use.

Does marijuana use cause cancer?

Marijuana smoke contains known carcinogens, in concentrations greater than their concentration in tobacco smoke. What is not clear is whether exposure causes cancer. Marijuana users typically inhale more deeply than cigarette smokers, but marijuana users consume far smaller quantities of marijuana than regular cigarette smokers consume of tobacco: while a pack a day (twenty grams of tobacco) is a typical cigarette habit, four grams a day is an extremely heavy marijuana habit. And, once again, these risks involve smoking; there are other ways to consume marijuana (see chapter 2).

What is lacking is clear epidemiological evidence from population studies showing that groups who smoked marijuana had higher rates of cancer than otherwise similar groups that abstained. The published research shows mixed results.

A 1997 study by Kaiser Permanente researcher Stephen Sidney and colleagues followed 65,000 individuals for an average of eight years to examine cancer incidence. They found that using marijuana in the past or being a current marijuana user did not increase the risk of respiratory cancer. Another large study by University of Utah professor Mia Hashibe, UCLA professor Donald Tashkin, and colleagues showed that marijuana does not increase the risk of lung or upper-aerodigestive-tract cancers, after accounting for cigarette smoking. (Controlling for tobacco smoking is important but tricky; 97 percent of adults who currently use marijuana have used tobacco at some point in their lives, so it is hard to study marijuana-only users, and there's at least some risk that increased marijuana smoking might encourage increased tobacco smoking.)

On the other hand, a study by Sarah Aldington and colleagues affiliated with the Cannabis and Respiratory Disease Research Group found that smoking the equivalent of a joint a day for a year increased the probability of lung cancer by 8 percent (i.e., 8 percent of the very small baseline probability, not an 8-percentage-point increase in the chance of getting cancer).

A 2015 epidemiologic review of marijuana and cancer by University of Utah's Yu-Hui Jenny Huang, UCLA's Donald Tashkin, and colleagues concluded:

> Studies on head and neck cancer reported increased and decreased risks, possibly because there is no association, or because risks differ by human papillomavirus status or geographic differences. The lung cancer studies largely appear not to support an association with marijuana use, possibly because of the smaller amounts of marijuana regularly smoked compared with tobacco. Three testicular cancer case-control studies reported increased risks with marijuana use. . . . For other cancer sites, there is still insufficient data to make any conclusions.

In part, the answer to the cancer question depends on the level of proof one demands. There are literally hundreds if not thousands of careful studies showing that smoking tobacco causes cancer. The literature on marijuana and cancer does not even begin to approach that level of evidence.

However, tobacco is the exception, not the rule, in being so well studied and the number of cancers caused being so large. In many contexts we do not wait for epidemiological studies before drawing conclusions. Food manufacturers are not allowed to add known carcinogens to their products regardless of whether there are epidemiological studies documenting an increase in cancer at the population level. On the other hand, cigarettes have not been banned, despite the overwhelming evidence that they cause cancer and a host of other ailments.

But the debate about marijuana and cancer is more complicated than just assessing whether or not smoking marijuana causes cancer. A number of studies suggest that some cannabinoids can inhibit the growth of tumors. (This is a separate issue from the use of marijuana in managing cancer symptoms and chemotherapy side effects, discussed in chapter 5.) Most of this research has been done in the laboratory, with cells in petri dishes or with animals, and there are questions about how the results might translate to humans.

How much harm does secondhand marijuana smoke cause?

Since marijuana smoke contains carcinogens and other irritants, it is possible that secondhand marijuana smoke could pose health threats to those who spend a lot of time around heavy users. Again, quantity matters: the average past-month marijuana smoker consumes less than two hundred grams a year, while the average cigarette smoker goes through two hundred grams of tobacco (ten packs) in two weeks. Less smoke suggests less secondhand risk. While there have been thousands of studies on the impact of secondhand tobacco smoke, the literature is almost silent when it comes to secondhand marijuana smoke.

Since marijuana remains illegal in many states and at the federal level and since drug tests are used in employment, schooling, and criminal justice settings, there is at least in theory another potential secondhand risk: that someone could test positive for marijuana after being around someone else who was smoking marijuana. To address this question, a group of researchers at Johns Hopkins University tested the effects of what they described as "extreme exposure" to secondhand marijuana smoke. The researchers put twelve people in an unventilated 10' by 13' room. Six participants were allowed to smoke as much as they wanted for sixty minutes; the other six were told to abstain. The smokers had access to pre-rolled joints that were 11.3 percent THC, and on average the smokers consumed 2.6 grams, which is more than even daily or near-daily users usually consume in a day. After an hour, a series of tests were conducted on all of the participants, and the authors concluded, "Exposure to secondhand marijuana smoke in an unventilated chamber the size of a small room produced minor increases in heart rate, mild to moderate subjective drug effects, and minor, but detectible, levels of performance impairment on some behavioral/cognitive assessments."

Even in this extreme situation involving an unventilated room, only one of the nonsmokers "failed" a urine test using the conventional level of 50 ng/ml; several others failed at a lower 20 ng/ml level. Further, when the study was repeated with a ventilated room, exposure was significantly reduced as "evidenced by much lower (in some cases undetectable) levels of cannabinoids in blood and urine and the absence of subjective and behavioral/cognitive effects." Thus, the problem of false-positive drug tests, like the problem of intoxication from secondhand smoke, is likely to be minor.

Is marijuana a "gateway drug"?

Few topics related to drugs have stirred more acrimonious debate than the gateway hypothesis. To the extent that there is any consensus in the professional literature, it is that claims about causal mechanisms rooted in pharmacology have been overstated in the past. But that doesn't prove that the problem is imaginary.

Adolescents who use marijuana—particularly those who start young—are much more likely to go on to use other drugs than their non-using peers.

What is less clear is whether marijuana use causes subsequent use of other drugs or whether it is merely a signal indicating the presence of underlying social, psychological, or physiological risk factors—such as weak parental supervision, a taste for intoxication, or a willingness to take risks—for both early marijuana use and later hard-drug use. There have been some rigorous studies with twins (comparing one who used marijuana with the other, who did not) that implicitly control for genetics and unmeasured family background, and some find evidence consistent with the gateway hypothesis. But since even "identical" twins aren't identical human beings, the question is how much of the correlation reflects causality.

Since most people have opportunities to try marijuana before they have opportunities to use harder drugs, marijuana use might precede hard-drug use even if both are caused by the same underlying personality traits. Indeed, Andrew Morral and colleagues at RAND's Drug Policy Research Center have shown that such explanations are completely consistent with available data.

However, the fact that causal connections are not needed to explain the observed correlations does not mean there is no causal connection. At least two very different mechanisms might produce a causal "gateway" effect. One is the consequences of the drug use itself. For example, trying marijuana might increase the taste for other mind-altering experiences or lead users to revise their judgments about other substances, inferring that they are more pleasurable or less risky than previously supposed. (The extent of this effect might depend in part on how much drug prevention education stresses the differences among drugs as opposed to their commonalities.)

The causal effect could also be rooted in social interactions. If acquiring and using marijuana leads to greater contact with peers who use and favor the use of drugs generally, those peer interactions might influence subsequent behavior. One version of this conjecture is that those peers could include people who sell other drugs, reducing the difficulty of locating potential supplies. (Note that, if this hypothesis is valid, legalizing marijuana might attenuate the gateway effect by divorcing the marijuana supply chain from the supply chains for other currently illicit drugs.)

The same logic applies to the two drugs that often come before marijuana in the developmental sequence: alcohol and nicotine. Early use of those drugs is a strong predictor of heavy marijuana use and of progression to harder drugs.

It also makes sense to distinguish the very common experience of having tried marijuana from the less common heavy use of marijuana; their effects on later drug use are not necessarily similar. Drug dependency leaves its mark on the brain for some time after actual drug-taking stops. It is possible—but not proven—that one of its effects might be increased vulnerability to dependency on other drugs (or potentially addictive nondrug behaviors such as gambling). Since the question is still open, a degree of humility is in order. That applies especially when we try to project our current knowledge—all of it gathered under prohibition, and much of it involving materials with lower levels of THC than today's marijuana, used by people who started later in life than today's typical user—to the effects marijuana might have as a legal drug. After legalization, any gateway effect could be stronger if the "vulnerability to dependency" story is right and if legalization turns out to increase the rate of progression to very heavy use, or weaker insofar as the gateway effect stems from illegal marijuana bringing youth into contact with suppliers of other illegal drugs or from false generalization by users from marijuana to other currently illegal drugs.

How does marijuana affect brain development?

A parallel issue concerns the lasting effects—if any—of using marijuana before the brain is fully developed. The associations are clear. For example, researchers at the University of Maryland report that adults who first used marijuana before age 15 were nearly five times more likely to meet clinical criteria for abuse or dependence of an illegal drug (whether marijuana or some other drug) than those who first used marijuana when they were 18 or older. But as with the gateway hypothesis, it is very hard to know how much of the association is causally attributable to early marijuana use, as opposed to being merely a correlation explained by common causes.

There are concerns that heavy use of marijuana can negatively influence brain development, especially among adolescents. So far, the research conducted with humans has been cross-sectional, meaning that the brain development of marijuana users and nonusers is compared at one point in time. Such studies do not allow researchers to draw conclusions about causality. There have been more rigorous studies conducted with animals which suggest that there could be a causal relationship between marijuana and brain development, but not everything true of lab rats turns out to be true of humans.

The studies on humans do tend to find brain changes associated with use. A recent review of the literature concluded that "regular cannabis use is associated with alterations in medial temporal, frontal and cerebellar brain regions." Harvard neuroscientist Jodi Gilman and colleagues conducted one of the studies in this literature that has generated the most interest. After scanning the brains of marijuana users and nonusers, they concluded, "The results of this study indicate that in young, recreational marijuana users, structural abnormalities in gray matter density, volume, and shape of the nucleus accumbens and amygdala can be observed." However, the researchers are clear that their study does not provide causal evidence and that they cannot rule out alternate explanations, such as early exposure to alcohol. (Moreover the definition of "recreational" included some subjects who probably met criteria for substance use disorder; the danger of generalizing from heavy users to all users is omnipresent in this research).

But if it turns out that marijuana use changes brain development, we must then ask, "Are these changes serious enough to lead to behavioral or intellectual consequences?" A new research project funded by the National Institute on Drug Abuse (NIDA), the Adolescent Brain Cognitive Development (ABCD) Study, should give us more insight into this question. The ABCD study will follow ten thousand teenagers for at least a decade, regularly interviewing them, conducting brain scans, and collecting biological data such as blood, urine, and genetic information. But, unfortunately, results won't be available for years.

Does using marijuana lead to cognitive impairment
and a reduction in IQ?

Being under the influence of marijuana can impair verbal and working memory, attention, and psychomotor performance. For some
users these cognitive effects are a feature of the experience, not a
bug. For employers and teachers, these effects can present important challenges. Compared to past-month alcohol users, past-month
marijuana users are much more likely to become intoxicated every
day or nearly every day, increasing the importance of any adverse
acute effects of intoxication on performance.

Some of the adverse performance effects may persist hours or
even days after intoxication in the conventional sense is over. For
example, a recent study found that "cannabis users have an increased
susceptibility to memory distortions" even some time after they no
longer feel intoxicated.

While there are debates about the practical importance of these
short-term effects, their existence is not really in dispute. The real
controversy concerns whether prolonged marijuana use can lead
to lasting reductions in cognitive functioning. Reviews of the academic literature on this topic suggest that the measured relationship is fairly weak and somewhat inconsistent. If there are effects,
they appear most likely to occur with very heavy users who started
using marijuana at an early age. There is great variation in these
studies with respect to how they measure cognitive functioning,
what populations they examine, and their ability to rule out alternative explanations.

One study stands out from this muddled literature in terms of
the attention it has received. Arizona State University psychologist Madeline Meier and colleagues reported that persistent (over
decades) daily or near-daily marijuana use among a cohort of 1,038
New Zealand residents born in the early 1970s was associated with
a reduction in IQ measured many years later. This was a rigorous
study that was able to demonstrate a dose-response relationship
with changes in IQ at the individual level, since the researchers had
also measured the subjects' IQ before they started using marijuana.
The authors were very careful to rule out many alternative explanations, and the study was published in a highly respected journal. Nevertheless, other researchers were quick to point out there

is really no way to rule out the possibility that some other unmeasured factors or personality traits might have caused both the cognitive decline and the marijuana use.

This study, the subsequent critiques, and responses to those critiques will likely play an important role in legalization debates in 2016 and beyond. After assessing the available research and the back-and-forth about this recent study, we and five other colleagues concluded, "It is premature to argue that long-term cognitive impairment has been clearly established, but just as premature to argue that the risks are nonexistent."

Does marijuana use affect education and employment?

One of the many concerns about adolescent substance use is that it could lead to worse performance in school. If students come to school intoxicated, it may be harder for them to pay attention and learn. Some parents also worry that substance use will increase the chance their kids will get caught up with a crowd that does not take school seriously.

There is clearly a correlation between marijuana use and poor performance in school. For example, a paper by University of New South Wales professor Ed Silins and colleagues combined three longitudinal surveys from Australia and New Zealand to examine the effect of marijuana use before the age of 17 on a number of outcomes. Even after controlling for several covariates, they found daily marijuana users were much less likely to complete high school or attain a college degree than nonusers. In addition, they also found a dose-response relationship with respect to intensity of marijuana use.

Yet the standard caution about causality also applies to these studies. A review of this literature by Michael Lynsky and Wayne Hall suggests that if there is a causal relationship (and they believe pot use does increase the risk of leaving school early), it is not because marijuana permanently impairs cognitive function; rather, it probably has to do with the social context in which marijuana is used. Specifically, they propose that early marijuana use appears to be associated with "adoption of an anti-conventional lifestyle characterized by affiliations with delinquent and substance-using peers, and the precocious adoption of adult roles including early school leaving, leaving the parental home and early parenthood." Work by

RAND statistician Dan McCaffrey and colleagues also suggests that the relationship between marijuana use and dropping out could be driven by an affiliation with deviant peers. If this is the mechanism, then the net effect of legalization on educational outcomes isn't obvious: it might increase marijuana use but at the same time weaken its relationship with deviance.

As for research on the effect of marijuana use on employment and worker productivity, the findings vary dramatically. Some studies find no effect; one finds that marijuana use reduces the probability of employment; another finds that off-the-job marijuana use actually increases wages; and a third shows that the same methodological approach yields precisely opposite findings depending on whether data from 1991 or 1992 are used. A review of this literature one of us did with RAND economist Rosalie Pacula identifies a number of reasons for the disparate findings, including that these studies do not always examine the same age groups or use the same definitions of marijuana use. So the question of the marijuana/employment relationship is far from settled.

Even with the shift in attitudes about marijuana, it is still possible for users to be punished by their employers if they fail a urine test. The military and most law enforcement agencies have policies against the use of marijuana and other drugs. But this is also an issue for civilians, even in states that have legalized. In a recent case involving someone who failed an employer-ordered drug test because of his medical-marijuana use, the Colorado Supreme Court ruled that businesses are allowed to fire employees for using marijuana off the clock because it is still prohibited under federal law.

Does using marijuana cause schizophrenia and other mental health problems?

There is a literature suggesting that marijuana use elevates the risk of schizophrenia and psychotic symptoms. Before exploring the evidence, it is important to clarify some terms.

There is a common misunderstanding that schizophrenia means having multiple personalities, but schizophrenia and multiple personality disorder are entirely distinct diagnoses. As far as we know, no one claims that marijuana use has anything to do with multiple personality disorder (which in any case is extremely rare).

Rather, schizophrenia is a debilitating mental health condition characterized by persistent psychotic symptoms (e.g., auditory hallucinations, the delusion that someone is controlling you), making it very difficult for those who suffer from the disorder to distinguish between real experience and illusion. It is often a lifelong condition that can be marked by cognitive impairment, depression, or apathy, derailing the lives of those who are diagnosed as well as those of their family and friends. Fortunately, it's relatively rare; past-year prevalence for adults in the United States is roughly 1 percent.

Experiencing psychotic symptoms at some point in one's life is much more common. Psychotic symptoms are not benign, but there is a world of difference between experiencing these symptoms occasionally and having schizophrenia. And there are a range of schizophrenia symptoms, including not only hallucinations and delusions but also others, such as jumbled speech and trouble paying attention, which are not so terribly different than familiar and expected effects of acute marijuana intoxication.

Statistically, there is a strong association between regular marijuana use and the emergence of psychotic symptoms. But does that mean that marijuana use causes psychotic symptoms, or that these symptoms can cause people to use marijuana, or that some third factor causes both?

Most of the research addressing this question follows individuals (usually starting in childhood) for several years and regularly inquires about substance use and mental health. A systematic review of these studies by University of Bristol psychologist Theresa Moore and colleagues examined the effect of marijuana consumption on symptoms associated with affective disorders such as depression and psychotic disorders such as schizophrenia. With respect to affective disorders, the authors concluded that the evidence was not consistent and some studies did not adequately rule out other explanations for the association. But they found stronger evidence implicating marijuana in causing psychotic symptoms. Pooling the results of seven longitudinal studies, they found that those who had ever used marijuana before were more likely to experience psychotic symptoms in the future. The effect was stronger when examining more frequent users, thus suggesting a dose-response mechanism. A more recent longitudinal study by Maastricht University Medical Center researchers Rebecca Kuepper, Jim van Os, and their

colleagues concluded, "Cannabis use is a risk factor for the development of incident psychotic symptoms . . . [and] continued cannabis
use might increase the risk for psychotic disorder by impacting the
persistence of symptoms."

But even if marijuana does increase the risk of psychotic symptoms, how important is that increase? Over a lifetime, between one
in four and one in five people experience psychotic symptoms at least
once. Moore and colleagues found that marijuana use increased that
risk by at least 40 percent, with the figure increasing for those who
used marijuana more often. The risk can be even higher for those
with a family history of psychotic disorders.

There are other approaches for examining the relationship
between marijuana and psychosis. For example, some researchers
examine whether large changes in marijuana use (e.g., measured in
household surveys) are correlated with changes in population-level
rates of schizophrenia as reflected in registry data. Analyzing eight
different age cohorts in Australia, University of New South Wales
professor Louisa Degenhardt, formerly of the Burnet Institute, and
colleagues found that there was no evidence of an increase in schizophrenia during the thirty years when there was a steep increase in
marijuana use.

The United Kingdom's Advisory Council on the Misuse of Drugs
(ACMD) conducted its own analysis and found that the prevalence
and annual incidence of schizophrenia and psychoses decreased
from 1996 to 2005. Past-month marijuana use increased from 1996 to
2002, but then fell from 2002 to 2006. Based on its review of the literature, the ACMD concluded that the "evidence points to a probable,
but weak, causal link" between cannabis use and psychotic disorders; however, the ACMD argued there is "unequivocal evidence
that the use of cannabis by people with schizophrenia increases the
likelihood of relapse, manifested by a worsening of symptoms and
often accompanied by a refusal to continue treatment."

There have also been biological studies that randomly assigned
subjects to different levels of intravenous THC (including a placebo).
These studies find that THC increases the probability of experiencing
psychotic symptoms for both healthy subjects and those with schizophrenia. In their review of the longitudinal and biological studies
with humans, psychiatrist Deepak D'Souza and colleagues at the
Department of Veterans Affairs conclude: "Exposure to cannabis is

neither a necessary nor a sufficient cause of schizophrenia. . . . More likely, cannabis exposure is a component or contributing cause that interacts with other known (genetic, environmental) and unknown factors." Based on the available evidence about marijuana and psychoses, Wayne Hall and Louisa Degenhardt go as far as to say, "If we had similar evidence of an association between using a pharmaceutical drug and an adverse effect, the drug would either be withdrawn from the market or would only be prescribed with clear warnings about the risk to patients and prescribers."

As more work is done exploring the links between marijuana use and mental health problems, we hope more attention is paid to the amount and type of marijuana used. As noted in chapter 1, there is reason to believe that the ratio of THC to CBD in marijuana could affect the mental-health consequences of consumption. That might suggest that contemporary marijuana is more dangerous than the marijuana whose use is reflected in historical statistics. On the other hand, it might also suggest that legalization with controls on potency and on cannabinoid ratios might lead to less mental illness in total than continued prohibition and a black market dominated by high-THC, low-CBD product.

Does using marijuana influence crime and delinquency?

The rate of marijuana use is higher among offenders than among non-offenders, but the conventional wisdom in the academic community is that both behaviors result from the same common causes, rather than from marijuana causing criminal offending. Heavy heroin and cocaine users who aren't rich may need to steal to support their habits, but a heavy heroin or cocaine habit can easily consume $15,000 per year; it's very hard to smoke up that much money in the form of pot.

Marijuana use by itself does not tend to induce violent crime; in fact, some studies suggest the opposite. A review of the evidence in a National Academy of Sciences study on violence concluded, "The majority of the evidence in experimental studies with animals and humans, as well as most data from chronic users, emphasizes that cannabis preparations (e.g., marihuana, hashish) or THC *decrease* aggressive and violent behavior" (emphasis added).

As for other types of crime, Trevor Bennett, a criminologist at the University of Glamorgan, and his colleagues systematically reviewed thirty studies about drug use and crime and found the association was much stronger for hard drugs like crack, heroin, and powder cocaine than it was for marijuana. While the association between marijuana use and general criminal offenses was positive and "statistically significant," the effect was small. In fact, one of Bennett's coauthors, David Farrington of Cambridge University, argued elsewhere that their results about the statistical association for marijuana should be thought of as inconclusive.

A number of longitudinal studies have examined the relationship between adolescent marijuana use and measures of future criminality. Those finding a positive correlation cannot escape the criticism that an unobserved third factor may be driving both results, but some studies are still more persuasive than others. In a particularly advanced statistical analysis, Johns Hopkins researcher Kerry Green and her colleagues found that in a cohort of urban African Americans, using marijuana more than twenty times before age 16 was positively correlated with adult property crime, even after accounting for dropping out of high school, progression to the use of harder drugs, and several other variables. The authors make it very clear that because of potential unobserved confounders, their results are consistent with a causal story but are not definitive evidence of a causal relationship.

Of course marijuana use under prohibition directly causes crime and delinquency in the form of violations of drug laws. And it's possible that the experience of arrest and even brief confinement, plus the consequences of acquiring an arrest record, might push some youngsters down the wrong path. (For example, the fear of arrest tends to decrease after a first juvenile arrest.)

Legalization would reduce marijuana-related arrests but not eliminate them; some activities, such as sales to minors, would remain banned. There are about as many alcohol-related arrests (for public drunkenness, minor-in-possession, DUI, etc.) per dependent alcohol user as there are marijuana arrests per person dependent on marijuana (see chapter 6).

Does marijuana cause automobile crashes?

Being stoned impairs driving performance. Both sides of the legalization debate agree that no one should drive under the influence of marijuana. The question is just how dangerous it is. The answer seems to be that driving stoned isn't as dangerous as driving drunk, but driving under the influence of both drugs is worse than either by itself.

How much marijuana adds to the risks of driving, both in terms of the risk of a crash and in terms of the contribution of marijuana to the overall rate of accidents and fatalities, turns out to be a hard question to answer precisely.

Marijuana is unlike alcohol in that its metabolites stay in the body for a number of days after intoxication. If someone is in a traffic accident and has a positive urine test for marijuana, that shows past use but not necessarily current intoxication; to measure the current level of the drug requires a mouth swab or a blood test, and even those are harder to interpret than a breathalyzer test result. That makes it harder to study the effects of stoned driving. The experimental research on marijuana-impaired driving examines how drivers under the influence of marijuana performed in driving simulators or on closed courses. Being stoned seems to interfere more with the mechanical process of driving and the ability to respond to unexpected situations than it does with judgment.

The "culpability studies" approach analyzes multicar accidents to determine which driver caused the crash, and then assesses whether the responsible driver was more likely than the other driver to have been using marijuana. The early reviews of these studies did not find that those with cannabinoids in their blood were more likely to be culpable, but more recent (and more sophisticated) studies show that marijuana does increase crash risk, with higher doses creating greater risks; adding alcohol makes things worse.

Pulling together a large literature with a variety of conflicting findings, it appears that driving while intoxicated on marijuana has a relative risk of about two: that is, being stoned roughly doubles the risk of a crash, compared to being sober. That's considerably smaller than the risks of driving drunk, which range from about a factor of six at the legal limit of 0.08 percent blood alcohol content to a factor of more than thirty at 0.15 percent. That difference may result from the fact that alcohol is more likely than marijuana to make its users reckless and aggressive.

Unfortunately, many marijuana users underestimate the risks of stoned driving, and surveys suggest that they actually get behind the wheel after smoking much more often than drinkers do when drunk. That presumably raises the total contribution of stoned driving to overall accident risks.

The lack of a marijuana equivalent of an alcohol breath test also poses problems for enforcing the laws against it. Some states have "zero tolerance" laws which define someone as under the influence of a controlled substance if there is evidence of *any* THC in the body. Under such laws someone could be punished for intoxicated driving as a result of marijuana use days before the incident. Other states define a threshold level of THC in blood, just as the drunk-driving laws define a threshold amount of alcohol. Still, someone can be legally "under the influence" according to that rule without being actually impaired. On the other hand, experience with alcohol has shown the enormous difficulty of trying to prove impairment by observing behavior.

Does mothers' prenatal marijuana use affect their babies' health?

The stakes, passions, and uncertainties surrounding marijuana's health effects are all greatly multiplied when it comes to the effects of prenatal exposure. NIDA director Nora Volkow and colleagues noted in a recent article that "our understanding of the long-term effects of prenatal exposure to marijuana in humans is very poor."

Such exposure is not rare; researchers with the Centers for Disease Control and Prevention note that 4 percent of pregnant women self-report using marijuana in the month before they were surveyed. The number jumps above 7 percent for those in the first trimester, presumably because some used before they knew they were pregnant. Given stigmatization of behaviors that risk fetal health, rates of underreporting are likely to be even higher among pregnant women than in the general population, so the actual rates of prenatal use are probably higher than those reported in surveys.

How bad is that for fetal development? The available evidence is mixed. Prenatal exposure may adversely affect neurodevelopment; that has been shown both by studying the biological effects directly and by following the early lives of children whose mothers did or did not use marijuana while pregnant. The two major research projects which followed expectant mothers and their children after birth both found an association between prenatal marijuana exposure and poorer cognitive development, attention, and executive functioning. As always, it's hard to separate out the effects of marijuana on the fetus from those of the behavioral differences between women who keep smoking pot after getting pregnant and those who either don't smoke at all or stop. The fact that women who smoke marijuana are more likely to also smoke tobacco—a known source of fetal damage—further complicates the interpretation of the results.

One perhaps surprising finding from one of the projects is that prenatal marijuana exposure predicts the child's marijuana consumption at age 22, even after accounting for the parent's marijuana use when the child reaches that age. Whether or not this novel finding will be replicated in other studies remains to be seen.

Should mothers who use marijuana breastfeed their babies?

There is a sharp debate about whether mothers who occasionally use marijuana should avoid breastfeeding. The debate is not over whether it is a good idea for mothers who breastfeed to use marijuana. In 2012, the American Academy of Pediatrics published a policy statement about breastfeeding, arguing that street drugs, including marijuana, "can be detected in human milk, and their use by breastfeeding mothers is of concern, particularly with regard to the infant's long-term neurobehavioral development and thus are contraindicated." So recommending that women who breastfeed should not use marijuana is not controversial.

However, given the well-documented advantages of breastfeeding, there is debate about whether to recommend that mothers who cannot or will not stop using marijuana should refrain from breastfeeding.

In 2015, the Academy of Breastfeeding Medicine—a group of physicians dedicated to the promotion of breastfeeding—released revised guidelines, noting, "The lack of long-term follow-up data on infants exposed to varying amounts of marijuana via human milk, coupled with concerns over negative neurodevelopmental outcomes in children with in utero exposure, should prompt extremely careful consideration of the risks versus benefits of breastfeeding in the setting of moderate or chronic marijuana use." While recommending that doctors ask mothers to abstain from marijuana while breastfeeding, the academy argued, "Information regarding long-term effects of marijuana use by the breastfeeding mother on the infant remains insufficient to recommend complete abstention from breastfeeding initiation or continuation [for mothers who use marijuana] based on the scientific evidence at this time."

This position has caused a stir, with Dr. Lauren Jansson of Johns Hopkins University's Center for Addiction and Pregnancy and her colleagues arguing that the recommendation is "erroneous and disappointing" because of concerns about THC affecting infants' cognitive development. Not surprisingly, this prompted a response from the original authors, and the debate will likely continue.

How does parental marijuana use influence child welfare?

As Harold Pollack of the University of Chicago has observed, parental substance use is as much a pediatric issue as an obstetric one: the impact of the drug on parental (especially maternal) behavior after the child is born may be more important than the impact of whatever drugs reach the developing fetus.

Unfortunately, there also does not appear to be much research examining the effect of parental marijuana use on children, even though it affects large numbers of children. There are about seven million people under 18 who live with a parent who is a current marijuana user; more than three million of them live with a parent who used marijuana on twenty or more days in the past month, and one million with a parent who meets diagnostic criteria for marijuana abuse or dependence.

Current marijuana use by parents is associated with a greater risk of tobacco, alcohol, and marijuana use among their adolescent children; however, the jury is still out on whether this is a causal relationship.

Another potentially worrisome correlation was identified by UC San Diego sociologist Davis Phillips and colleagues. They found that deaths from sudden infant death syndrome (SIDS, or "crib death") spike the day after April 20—which some users treat as a marijuana-smoking holiday—as they do on New Year's Day and on weekends. There are a number of hypotheses (e.g., parental caretakers are more likely to sleep in, exposure to smoke, concurrent use of alcohol), but at this point no one has nailed down the mechanism. The effect is too big to be merely random.

While parental substance use is the main reason that children are removed from their homes, the conventional wisdom is that marijuana is not an important contributor when compared to alcohol, cocaine, methamphetamine, and other drugs. That said, parents arrested for marijuana may attract attention from Child Protective Services, and in some states a misdemeanor marijuana conviction can create serious problems for those seeking to adopt or foster a child.

Is marijuana really safer than alcohol?

Marijuana is much safer than alcohol in two very important respects: alcohol use is much more likely to lead to fatal overdose and to trigger violence. More generally, alcohol clearly kills more people. But a substance can be safer in some ways, yet riskier in others.

For example, a sufficient dose of heroin can kill even a healthy person, while almost no one dies of acute cigarette overdose. Yet the long-term consequences of smoking kill over 425,000 smokers in the United States each year; by contrast, chronic use of (pure) heroin causes no significant organ damage. (Heroin users' poor health has more to do with poverty, dirty needles, and impurities than with pure heroin itself.) So heroin is worse on one outcome (acute effects), and cigarettes are worse on another (chronic organ damage).

Likewise, marijuana may cause some problems at rates that match those of alcohol, even if alcohol is much worse in terms of violence and acute toxicity. For example, among the 20 million past-month marijuana users recorded in 2012, 14 percent meet DSM-IV criteria for marijuana dependence (2.7 million out of 20 million). The corresponding proportion for past-month alcohol users, based on the same survey, questions, and estimation methods, is only 6 percent (8.8 million out of 131 million). Both the 14 percent and the 6 percent may be underestimates, but since they are derived in the same manner, the relative rate (14 percent/6 percent, or 2.4 to 1) is less vulnerable to reporting bias and suggests that marijuana may be associated with more dependence per month of use, at least as used in the United States at the time of that survey. (This wouldn't be true if instead we compared marijuana use to binge drinking: i.e., to getting drunk.)

Table 3.1 Rates of Problem Mentions per Past-Month User of Marijuana and Alcohol

Abbreviated question wording	Marijuana		Alcohol		Relative rate
	Number reporting problem (millions)	Number per past-month user	Number reporting problem (millions)	Number per past-month user	
Needed to use more to get desired effect	4.75	0.25	10.30	0.08	3.3
Spent a lot of time getting or using the drug	9.67	0.51	21.27	0.16	3.2
Drug caused serious problems at home, work, or school	1.49	0.08	3.85	0.03	2.8
Drug took time from work/school/other important activities	2.26	0.12	6.18	0.05	2.6
Tried to limit use but failed	1.49	0.08	6.30	0.05	1.7
Tried to cut down but failed	1.36	0.07	6.10	0.05	1.6
Drug caused problems with emotions, nerves, or mental health	2.11	0.11	9.75	0.07	1.5
Continued use despite those problems	1.33	0.07	5.96	0.04	1.6
Drug caused problems with family or friends	1.59	0.08	7.45	0.06	1.5
Continued use despite those problems	1.22	0.06	5.09	0.04	1.7
Using same amount had less effect	1.94	0.10	11.35	0.08	1.2
Drug put you in physical danger	1.28	0.07	10.84	0.08	0.8

Data source: Authors' analysis of National Survey on Drug Use and Health

Dependence is inferred based on questions about substance-related issues arising within the past year. Table 3.1 lists the questions for which the number answering yes (for either substance) was at least 5 percent of the number of past-month users. For each question and substance, Table 3.1 gives the number saying yes, the rate per past-month user, and in the last column the relative rate (how much more common the problem was per marijuana user than per alcohol user).

Problem rates were relatively higher for marijuana in domains concerning life functioning, such as "Did your use cause serious problems at home, work or school?" There were no appreciable differences for items related to physical danger or health (although the latter was rare for either substance). Similar analyses with data on high-school students finds that marijuana users reported more problems with lower energy and decreased school or job performance, while alcohol users reported more adverse effects on relationships with friends and significant others.

Of course legalization might change the relative riskiness of the substances if some problems are exacerbated by the illegality of marijuana (e.g., legalization should reduce time spent trying to obtain the drug). Legalization might also make marijuana look relatively better if it increased the number of occasional users who did not experience problems, or worse if the increase in use continues to come mostly from greater intensity of use, not increases in prevalence. Only time will tell. But while marijuana may be safer than alcohol in some respects, there are dimensions along which marijuana as used today appears to be just as problematic, and absolute statements about one substance being safer than the other ought to be avoided.

Additional Reading

Caulkins, Jonathan P., Beau Kilmer, Mark A. R. Kleiman, et al. "Considering Marijuana Legalization."

Compton, Richard, and Amy Berning. *Drug and Alcohol Crash Risk.*

Hall, Wayne. "What Has Research Over the Past Two Decades Revealed About the Adverse Health Effects of Recreational Cannabis Use?"

Hasin, Deborah S., et al. "Prevalence of Marijuana Use Disorders in the United States Between 2001–2002 and 2012–2013."

Hedlund, James. *Drug-Impaired Driving: A Guide for What States Can Do.*

Huang, Yu-Hui, et al. "An Epidemiologic Review of Marijuana and Cancer: An Update."

Jaques, Siobhan C., et al. "Cannabis, the Pregnant Woman and Her Child: Weeding out the Myths."

Kleiman, Mark A. R., Celeste J. Miller, and Jeremy A. Ziskind. "Driving While Stoned: Issues and Policy Options."

Room, Robin, et al. *Cannabis Policy.*

Volkow, Nora, et al., "Adverse Health Effects of Marijuana Use."

4

WHAT IS KNOWN ABOUT
THE NONMEDICAL BENEFITS
OF USING MARIJUANA?

Astoundingly little. Much is claimed, but little is known.

One thing is certain: people across the globe have enjoyed it for thousands of years, and more than 100 million do so today. Users report that getting high is relaxing and pleasurable, and that it contributes to other pleasures, including food, music, dancing, art, conversation, humor, and sex.

Some believe that marijuana intoxication enhances their creative work in fields ranging from music to mathematics, or that the experience of having been stoned in the past gives them access, in their nonstoned hours, to a usefully different style of thought.

But even simple, easy-to-test claims such as "Marijuana users who like Mozart enjoy listening to Mozart more with marijuana than without" lack anything approaching good scientific evidence to support them.

Of course, even if we knew more than we do about the benefits, we'd still need to know about the harms. The same drug can be both helpful and harmful: helpful at some times and harmful at others; helpful when used carefully but dangerous if abused; helpful to some people and harmful to others. Perhaps the least constructive—albeit common—approach to writing about marijuana is to start from the desire to "prove" that it is either the source of all evils or the cure for all ills.

Why don't we know more about the benefits of marijuana use?

Studying the benefits of intoxication is inherently difficult; most of them are personal, subjective, and hard to observe. There are several additional challenges unique to studying marijuana intoxication, including a frustrating set of administrative rules (see chapter 5).

A more fundamental challenge that pertains everywhere, not just in the United States, is that while THC is the primary psychoactive agent, cannabis products also contain varying amounts of scores of other psychoactive chemicals (e.g., CBD) that modulate or otherwise interact with THC. For example, one recent review of forty-five neuroimaging studies of the effects of cannabinoids on brain functioning found that THC and CBD generally have opposing effects in both human and animal subjects. Such findings greatly complicate research, because they imply one has to study various combinations of the many cannabinoids, not just varying doses of THC, and also because they limit the value of much of the older research with plant-based marijuana material: those studies rarely documented the amounts of other cannabinoids administered to the subjects.

The ratios of these active agents can vary dramatically across strains and over time. The very-high-THC preparations that dominate the contemporary market for expensive marijuana tend to have high ratios of THC to CBD, and it is possible that high-ratio products increase the risk of panic attacks and dysphoria. So asking about, or trying to study, the benefits (or harms) of marijuana generically is a little bit like asking what wine tastes like, as if merlot and champagne were interchangeable. Furthermore, even for a single well-defined cannabis product, the effects still vary from individual to individual and from occasion to occasion.

It's possible to compare users to non-users on a variety of dimensions, but such comparisons don't give usable estimates of the impact of marijuana use: those who choose to use the drug—especially while it remains illegal—surely differ systematically from those who choose not to use it.

We can study the immediate effects of being under the influence, but those results don't tell us much about the lasting effects, and especially the effects of long-term heavy use. And of course the opinions of heavy, chronic users about the effects of their favorite drug need to be taken with a grain of salt, or maybe two. (Testimonials from people who once used marijuana but have stopped, and who still say that their past use enhances their current lives, perhaps deserve more respectful attention, but there doesn't seem to have been any systematic attempt to collect such retrospective evaluations.)

Thus even under the best of conditions it would be difficult to study the benefits of marijuana use.

Would there be more high-quality research if marijuana were legal nationally?

National legalization would remove some administrative barriers to doing research on marijuana, but it's not clear who would fund objective studies about nonmedical benefits. And rules about protecting human research subjects would continue to make it difficult for scientists to offer marijuana to those who had never used it. In the absence of carefully gathered before-and-after data—ideally on subjects chosen at random to receive marijuana or not—it will remain hard to discover which of the impacts outlast the period of intoxication.

So legalization may not bring a wealth of reliable new knowledge; after all, much of what passes for "research" about (entirely legal) nutritional supplements and herbal remedies doesn't pass the scientific giggle test. The licit marijuana industry might prove no more reliable a source of knowledge about marijuana than the nutraceutical sector is about its products, or than cigarette companies are about the effects of smoking.

Is there a "stoned" way of thinking?

Some of the argument about marijuana policy has to do with the adverse side effects of use: accidents, health damage, and drug dependency. But that cannot fully account for the passion of some partisans on both sides of the question. Lurking in the background is the question of whether the *intended* effects of pot smoking ought to be regarded as valuable or harmful.

William Bennett, who as the director of the Office of National Drug Control Policy under George H. W. Bush was the first legislatively authorized "drug czar," once said of marijuana legalization, "Why in God's name foster the use of a drug that makes you stupid?" Since this comment was made well in advance of the (hotly contested) finding that long-term intensive pot smoking permanently lowers IQ scores, presumably Bennett was describing the acute, intoxicated state. In his view, those effects could be summed up as being "stupid."

At the other end of the spectrum, natural-health physician Andrew Weil's book *The Natural Mind* offers a spirited defense of what Weil calls the "stoned" way of thinking. He identifies "stonedness" with "states of consciousness other than the ordinary, ego-centered waking state" such as dreaming or meditative calm. "Straight" thinking, on this account, has five tendencies: dominance of the intellect; attachment to the senses and thus to external reality; attention to form over content, leading to materialism; a focus on differences rather than similarities; and "negative thinking, pessimism, and despair." Weil depicts straight thinking as literal-minded, linear, unsubtle, humorless, and hubristic (mistaking "our perceptions of reality for reality itself"), and as leading to such misguided (in Weil's view) activities as the use of insecticides and antibiotics, Western medicine, and political action.

Table 4.1 tries to assign the members of several pairs of opposites to one side or the other of the "straight" versus "stoned" division as we understand Weil's conception of the distinction. Our goal is to set the stage for considering whether occasional marijuana intoxication is good or bad by trying to describe what mental processes, attitudes, and actions it is imagined to produce.

Is "stoned thinking" valuable?

Some will find themselves consistently preferring one or the other side of Table 4.1; others will be more inclined to seek an appropriate balance. If occasional pot smoking does indeed promote "stonedness" in this sense, then (nondependent) use might seem like a net benefit to those who think that contemporary society is too rigid and uptight and insufficiently tolerant and creative. It would seem like a net cost to those who think that our problems result more from an excessively permissive, insufficiently conscientious culture. Even if there were an objective truth of the matter (which seems like a terribly "straight" thing to claim), there is no reason to think that the "right" answer should be a constant over time, or across

Table 4.1 A Table of Oppositions

Straight	Stoned
Authoritarian	Permissive
Prose	Poetry
Straightforward	Subtle
Serious	Humorous
Conscientious	Creative
Hierarchy	Equality
Exchange	Gift
Business	Pleasure
Ant	Grasshopper
Artificial or synthetic	Natural
Apollonian	Dionysian
Precision	Approximation
Analytical	Holistic
Sequence	Recursion
Certainty	Doubt
Football	Ultimate Frisbee
Frank Sinatra	John Coltrane
John Wayne	Jack Nicholson
To-do lists	Living in the moment
Top-ten lists	Tables of oppositions

population subgroups. Perhaps this helps explain why sensible people can have such diametrically opposed—and passionately felt—opinions about marijuana use.

In philosophic terms, the attack on "straight thinking" reflects an often-stated critique of a certain kind of rationalism (often associated with Descartes): a style of thinking typical of both contemporary science and the contemporary practice in business and statecraft. In terms of the psychology of personality, Weil's "Straightsville" would be characterized as having deficient openness, excessive negative affect, and too rigid a form of conscientiousness. In theological terms, legalistic traditions and organized religion tend toward the "straight" while mystical traditions and private spirituality tend toward the "stoned." In generational terms, the baby boomers and the cultural Sixties were "stoned," compared to the "straight" Depression/World War II and Korean War generations and the cultural Fifties. The culture war that now plays such a role in American political life has a "straight" versus "stoned" dimension. And that is part of what makes marijuana and marijuana legalization so controversial, even in the absence of any strong evidence that smoking pot has any actual link with "stonedness" in Weil's sense.

But is Weil's description really about the effects of using marijuana, or does it rather portray the cultural and personality traits of the people who pioneered widespread marijuana use in the 1960s? In the 1960s, high-school students who self-reported marijuana use were more likely than their non-using peers to report that they planned to go on to college. Stereotypically, bookworms smoked pot while jocks drank beer. It was an easy leap, but not a valid one, from that observation to the idea that pot might make its users more reflective. Over the intervening years, pot has moved down the socioeconomic ladder—the association between regular marijuana use and educational attainment is now negative—but perceptions about it may still be caught in a cultural lag.

The rise of the Sixties counterculture certainly was contemporaneous with the rise of marijuana use, but so many other things were changing at that time that it is hard to sort cause from effect. The same is true at an individual level: there are studies that find more creative or "stoned" styles of thought among those who have used marijuana, but is the right explanation for such a correlation that getting high leads to openness and intuitive thinking, or that openness and intuitive thinking lead to getting high? The answer might vary from time to time, place to place, and group to group.

Thus it is entirely possible that the hopes of the advocates and the fears of the opponents are equally ungrounded.

Does marijuana use enhance creativity?

Maybe. Maybe not. The scholarly literature offers no definitive answer.

Marijuana's effect on creativity is perhaps the most discussed of its potential nonmedical benefits, an effect famously endorsed by Apple guru Steve Jobs, and one that seems eminently plausible given THC's documented effects on reducing inhibitory control. Yet the research evidence for this claim is tenuous. Type the search terms "(CANNABIS or MARIJUANA) and CREATIVITY" into PubMed—the primary database for serious studies in biology and medicine—and one gets a grand total of twenty hits. Ten of the twenty are old (from 1980 or before). Many shed no light on causality, merely documenting correlations or noting the quest for creativity as a motivation for using. Of the two modern experimental studies, one found that marijuana improved verbal fluency—but only in those in the lowest quartile of baseline creativity scores. The second found no effects on divergent-thinking tasks at low doses of THC and adverse effects at higher doses.

Certainly some people believe that they are more creative under the influence, but those opinions cannot be accepted at face value; many people also believe that they sing better while drunk. On the other hand, the role of marijuana in the cultures of jazz, reggae, hip-hop, and Beat poetry is harder to dismiss.

The effects of marijuana on mental functioning are complex and poorly understood, but it is possible to lay out a mechanistic explanation of how marijuana might enhance creativity. While the user is under the influence, chemicals alter the experience of time and the "gating" process that filters out most sensory input before it reaches consciousness. Marijuana also interferes with short-term working memory and the "executive function" that allocates attention across topics and activities: performance on what psychometricians call "divided attention" tasks degrades sharply. The person who begins a sentence and forgets what he is saying before reaching the end of it is a staple of stoned humor.

These alterations seem to enhance some kinds of sensual experience; colors, sounds, tastes, textures, and aromas may seem more intense, and may actually (this is not known) be more sensitively perceived. Slowing of the time sense may allow more attention to the details of music, whether listening or performing.

Altered gating may occur at the level of thoughts as well as sensations. If creativity is defined as the capacity to make valid but non-obvious connections between seemingly disparate elements, then it is not hard to see how a less stringent set of filters might enhance it.

One of the most widely reported effects of marijuana use is increased proneness to laughter. Insofar as laughter depends on the perception of incongruity, it's not hard to imagine that laughter and creativity might be helped or impaired by the same things. But the mere possibility of a connection is not evidence; we don't actually know whether people who smoke pot have more laughter in their lives overall.

Also unknown is the extent—if any—to which marijuana users can learn ways of thinking while under the influence that then become available to them while not actively high. If that were possible, it would constitute an important potential benefit of marijuana smoking, and thus of marijuana legalization. That makes the failure of the current research enterprise to address such questions (or the broader question of "stoned thinking") all the more frustrating.

Can marijuana use enhance athletic performance?

At first blush, or to anyone who remembers Zonker, the feckless, hapless Yale pass receiver from the early *Doonesbury* comic strips, this possibility seems far-fetched. But the International Olympic Committee banned marijuana as a potential performance enhancer in 1989, and the World Anti-Doping Agency has prohibited its use in competitive sports since 2004.

Although scientific studies tend to find negative acute effects on athletic performance, that fact has not stopped some from arguing that marijuana may give some athletes an advantage by improving concentration and reducing anxiety, fear, depression, and tension. For example, the *Wall Street Journal* recently published a piece titled "The Debate over Running While High," which featured anecdotes from some ultra-marathoners. One veteran runner reported, "The person who is going to win an ultra is someone who can manage their pain, not puke, and stay calm. . . . Pot does all three of those things." Yet the article also notes:

Pot's original inclusion on the Olympic banned list had more to do with politics and ethics than its perceived performance enhancement, said veteran drug tester Don Catlin, who founded the UCLA Olympic Analytic Laboratory. "You can find some people who argue that marijuana has performance-enhancing characteristics. They are few and far between," he said. "It's seen more as a drug of abuse than as a drug of performance enhancement."

What role does cannabis play in worship?

With a few notable exceptions, only a modest one.

Rituals involving cannabis seem to be quite ancient, but current ritual use is not widespread. Among Hindus, some devotees of Shiva regard cannabis use as pleasing to the goddess, and cannabis is used in some Sikh festivals. Cannabis is central to Rastafarian culture, and not only in church. Sufism—the mystical tradition of Islam—has a long relationship with cannabis use. A number of churches seem to have formed specifically to be able to claim a religious exemption from the drug laws; those claims have been rejected by the courts.

Overall, though, the tension between drug laws and religious freedom is not nearly so strong with respect to cannabis as it is with respect to hallucinogens.

So there's no real evidence of any benefits?

It's fair to say that evidence of measurable nonmedical benefits, and especially of lasting benefits, remains equivocal, and mostly not up to the standards used in evaluating claims of medical efficacy. But that laboratory-and-dataset approach is only one way of looking at the value of an activity. The other way—characteristic of economics rather than psychology or biomedical research—is to look at behavior in the market. Tens of millions of people enjoy using marijuana, as evidenced by their willingness to pay even the inflated prices generated by illicit markets and to face the legal risks and social stigma associated with being "drug users." Why? Answering that question may be complicated for those who are dependent, but it is simple for the majority of users who are not. Primarily they use it because they enjoy it.

But neither domestic law nor international treaty recognizes enjoyment as a reason to allow the use of otherwise banned drugs.

Why should mere pleasure count as a benefit?

Well, why *shouldn't* pleasure count as a benefit? Marijuana dependency is a real problem, and the demand for marijuana by those dependent on it isn't evidence that it benefits them. But that doesn't mean that the pleasures of ordinary use are imaginary, or that getting stoned somehow shows a defective character.

Some will protest that pleasure is all well and good, but it should not enter the equation when there is a real risk of serious injury or death. That line of reasoning should not persuade anyone who skis, climbs mountains, or rides motorcycles—or, for that matter, anyone who drinks alcohol. We have long known how much football, at every level from high school to the Super Bowl, damages its players' knees; now we're learning more and more about how much it harms their brains. Yet few propose making football illegal.

Economists have a straightforward way of evaluating the benefits consumers receive from the things they buy and use: the principle of "willingness to pay." Clearly, anyone who buys something is willing to pay its price rather than go without it. But many people who buy at the market price would have been willing to pay more, if necessary. The difference between the actual price of a good and the maximum a consumer would have been willing to pay for it is called the "consumer surplus."

The problem of drug dependency makes the evaluation of consumer surpluses more difficult. Marijuana, like any other drug when used as part of a pattern of dependent behavior, may actually create "consumer deficits" (a concept unknown to orthodox economic analysis). But the vast majority of marijuana users are not in the grip of dependency; they use the drug because they want to use it.

Slightly over 40 percent of the days of use in the United States involve people who self-report having tried to cut down or quit in the past year. Since not everyone who has a drug problem grasps that fact, and not everyone who acknowledges a problem tries to quit, that likely understates how much marijuana is used by people who use too much of the drug. Still, at least a large minority of the stoned hours are hours of enjoyment rather than entrapment. Counting people rather than hours, most users aren't abusers.

Prohibition raises prices and imposes nonmonetary costs. Those are sources of loss to actual and potential consumers—at least those who are not dependent. Removing those costs—letting people do more of what they like doing, at lower cost and with fewer risks, fears, and penalties—ought to count, by all the canons of ordinary economic reasoning, as potential benefits of making marijuana legally available. The sum of those gains, if the United States were to legalize marijuana, would be at least in the billions of dollars per year—perhaps in the tens of billions (see chapter 9).

Additional Reading

Erowid. "Cannabis Effects."

Grinspoon, Lester. *Marihuana Reconsidered.*

Huestis, Marilyn A., Irene Mazzoni, and Olivier Rabin. "Cannabis in Sport."

Weil, Andrew. *The Natural Mind.*

5

WHAT ARE THE MEDICAL BENEFITS OF MARIJUANA?

Is marijuana medicine?

Marijuana products used for medical purposes range from conventional cannabis flowers to synthetic cannabinoids produced in a lab. Even among plant extracts, there's a contrast between boutique oils made by individual farmers and processors (e.g., Charlotte's Web, which is discussed in chapter 13) and extracts produced to pharmaceutical standards (e.g., Sativex, which is roughly half THC and half CBD). Marinol, a pill consisting of pure THC, produced synthetically rather than from the plant, was approved for prescription use in the United States more than twenty years ago.

Few people object to the project of developing pharmaceutical products from cannabis, if those products can pass the strict scrutiny of the Food and Drug Administration. There are, though, complaints about how slowly that system moves, and about the regulatory barriers to developing such products.

The heated debate instead surrounds products on the other end of the spectrum, particularly smoked marijuana and the "medical edibles" that fill shelves at dispensaries. These cannabis-plant products, variable from batch to batch, are more like herbal preparations such as echinacea, ginkgo biloba, or St. John's wort than they are like conventional pharmaceuticals. Herbal products can rarely be marketed as medicines in the United States. The FDA did not even consider approving "botanical products" as drugs until the mid-2000s, and just a handful of the hundreds of applications have been approved (e.g., Veregen and Fulyzaq).

On the other hand, the United States generally takes a quite relaxed regulatory posture toward herbals that are marketed as "dietary supplements." The FDA does not require manufacturers to demonstrate the safety or efficacy of dietary supplements as long as the manufacturers make no medical claims concerning the product and the product does not have known toxic side effects. Marijuana—meaning the dried plant material—is an herbal product about which suppliers do claim medical benefits for treating everything from Alzheimer's to post-traumatic stress disorder. And although it has low toxicity, it is psychoactive and dependence-inducing, complications that do not pertain to ginger or milk thistle. Because it is a controlled substance under federal drug laws, it can't legally be supplied as an "herbal"; the only legal way to get a controlled substance is by prescription, and prescriptions can be written only for FDA-approved drugs. The medical-marijuana movement, and the associated industry, wants to relax those rules, in one way or another.

There is a deeper argument here: conventional Western medicine stresses giving known quantities of specific molecules, while other traditions place more reliance on plant materials containing a variety of chemicals. In some cases, the latter approach is probably superior. For example, vitamin C in fresh fruit is widely believed to have benefits not present in pure ascorbic acid; it seems some of the other chemicals in fresh fruit promote the work of the vitamin. Medical-marijuana advocates argue that similar "entourage effects" make herbal cannabis more medically useful than purified extracts. For example, the protective effects of CBD may help Sativex outperform pure THC. But suggestion is not evidence.

But isn't smoking unhealthy?

Yes, smoking is unhealthy. So is exposure to X-rays. Every medical procedure involves weighing side effects against therapeutic effects.

If some patient with terminal cancer gets substantial symptomatic relief from marijuana, the lung insult from smoking isn't a substantial objection to using it, any more than the stomach irritation from aspirin is a strong reason not to take that when you have a headache.

The data showing that marijuana smoking is harmful generally come from people who smoked many joints a day for years (see chapter 3). If it turned out that for some strain of marijuana taking

one puff at bedtime acted as a sleeping aid, taking that puff occasionally wouldn't pose any great health risk.

Of course, medicines (or delivery mechanisms) with fewer or less
serious harmful side effects are to be preferred. Many of the harmful effects of smoking can be avoided by vaporizing. A vaporizer
is a device that uses external heat—for example, from an electrical
resistance element—to transform the active chemicals in marijuana
from solids to gases (and to decarboxylate the inactive tetrahydro-
canabolic acid [THC-A] into the active delta-9-tetrahydrocannabinol
[THC]), allowing the patient or other user to inhale the chemicals
in the form of a vapor without the mix of toxic chemicals and par-
ticulates in smoke. Even elaborate vaporizers are cheap compared
to many medical devices. And vaping is not the only alternative to
smoking; medical-marijuana dispensaries (and retail stores) sell
THC-infused edibles of all kinds, as well as beverages, lotions, and
other THC-infused products. Sativex (a cannabis extract approved
as medicine in Canada and parts of Europe) is supplied as a sublingual spray. Thus the fear of smoking need not be an objection to the
use of marijuana as a medicine, even though in practice much of the
marijuana purchased as medicine is smoked.

What did the 1999 Institute of Medicine report (really) say?

A comprehensive review of marijuana's medical value published in
1999 by the Institute of Medicine (IOM) remains a standard reference,
and different parts of it are cited by opposing groups of advocates.
Concerning the efficacy of cannabinoids isolated from marijuana,
the IOM found therapeutic value "particularly for symptoms such
as pain relief, control of nausea and vomiting, and appetite stimulation," although the effects are "generally modest, and in most cases
there are more effective medications. However, people vary in their
responses to medications, and there will likely always be a subpopu-
lation of patients who do not respond well to other medications." So
the IOM concluded that "scientific data indicate the potential therapeutic value of cannabinoid drugs, primarily THC, for pain relief,
control of nausea and vomiting, and appetite stimulation."

In contrast, the IOM viewed smoked marijuana as a "crude THC
delivery system that also delivers harmful substances," so "smoked

marijuana should generally not be recommended for long-term medical use. Nonetheless, for certain patients, such as the terminally ill or those with debilitating symptoms, the long-term risks are not of great concern." It recommended limited clinical trials of smoked marijuana, but the goal "would not be to develop marijuana as a licensed drug but rather to serve as a first step toward the possible development of non-smoked rapid-onset cannabinoid delivery systems." Since that would take some years, it recommended that in the meantime "patients with debilitating symptoms (such as intractable pain or vomiting)" could be provided with smoked marijuana on a short-term basis (less than six months)—perhaps as single-patient clinical trials—if:

- failure of all approved medications to provide relief has been documented;
- the symptoms can reasonably be expected to be relieved by rapid-onset cannabinoid drugs;
- such treatment is administered under medical supervision in a manner that allows for assessment of treatment effectiveness; and
- the treatment involves an oversight strategy comparable to an institutional review board process.

Critics condemned the IOM review for not considering the possibility that some standardized mixture of the full range of chemicals in the cannabis plant might be more therapeutically useful than a single chemical in isolation (such as THC) or the possibility that vaporization could provide the benefits of quick uptake through the lungs without the unhealthy smoke. Also, given the accumulating evidence concerning CBD, it may be that the IOM report, and indeed the bulk of the research literature that focuses on THC, has been missing some—perhaps much—of the potential benefit of the cannabis plant as medicine.

What is the state of the medical-marijuana literature today?

The research base is growing, but we still have a tremendous amount to learn.

ProCon.org is a nonprofit that attempts to provide unbiased reviews of evidence pertaining to controversial topics in a manner that is transparent to all via its website. Its reviews of evidence on medical-marijuana are widely cited in public debates.

As of August 2015, ProCon.org identified sixty peer-reviewed articles concerning the effectiveness of the marijuana plant or extracts, but excluding synthetic cannabinoids such as Marinol and Cesamet. The studies concern sixteen diseases or conditions, and ProCon.org characterized 41 (68 percent) of them as "pro" (providing evidence of effectiveness), 6 as "con," and 13 as "NC" for not clearly pro or con. Not all of the studies had a strong design. For example, one (coauthored by one of us) merely reported the attitudes and experiences of oncologists from a survey; it did not collect clinical data at all.

ProCon.org labeled 27 of the 60 studies as following a double-blind design, and classified 17 (63 percent) as "pro." However, 20 of those 27 more rigorous studies evaluated cannabis extracts, such as Sativex (a blend of THC and CBD that has been approved as a medicine in more than twenty countries but not yet in the United States). Only seven studied herbal marijuana (six by smoking, one by vaporizing). Among those seven:

- Two (both "pro") pertained to treating neuropathic pain in HIV patients.
- Three (all "pro") pertained to neuropathic pain more generally.
- One ("NC") pertained to ameliorating pain induced intentionally as part of the experimental process.
- One (labeled "con") found that smoked marijuana adversely affected balance and posture of patients with multiple sclerosis (even more than it adversely affected healthy controls).

Overall, ProCon.org identified seventeen double-blind clinical trials that found beneficial effects, but mostly from extracts such as Sativex. The only condition for which it identifies such clinical evidence concerning marijuana plant material is neuropathic pain, for which there were five such studies.

In June 2015, a well-publicized meta-analysis about medical-marijuana was published in the *Journal of the American Medical Association*. The authors reported the results for various medical conditions and distinguished what they called "smoked THC" from three classes of approved pharmaceuticals: nabiximols (Sativex), dronabinol (Marinol), and nabilone (Cesamet). To rate the overall quality of the evidence for factors such as risk of bias, imprecision, and the magnitude of the effect, they used four categories: very low-, low-, moderate-, or high-quality. They concluded:

- "[T]here was moderate-quality evidence to suggest that cannabinoids may be beneficial for the treatment of chronic neuropathic or cancer pain (smoked THC and nabiximols) and spasticity due to MS (nabiximols, nabilone, THC/CBD capsules, and dronabinol).
- There was low-quality evidence suggesting that cannabinoids were associated with improvements in nausea and vomiting due to chemotherapy (dronabinol and nabiximols), weight gain in HIV (dronabinol), sleep disorders (nabilone, nabiximols), and Tourette syndrome (THC capsules); and
- very low-quality evidence for an improvement in anxiety as assessed by a public speaking test (cannabidiol).
- There was low-quality evidence for no effect on psychosis (cannabidiol) and very low-level evidence for no effect on depression (nabiximols)."

It is important to note that only 2 of the 79 studies the authors judged to be of sufficient quality to include pertained to smoked THC; none pertained to edibles. The evidence base concerning the forms customarily supplied by state-legal medical-marijuana programs is very slim. Most of the serious studies pertain to pharmaceutical-grade cannabinoids.

Some other systematic reviews of the effect of cannabinoids have looked specifically at epilepsy, dementia, schizophrenia, and HIV/AIDS morbidity/mortality, but for each review few trials met methodological standards for inclusion.

Absence of evidence is not evidence of absence of effectiveness. There have been few clinical trials involving smoked or vaped marijuana, largely because of prohibition, medical research culture, and hurdles to conducting these studies (discussed later in this chapter). But even if a study shows that cannabinoids do produce medical benefits, one should not assume that it is the best treatment available.

As the University of Queensland's Wayne Hall and the University of New South Wales's Michael Farrell noted in a recent review:

Controlled clinical trials indicate that cannabinoids have some efficacy in controlling emesis in cancer patients, in stimulating appetite in AIDS patients and in relieving pain. Much of this evidence comes from studies that are 30 years old and for many of these indications the medical need for cannabinoids has been reduced by the development of more effective drugs. If the cannabinoids have a medical role in these indications, it is as second or third line treatments, or as an adjunctive treatment.

Whether the product innovation, chemical testing, and labeling that result from marijuana legalization turn out to improve the medical utility of the material remains to be seen.

Does marijuana have legally recognized medical value in the United States?

That depends on whom you ask. Many states say yes, but medical status under federal law is not determined by plebiscite or state actions. The federal Controlled Substances Act, as interpreted by the DEA and the FDA (an interpretation upheld by the courts), requires that a drug meet five conditions to be accepted as a treatment in the United States:

1. The drug's chemistry must be known and reproducible;
2. There must be adequate safety studies;
3. There must be adequate and well-controlled studies proving efficacy;
4. The drug must be accepted by qualified experts; and
5. The scientific evidence must be widely available.

Some pharmaceutical cannabinoids meet these criteria, but the DEA insists that marijuana in the usual sense—meaning dried plant material—does not. Indeed, General Barry McCaffrey, the Clinton administration's drug czar, once referred to it as "Cheech and Chong medicine." However, the federal government also controls access to marijuana for research purposes, and therefore gets to decide whether many of these conditions could ever be met. It is fair to say that federal agencies involved have been less than enthusiastic about medical research on whole-plant cannabis, and have put a number of barriers in the way of those who wanted to do such research. The situation is different outside the United States.

Even in states that allow access to marijuana for medical purposes, doctors still may not prescribe marijuana and pharmacies may not dispense it (as pharmacies operate under DEA license). Instead, clinicians provide recommendations to their patients, who then obtain marijuana products through cooperatives and other dispensaries, or by growing it themselves or having a caregiver grow on their behalf. The particulars of these states' various regimes vary enormously (see chapter 13). "Recommendations" tend to be far less specific than prescriptions, reflecting the limited knowledge in the area as well as complicated legal rules. It is rare for the recommendation to specify—as any prescription must—what material is to be used, in what quantity, and how often. That increases the skepticism about whether "medical-marijuana" is truly medical: "I recommend that you inhale or ingest, on no specific schedule, some random amount of an unspecified and unregulated substance" is not really a very good substitute for "Take 100 mg. of amoxicillin three times a day, with meals, for seven days."

Why isn't marijuana available as a regular prescription drug in the United States?

1. Because no one has done the work necessary to make marijuana a prescription drug, with the federal government obstructing the process at every step of the way.
2. Because "marijuana" isn't the name of a specific drug.

A regular prescription drug must be approved as "safe and effective" by the FDA. The FDA doesn't do its own testing. It's up to the sponsor of a new drug application—in the usual case, a pharmaceutical company—to do, or pay for, the research to show safety and efficacy (in hopes of being able to profit from exclusive rights to sell the drug).

The drug must succeed in two large-scale ("phase III") clinical trials. These are usually randomized controlled trials (RCTs), in which the candidate drug is compared either to a placebo (something expected to have no actual chemical effects) or some active comparison drug in treating a group of patients randomly assigned to the experimental condition (the new drug) or the control condition (the placebo or comparison drug). To avoid expectancy effects—just thinking you're getting what might be a wonder drug can make you feel better—neither the patients nor the experimenters knows which patient is getting which drug. That's the famous "double-blind" design. (The real gold standard is "triple-blind," which keeps the statisticians analyzing the outcome data in the dark as to whether group A or group B got the candidate drug.)

Those clinical trials need to test exactly the medicine that would be used by actual patients. So the producer and sponsor of the drug must show they can meet the standards of "good manufacturing practice" (GMP): that is, that they can reliably produce something of known, and repeatable, composition and dosage. That's harder with a plant containing an ensemble of active chemicals than it is with a single chemical compound, or a mixture of a small number of known molecules.

Developing GMP methods, running two big RCTs, and doing the endless paperwork required by the FDA typically cost tens to hundreds of millions of dollars. In the usual case, the sponsor has a patent on the candidate drug, and expects to recoup that investment by charging monopoly prices on the drug until the patent expires. Marijuana of the sort that millions of people have been using for decades cannot be patented as a novel innovation, precisely because it has been used by millions of people for decades, though there may be opportunities to patent the cloning process, methods of extraction, or other aspects of the product.

Furthermore, marijuana is not one well-defined thing. There are myriad forms with varying ratios of many different active chemicals. So the first step in developing a prescription marijuana medicine would be to decide on a level of THC and other active agents, including CBD, that will constitute one dose of the new medicine, and then to figure out a way to grow and blend the plant material so that every dose has precisely that same mix of chemicals. (It's possible but not certain that a strain of marijuana or blending process could be patented; the US Patent and Trademark Office has yet to grant such a patent.)

To get to that point—at which clinical trials could even be designed, and permissions applied for from the FDA and from the institutional review boards that protect the human subjects of medical research—the sponsor would need a supply of marijuana. But—catch-22!—the DEA has licensed only a single producer of marijuana for research (the University of Mississippi). This producer is under contract with NIDA and is forbidden to sell to anyone but the government. Thus opponents of "marijuana as medicine" are being somewhat disingenuous when they argue that it hasn't passed FDA scrutiny.

But we live in interesting times, and some of these administrative hurdles are now being lowered. At a Senate hearing in June 2015, Nora Volkow, director of the National Institute on Drug Abuse, recommended ending NIDA's longstanding monopoly on the cultivation of marijuana for research purposes. And in the same month, the Office of National Drug Control Policy announced it had removed the Public Health Service review on marijuana research projects, a process that had caused years-long delays and sometimes resulted in flat refusals, and which likely deterred some researchers. In December 2015, the DEA eased some regulatory requirements for researchers working with CBD.

There are also comprehensive bills about medical-marijuana pending in both the House and Senate. If passed, the bipartisan Compassionate Access, Research Expansion, and Respect States Act of 2015 would reschedule marijuana, expand its availability as medicine, and reduce barriers to research. This would mark the most significant federal marijuana policy reform since prohibition, although it is important to stress that simply moving marijuana to Schedule II would have no bearing on its legality for either medical or recreational use; a Schedule II drug can't be provided except under prescription, and no prescription can be written for a drug the FDA has not approved. (If the FDA approves a drug, it is automatically removed from Schedule I.)

What is happening with medical-marijuana outside the United States?

Quite a bit.

As mentioned above, the pharmaceutical Sativex, a cannabis extract containing roughly equal quantities of THC and CBD, delivered as a sublingual spray, has been approved for use in more than twenty countries, although not yet in the United States.

There are also countries that permit herbal marijuana to be used for medicinal purposes; Canada has a small, tightly regulated and government-supervised medical-marijuana program that runs alongside a much larger, informal system that operates out of bricks-and-mortar dispensaries, not unlike those in many US states. In the Netherlands, doctors can prescribe specific strains, which patients can then pick up at pharmacies. The program is relatively small, with one report suggesting that from 2007 to 2013 only about five thousand individuals participated, even though the Dutch Office of Medical Cannabis does not limit the ailments or conditions for which doctors can prescribe marijuana. It merely requires that "standard treatments and registered medicines are not having the desired effect or are causing too many side effects." It may be that legal access to recreational marijuana makes separate access for medical purposes moot for most patients (albeit not for minors).

Israel (where THC was first isolated in 1964) has allowed access to medical-marijuana since the 1990s, and the Health Ministry launched a large-scale program in 2007 which currently serves thousands of patients (one report from the *Washington Post* suggests the number of patients could reach thirty thousand by 2016). Israel receives international attention for Sheba Medical Center, a government-run hospital which piloted a program in 2009 that allowed patients to use medical-marijuana in a common smoking room or in a room with a window if they were bedridden. The hospital still permits medical-marijuana for designated patients and was featured in Dr. Sanjay Gupta's CNN special, *Weed* (discussed in chapter 13). Israel continues to invest in medical research, including clinical research on whether CBD can reduce tumors in humans.

If there are pharmaceutical cannabinoids, is there any reason to use plant material?

Quite possibly, and for two distinct reasons. First, the FDA approval process is slow even under normal circumstances, so one might want to make herbal marijuana products available on an interim basis until the "real medicines" based on marijuana get approved. That is one argument for the recent wave of "high-CBD/low-THC" laws (discussed further in chapter 13).

The second is that pharmaceuticals based on marijuana now focus on THC and CBD, which are just two of the dozens of cannabinoids found in the cannabis plant. There could be other cannabinoids that are beneficial in their own right, and there is also the notion (discussed above) of "entourage effects": perhaps a mixture of cannabinoids and other compounds might be superior to any one molecule taken by itself.

That process of isolating, or isolating and modifying, the active agents in plant materials, and producing pure chemicals to be given in pill form, has characterized Western pharmacology for more than a century. Indeed, one difference between a "real" doctor and a naturopath or a traditional healer is that the university-trained MD uses refined chemicals rather than crude plant materials.

But those are facts about medical anthropology—about the practices of the officially recognized healers in the currently dominant culture—not about the way the human body heals. It's scientifically easier to study the effects of pure chemicals than to study the effects of complex and variable plant materials. That makes those pure chemicals easier to shepherd through the FDA process and makes them appear more "scientific" than the roots, leaves, and berries they displaced. In some cases there are real clinical advantages to the more precise knowledge available from the studies that can be done with pure chemicals and the more precise dosage control available when every pill in a bottle is exactly the same as every other pill in that same bottle. Certainly the history of the nutritional supplement industry, with its plethora of scientifically dubious claims and its paucity of reliable information, shows the risks of straying too far from rigorous experimental technique.

But, as noted above, pure vitamins don't replace fresh fruits and vegetables, and many believe that real vanilla—containing many different molecules—tastes better than pure vanillin. There's no reason in principle that one or a few isolated cannabinoids must outperform the mixture of dozens of different cannabinoids in the natural plant. Marinol turned out not to be very helpful for many patients; pure THC, taken by mouth, is simply not a very good medicine. Sativex, with its high CBD content reducing the risk of dysphoria and panic, seems better, at least in some uses. Nothing guarantees that something else won't be still better than Sativex, or that anything is as good as (some version of) the crude material.

But whether the right way to use marijuana as medicine is as a blend of natural plant materials or as a mixture of pure extracts is an empirical problem, not one of principle. It cannot be sensibly answered by starting with the prejudice that pure chemicals are medicine while flowers are mere witch-doctoring, or the opposite prejudice that what grows in the soil gives health while chemicals are poisons.

Additional Reading

Belackova, Vendula, et al. *Medicinal Cannabis in Australia—Framing the Regulatory Options.*

Hall, Wayne, and Michael Farrell. *Inquiry into Use of Cannabis for Medical Purposes.*

Netherlands Office of Medical Cannabis. *Medical Cannabis: Information for Patients.*

Whiting, Penny, et al. "Cannabinoids for Medical Use: A Systematic Review and Meta-Analysis."

6

HOW STRINGENT IS MARIJUANA ᵍ ENFORCEMENT IN THE UNITED STATES?

Does it make sense for marijuana to be a Schedule I substance?

Yes, until the federal process finds it has medical value.

The Controlled Substances Act (CSA) divides abusable drugs into five groups, called "schedules," numbered from I to V. Schedule V includes only medications such as cough syrup with small amounts of codeine, which have very limited dependence liability. Schedule I includes heroin, which is arguably the most dangerous illegal substance, and also marijuana.

Some lampoon this apparently indefensible lumping of marijuana into a category that includes the most dangerous substances. This argument makes for great theater, but it (perhaps strategically) misrepresents the structure of the scheduling system.

The CSA scheduling criteria do embody a logical flaw. Each schedule is defined by a three-prong test concerning: (1) Potential for abuse, (2) Existence or absence of accepted medical use, and (3) Dependence potential or safety for use under medical supervision. If the law were well-written, these tests would form a mutually exclusive and collectively exhaustive partition; every controlled substance would fall in one and only one schedule. Yet by a literal reading some substances do not fit in any of the schedules at all.

For those seeking to understand the Act, here is the way to think about it. The CSA first divides all substances to be controlled into two big bins, one for those with no currently accepted medical use

(Schedule I) and another for those that are currently used as medicine (Schedules II–V).

The medicines are further subdivided based on their dependence liability. Schedule II contains substances like cocaine that have currently accepted medical value but whose abuse "may lead to severe psychological or physical dependence." Schedules III and IV contain medicines with "moderate" and "limited" dependence liability, respectively, and Schedule V is for medicines whose dependence liability is even more limited than those in Schedule IV.

The different schedules for the medicines impose different degrees of regulatory restrictions deemed appropriate based on the varying dependence liability. For example, prescriptions for Schedule II substances may not be refilled; those for Schedule III and IV may be refilled, but only a limited number of times. Also, the CSA limits the number of companies that can produce Schedule II substances, in order to prevent diversion to nonmedical use, whereas similar restrictions do not apply to the production of Schedule III–V drugs. Likewise, Schedule V substances are exempted from warning-label requirements that apply to medicines in Schedule II–IV. And so on. There is no need for such nuanced distinctions among Schedule I substances, because they do not have any recognized medical use.

In retrospect, legislators may wish they had named the categories Schedule I and Schedules IIa, IIb, IIc, and IId, rather than numbering them sequentially as Schedules I–V. The sequential numbering invites the misunderstanding which is sometimes exploited in policy debates.

In addition to using one set of sequential labels for what is actually a two-part test, the scheduling criteria themselves are poorly worded. The line which opens the door to mockery says that Schedule I is only for substances having a "high" potential for abuse. So the act literally has no place in which to put nonmedicines whose potential for abuse is only medium or medium-high. But Schedule I is better understood as the place for all substances with enough abuse liability to warrant control and which have no currently accepted medical use. If a substance with no current medical use is to be scheduled at all, it must go in Schedule I; there is simply no other place for it. It does not mean the substance necessarily has very high dependence liability; after all, FDA-approved pure THC, sold as a pharmaceutical, is in Schedule III, not Schedule II.

(Note: the "dangerousness" of the drug never enters into the scheduling calculus. So the fact that marijuana does not lead to poisoning deaths is irrelevant to scheduling decisions under the current law. That may be a flaw with the law, but not with how it is interpreted or implemented.)

There remains the question of whether marijuana has a currently accepted medical use. Obviously, many states have laws allowing medical use, and chapter 5 discusses the plant's medical value. However, for purposes of scheduling, the CSA outlines a specific process for determining whether medical use is "accepted," and to date whole cannabis plant material has not passed this test. (Pharmaceutically pure cannabinoids have.) That test and its drawbacks are discussed more in chapter 5.

The DEA does not decide these things unilaterally. The CSA stipulates that before making a scheduling decision, the Attorney General must request from the Secretary of the Department of Health and Human Services a scientific and medical evaluation and that:

> The recommendations of the Secretary shall include recommendations with respect to the appropriate schedule, if any, under which such drug or other substance should be listed. . . . The recommendations of the Secretary to the Attorney General shall be binding on the Attorney General as to such scientific and medical matters, and if the Secretary recommends that a drug or other substance not be controlled, the Attorney General shall not control the drug or other substance.

Who gets arrested for marijuana possession?

600,000 for possession

All sorts of people, and in large numbers.

In 2014 there were 1.6 million state and local arrests for drug violations, constituting about an eighth of all arrests nationwide. Forty percent of those drug arrests were for marijuana possession, and 5 percent for marijuana sale/manufacturing. That's roughly six hundred thousand arrests for marijuana possession. (Because some people are arrested more than once a year, the number of individuals arrested must be somewhat smaller.)

By comparison, there were 1.9 million arrests for public drunkenness, sales to a minor, driving under the influence, and other violations of liquor laws. Arrest rates for marijuana possession vary by region, being three times as high in the South (260 arrests per 100,000 people) as in the West (85 per 100,000 people) though the West has a higher prevalence of marijuana use.

Figure 6.1 shows that the number of arrests has varied substantially over time. The number of marijuana-possession arrests (solid line) ebbed in the 1980s, soared in the early 1990s, rose to a peak of 775,000 in 2007 and fell 20 percent since. It is worth noting that these trends mostly predate legalization. (Before 2014 only Colorado and Washington had legalized, and they account for less than 4 percent of the nation's population.)

Figure 6.1 also shows the number of possession arrests per day of use through 2013 (dashed line), scaled to fit on these axes. Use fell sharply through 1992 and rebounded just as sharply since, with a pause from 2002 to 2007. So a portion of the run-up in arrests was just keeping pace with expanding use, and the decline in arrests since 2007 is even more pronounced if one corrects for the increased use. As Stanford psychiatry professor Keith Humphreys recently

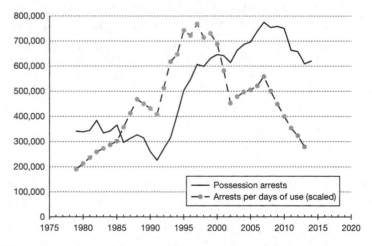

Figure 6.1 Marijuana Possession Arrests in the United States, 1979–2013, in Total and per Day of Use (scaled)

Federal Bureau of Investigation and National Household Surveys noted, the number of possession arrests per day of use fell by 50 percent between 2007 and 2013.

An "arrest" can mean anything from handcuffs, a trip downtown, booking, and a jail cell at one extreme to just getting a ticket or summons to appear before a judge at the other. "Custodial" arrests—the ones with handcuffs—aren't usually counted separately.

Although the number of people arrested for marijuana possession appears strikingly high, more than thirty million Americans report using marijuana each year; less than 2 percent of users are arrested for possession in the course of an average year. Users report about 3.4 billion days of use per year in surveys, so there is about one marijuana-possession arrest per 5,500 days of use reported. Of course, over many years of heavy use, those small per-incident risks cumulate to a more substantial risk of getting arrested at least once. And the risk of arrest varies greatly among users and occasions. Relatively few of those arrests result from police decisions to proactively seek out and arrest marijuana users; many are by-products of other actions—mostly by uniformed patrol officers rather than drug detectives—ranging from traffic stops and street-corner stop-question-and-frisks to arrests for serious crimes. So 2 percent per year greatly overstates the average arrest risk for someone who uses marijuana but does not otherwise attract police attention. Unfortunately, being a young black male in a high-crime neighborhood often does attract police attention, even if the man in question doesn't actually do anything unusual, and the ratio of user arrests to use-days is higher for African Americans than for others.

Fluctuations in the number of marijuana arrests can reflect factors beyond the prevalence of marijuana use or changes in drug enforcement generally. A study by Bernard Harcourt and Jens Ludwig of the University of Chicago found that marijuana arrests in New York City changed dramatically after the New York Police Department ramped up "order maintenance" policing in the 1990s. Harcourt and Ludwig found that arrests for smoking marijuana in public view multiplied twenty-five-fold, from fewer than two thousand arrests in 1994 to more than fifty thousand in 2000. The goals behind the surge in arrests were maintaining public order and discouraging gun-carrying, not suppressing marijuana use.

Marijuana arrests in New York City then plunged in 2015, not because of any change in marijuana laws or use but because order-maintenance policing had become so controversial. That policing strategy has been associated with sharp declines in crime, but also with racially disparate impact. An investigation by the New York State Attorney General's Civil Rights Bureau found that the disparities were particularly pronounced with respect to marijuana arrests.

Race is not the only risk factor. A study by Holly Nguyen and Peter Reuter of the University of Maryland found that men are more likely than women to be arrested for marijuana possession, and younger people more than their elders. Some part of the risk differences may be due to differences in the way that marijuana is bought and used. RAND behavioral scientist Rajeev Ramchand and colleagues observed that, controlling for other factors, African American marijuana users were twice as likely to buy outdoors and three times as likely to buy from a stranger than other users, which might help explain part of why the marijuana arrest rate for African Americans is 2.5 times as high as would be predicted based on their prevalence of use alone. Nevertheless, such factors do not fully explain the disparities, some of which stem from the concentration of police resources in high-crime neighborhoods.

What happens after those possession arrests?

Much less than some marijuana activists claim, but enough to represent a substantial cost of the current policies (and thus a potential gain from decriminalization or legalization).

As noted above, "arrest" for a misdemeanor such as marijuana possession often means receiving a notice to appear in court, not being physically restrained, and no one knows how many of the approximately six hundred thousand annual marijuana-possession arrests are noncustodial.

Not all marijuana arrests lead to prosecution; prosecutors often drop charges. Even after conviction (usually by means of a guilty plea rather than a trial), what happens depends on the age of the offender, number of prior arrests, amount of marijuana possessed, and the jurisdiction.

Custodial arrests could be reduced by changing the legal status of marijuana possession, either by making it a civil infraction (one meaning of the term "decriminalization") or by entirely legalizing possession for adults (as the District of Columbia, Alaska, Colorado, Oregon, and Washington have done).

In Alaska as early as 1975, possessing up to four ounces in a private residence was not considered a criminal act and carried no penalty. In other states, including California, Maine, Massachusetts, and Nebraska, possessing up to one ounce is considered a civil infraction or petty act that has no jail time attached, although users risk fines ranging from $100 (California and Massachusetts) to $350–$600 (Maine); Colorado was already as lenient as California even before it legalized marijuana in 2012.

In some states, fines increase for repeat offenders. Mississippi goes relatively easy on first-time offenders, with only a fine of $250 and no jail time, but incarceration is an option for repeat offenders. New York State punishes possession of small quantities (twenty-five grams or less) with a $100 fine for a first offense, increasing to $200 for a second offense; third and subsequent offenses trigger a fine of $250 and jail time of up to fifteen days. Florida is at the other extreme. It limits the personal-consumption exception to twenty grams, so carrying a full ounce could in theory trigger up to five years in prison and a fine of $5,000. Again, actual sentences aren't usually as harsh as the legal maximum; even in Florida, first-time offenders may be merely fined and put on probation.

Federal statutes also go easy on first-time possessors of small quantities. However, that leniency is largely symbolic, since, outside of federal lands (such as national parks) and at the borders, federal agents rarely work cases involving anything less than hundreds of pounds of marijuana.

Possession of larger quantities can be a misdemeanor or a felony depending on the amount (thresholds vary by state) and the location of the arrest. Many states impose stiffer sentences for possession in proximity to a school; as Will Brownsberger (then with the Harvard Medical School Division on Addictions) demonstrated, school-zone laws make the penalties systematically harsher in crowded urban neighborhoods than in less densely populated suburbs, contributing to racial disparities.

There is little evidence of a systematic relationship between statutory marijuana penalties and marijuana use, perhaps because of the large gap between the text of the laws and the sanctions actually imposed, which depend on risk of detection, probability of a sanction if detected, and magnitude of punishment if sanctioned.

Very few people convicted only of simple marijuana possession are incarcerated for any significant stretch. The vast majority face only a fine or are placed under community supervision. On the other hand, those already on probation or parole for other offenses, especially felonies, can, and sometimes do, go to prison if a drug test comes back "dirty." In one sense, you could say that those people were being punished for first breaking the law and then violating the rules of their conditional release. (Probationers and parolees can also be required to abstain from alcohol.) But it's still true that some probationers and parolees are going to prison—or back to prison—as a result of smoking pot.

In many cases, the impact of a fine, or even a day in jail, is small compared to the impact of a record of arrest and conviction on everything from employment opportunity to child custody. To accurately measure the full cost of user arrests, we would have to know for how many individuals an arrest for marijuana possession was the first blot on a previously clean criminal history.

How harshly are marijuana producers and traffickers punished?

While arrests for simple possession dominate the numbers, serious sanctions are reserved for production, trafficking, and sale—and sometimes also for possessing very large quantities (e.g., when holding or transporting a stash for a dealer).

Arrests for marijuana production, trafficking, and sales have been flat since 1980 in per capita terms, fluctuating between 25 and 35 arrests per 100,000 people. In 2013, that translated to 84,000 arrests.

The risk of arrest or incarceration varies with circumstances. Dealing that takes place discreetly behind closed doors, especially retail distribution embedded within social networks, carries little risk of arrest, in part because neighbors and passersby don't notice and don't call the cops. The greater risk comes from growing or from selling outdoors, and the tougher sanctions come from distributing large quantities (even if the defendant had only a small role within an organization transporting larger quantities) or having a weapon.

The sentences can be harsh, at least on paper. Minnesota and Mississippi have the stiffest maximum penalties for possession of large quantities, imposing penalties of up to thirty years in prison. But even a "mandatory" sentence is mandatory only for the judge; prosecutors still have, and use, the discretion not to bring charges, or to bring lesser charges.

For heroin and cocaine, federal mandatory minimum sentences are triggered by relatively small quantities: one hundred grams of heroin, five hundred grams of powder cocaine, or twenty-eight grams of base cocaine (the category which includes crack). By contrast, federal mandatory sentences for marijuana are reserved for those possessing at least one hundred *kilo*grams or one hundred plants. So the quantity threshold triggering federal mandatory sentences for marijuana is literally one thousand times as great as it is for heroin. Some federal prosecutors' offices, especially in busy border jurisdictions, routinely refuse to prosecute smuggling cases except for extraordinarily large quantities, simply because they have limited resources and don't want to spend them all on marijuana cases.

How many people are in prison for marijuana offenses?

About forty thousand state and federal inmates have a current "controlling conviction" involving marijuana. That is less than 3 percent of the total; clearly legalizing marijuana by itself cannot make a major dent in the historically high rates of incarceration.

Perhaps half of those prisoners committed offenses related to marijuana alone. The vast bulk of them were involved in production or distribution; less than 1 percent of state and federal inmates are serving time for marijuana possession alone—and in many of those cases, the possession conviction was the result of a plea bargain involving the dismissal of more serious charges. Jacqueline Cohen of Carnegie Mellon University has shown that prisoners whose conviction charge was drug possession actually had more serious histories of violence than those convicted of violent crime; it takes an extraordinary criminal history to lead a judge to sentence someone to prison time for just possessing drugs. Whether an arrest results in incarceration is influenced by many intervening variables. One key determinant is criminal-justice status; an arrest while on probation or parole from a previous conviction is more likely to lead to incarceration than a similar arrest of someone who has no active criminal-justice status. The illegality of marijuana may contribute as much to the total burden of incarceration by extending the time served by people who have committed other crimes, including violent crimes, as it does by incarcerating people whose only convictions are for marijuana-related offenses. As a result, the question "How many people are behind bars today who would be free if marijuana were legal?" has no easily determined answer.

Additional Reading

Humphreys, Keith. "Even as Marijuana Use Rises, Arrests Are Falling."

Kleiman, Mark A. R. *Marijuana: Costs of Abuse, Costs of Control.*

Nguyen, Holly, and Peter Reuter. "How Risky is Marijuana Possession? Considering the Role of Age, Race, and Gender."

Sevigny, Eric L., and Jonathan P. Caulkins. "Kingpins or Mules."

PART II
NATIONAL LEGALIZATION AND ITS
CONSEQUENCES

7

WHAT ARE THE PROS AND CONS OF LEGALIZATION GENERALLY?

What does it mean to legalize a drug?

Legalization means allowing production, distribution, and selling of a drug. Possession and use would be legal for all or most adults, albeit subject to the general rules governing any form of commerce—for example, the prohibition on misrepresenting the characteristics of the product being sold—and perhaps also some product-specific regulations, as with alcohol and tobacco.

In a market society, most things are freely bought, sold, and used. A relatively few commodities and services—mostly linked to danger, pleasure, or both—are banned. It is currently a crime, for example, to produce, import, sell, or possess heroin or rocket-propelled grenade launchers. There are also prohibitions against trade in certain endangered species; in June 2013, Steven Patrick Garcia was sentenced to two years in prison after he sold $400 worth of hawk feathers and eagle wings to an undercover US Fish and Wildlife Service agent. Child pornography is banned both to protect the children in the pictures and (it is hoped) to prevent the viewers of such material from going out and molesting children. There are also laws against prostitution, gambling, and usury (loansharking), as well as bans on selling human organs.

At most times and for most goods and services, US federal and state laws agreed on what was prohibited and what was legal, or at least they did not conflict. (Sometimes one level of government has no laws concerning what another level bans.)

However, today we're in an odd limbo with four states having legalized marijuana sales but the federal government still banning it. That conflict creates a host of complications particular to this substance, time, and country. So this part of the book steps back and considers only the more coherent scenario of legalization at both the federal and state levels. Part III delves further into the awkward intermediate case that pertains today. As an historical aside, the roles have been reversed in the past: while some states started passing anti-marijuana laws in the 1910s, the drug wasn't effectively banned nationally until 1937.

What is the essential tradeoff between legalization and prohibition?

Under the free market system, when companies can cheaply produce items that consumers value highly, there will be a lot of consumption. That is a boon when it comes to books, but not when it comes to bazookas or crack.

It is tempting to ban certain products, but most prohibitions generate at least some evasion of the laws; there are even organ-selling syndicates. The black markets for illegal drugs are unusually large and, as a result, sometimes quite destructive.

So legalization is the opposite of prohibition. It avoids the costs of prohibition—criminal enterprise, the need for enforcement, and loss of liberty—at the risk of increased drug use and abuse.

Legalization helps those who want to use the newly legal drug and can do so in moderation (that is, without losing self-control): they gain the liberty to do as they choose, along with whatever benefits flow from their drug use, and in most cases get access to cheaper and safer products. It's also a gain to those who suffer from the illicit markets and from drug law enforcement. It's a win for the entrepreneurs who successfully step in to create and lead the newly legal industry. It seems like a loss for the criminal entrepreneurs they displace, but that is true only for those who get away with it. Legalization is a big gain for those who would have been caught selling illegally and gone to prison as a result.

However, compared to prohibition, legalization is likely to increase the number of people who suffer from substance use disorders. That's a loss for the people who wouldn't otherwise have become dependent—and for their friends, children, and other family members.

To legalize a drug, then—as the US federal government did with alcohol in 1933—is to choose the problems associated with increased levels of excessive consumption over the problems associated with illicit dealing and enforcement.

Thus, in deciding whether to make marijuana legal—and just how "legal" to make it—citizens and officials are constantly trading off one set of costs and risks against another. The right choices aren't always obvious.

What are the shades of legalization?

— likely to include restrictions

As noted, in a market society most things are freely bought, sold, and used. "Freely" shouldn't be taken too literally. There are still rules designed to prevent fraud, damage to third parties, and harm to children. For a legal commodity, though, those rules are meant to shape the market, not to shrink the amount of market activity. (Changes in smoking policy over the past generation have created an unusual intermediate case: while cigarettes remain legal, reducing cigarette smoking is now a proclaimed objective of national health policy in the United States.)

A newly legalized drug could be subject to specialized rules, perhaps of the sort that now apply to alcohol: limits on times and places of sale, special licenses for sellers, labeling rules, a ban on sales to minors, and excise taxes over and above ordinary sales, service, and property taxes. Legalization is a big jump away from prohibition, but regulations can adjust the intensity of the contrast. On the other hand, those regulations wouldn't enforce themselves, any more than the current prohibition does. The tighter the restrictions and the higher the taxes, the greater the risk that an illicit market will develop to evade them; there are vibrant markets for cigarettes smuggled into some high-tax states and countries from jurisdictions with low or no taxes.

Under prohibition, the laws can punish the suppliers, the consumers, or both. Some jurisdictions arrest commercial sex workers, but not their customers. Others focus enforcement on the demand side. Many arrest both. Similar dilemmas arise when trying to prevent companies from employing immigrants without proper work visas.

Drug laws often criminalize both sides of the illicit transaction, punishing users as well as dealers. Eliminating criminal penalties

Risk: burdensome regulations will feed black market.

for possessing amounts suitable only for personal use—and thus freeing users from the consequences of a criminal sanction—is called "decriminalization." In jurisdictions that have decriminalized, possession is still illegal, but those who are caught are subject only to a civil sanction, such as a fine.

A jurisdiction could remove civil as well as criminal penalties for possession while continuing to ban production and sale. That would go beyond decriminalization but still fall far short of what is normally meant by legalization, which encompasses production and distribution as well. Washington, DC, offers the closest contemporary example in the United States, having legalized possession and small-scale home production but not commercial production or sale.

The Volstead Act, which implemented alcohol prohibition, had no penalties for possession or use; it only punished manufacturers and sellers. So, ironically, the situation under alcohol prohibition was in some ways akin to that in Washington, DC, today, which is sometimes described as having partially legalized marijuana.

The logical problem with reducing penalties for possession is that it allows users to buy what dealers are forbidden to sell. That logical problem becomes a practical problem if reducing user sanctions increases demand, thereby creating more customers for criminal enterprises, more dealing-related violence, and potentially even more incarceration, since it is mostly sellers who fill prison cells. So, in order to judge the outcome of reducing enforcement risks for users, we would have to know how great an effect the threat of arrest has on potential drug buyers. That in turn depends on how vigorously the current prohibition is being enforced.

The conventional view, backed now by a fair amount of evidence, is that decriminalizing marijuana does not greatly increase use (for more on this, see chapter 11). Thinner evidence points to the same conclusion for decriminalizing other drugs in jurisdictions that were already fairly liberal in their treatment of drug users. The same might not apply, however, to hard drugs in the United States; legalizing cocaine in the United States would be expected to reduce Mexican and Colombian drug trafficking organizations' incomes and levels of violence, but decriminalizing cocaine might have the opposite effects by increasing demand for a product that only criminals can supply.

Finally, creating availability for medical use can be implemented in a way that softens prohibition of recreational use, but it need not be. Methamphetamine, for example, is a legal drug when prescribed by a physician and sold by a pharmacist, but it's still a crime to manufacture or sell it outside of pharmaceutical channels or to have it in your possession without a prescription. As chapter 13 explains, state-level medical-marijuana regimes do not much resemble the system operating under the Controlled Substances Act, which already allows methamphetamine, cocaine, and oxycodone to be used medically.

Why have drug laws in the first place?

Ideally, drug laws protect drug users from the risks of taking drugs, or protect other people (including family members) from the risks some drug users create. Although it does not always work out this way, the stated goal of US drug policy is to reduce "drug use and drug-related consequences." (In that phrase, "drug" means "illicit drug"; reduced drinking by adults is not an official policy goal.)

Intoxicating drugs, like other commodities, are often used without causing any harm. But they can also be used in ways that harm their users and others.

Drugs can damage users' health. The wrong dose, the wrong mix of drugs, or the wrong combination of drug and user can lead to injury or even death, and chronic use can lead to chronic illness: smoking, for example, is bad for the lungs. Intoxication can lead to dangerous behavior that harms the user, or to reckless or criminal behavior that damages other people. And users can lose control of their drug taking.

Prohibition makes drugs more expensive and less convenient to buy, and largely eliminates the marketing efforts that boost sales of licit goods. It also prevents the drug-producing industry from lobbying for policies that promote addiction. The result is reduced consumption and a reduced incidence of substance use disorder as compared to the levels that would exist under legalization.

Hence the extent of harm caused by using a substance is a crucial variable in determining how much benefit is created by prohibition's (partial) suppression of its use. That makes the case for marijuana prohibition weaker than the comparable case for cocaine or heroin;

marijuana use does create harms, but at a much lower rate than any of the other major illegal drugs (see chapter 3).

Why even consider legalizing a substance whose use creates harm?

The liberty to make our own decisions about our own lives—including decisions that seem unwise to other people—is valuable. Intoxicating drugs are hardly the only potentially dangerous consumer items or recreational activities. People get killed and crippled climbing mountains, jumping out of airplanes, sailing, scuba diving, playing football, and riding motorcycles. Those other forms of recreation can be riskier than using marijuana—at least in terms of the risk of sudden death—yet a proposal to ban any of them would generate outrage. Statistically, people also die of physical inactivity, overeating, and insufficient sleep, but laws mandating exercise, limiting calorie consumption, or imposing a national bedtime, with criminal penalties for noncompliance, exist only in dystopian fantasies; no serious person would support any of them.

It isn't obvious that the majority of the users who do not, and would not, abuse the drug deserve to be inconvenienced—to say the least—to protect against the consequences of less responsible users.

Moreover, drug laws create harms of their own, including the harms associated with illicit markets. Illicit markets are less consumer-friendly than regulated licit markets; it's much harder for a cocaine user than a beer drinker to determine precisely what he or she is about to ingest. Buyers and sellers in illicit markets cannot resolve their disputes through the courts or complain to the police if they are ripped off. As a result, they sometimes resolve their conflicts with weapons. Illicit markets can easily become social problems comparable to or greater than drug abuse itself. It is hard to know how much of the approximately $40 billion a year that is spent on marijuana in the United States ends up in the pockets of large-scale criminal organizations, but the answer is surely in the billions, and some of those groups, including the notorious Mexican drug gangs, are highly violent.

Laws need to be enforced; otherwise they become dead letters. And enforcing drug laws is inevitably an ugly process; without the victim-witness who testifies in a robbery or assault case, the drug police must engage in intrusive means of gathering evidence: undercover operations, the use of paid informants, or surveillance by technical means such as wiretapping. Because the evidence in a drug-dealing case is easy to destroy, police engage in surprise "dynamic entry" raids, crashing through doors early in the morning or late at night, guns drawn. Sometimes the raid is on the wrong house, and that can have tragic consequences if the homeowner acts to repel an apparent home invasion. Less dramatic, but far more common, are marijuana-possession arrests, of which there were about six hundred thousand in the United States in 2014. (Chapter 6 describes marijuana enforcement in detail.) That does not mean there are six hundred thousand instances of a vice squad intentionally building a case against a marijuana user; many marijuana arrests are the by-product of routine policing or the enforcement of other laws. Nevertheless, an arrest, even if it never leads to a conviction, sometimes means spending a night or more in jail awaiting arraignment, and a night in jail is much more dangerous than an evening stoned.

The risk of jail varies by state and is much lower than in the past. Six percent of Americans live in states that have legalized marijuana possession outright, another 35 percent live in states that have decriminalized marijuana, and still others live in states that protect users who have medical recommendations. Still more live in cities (such as Philadelphia and Pittsburgh) that have decriminalized—by passing local laws discouraging marijuana arrests—within states that still punish marijuana possession criminally.

Even in places that have not decriminalized, "arrest" often means receiving a notice to appear in court, not a custodial arrest with a trip to the booking facility or jail. On the other hand, an arrest record—even when the arrest is noncustodial, and even when it does not lead to a conviction—can follow someone for life, with all sorts of bad consequences including rejection for public and private employment.

Efforts to deter use seem a natural adjunct to prohibition; after all, if there were no users, there could be no dealers. But the result is that laws designed in part to protect people from their own behavior wind up making some of those who are not deterred worse off than they would have been in the absence of the laws. That's an argument for decriminalizing possession even if sales remain against the law.

Wouldn't the result of a policy that treated marijuana like alcohol be an improvement over the current mess?

It might. Then again, it might not. And what is "better" depends on judgments about the relative importance of different kinds of harm and benefit as well as estimates of the likely results of alternative policies. We have observed what marijuana use looks like when it's prohibited, but not what would happen under a full alcohol-style model. The state-level reforms kicked off by Colorado and Washington give us only hints, because state-only legalization could be very different than national legalization and, more importantly, because it will take a generation (or more) to observe the full effects of legalization on consumption patterns. Indeed, as of this writing, even the industries in Colorado and Washington have not fully matured—prices are still falling, and product mixes are changing—and there is no way to estimate the response of consumers to whatever market conditions finally emerge. Legalization under federal law would tend to depress prices further, and might lead to the emergence of large marijuana corporations promoting national or even international brands.

Quantitative estimates about a hypothetical world so different from the one we have actually observed are subject to much uncertainty, but two abusable drugs are already offered for sale more or less freely: nicotine and alcohol. The results aren't encouraging: those two drugs alone far exceed all the illicit drugs combined in the number of problem users and the resulting ill health and death (see chapter 9). Tobacco is thought to kill nearly half a million Americans each year and alcohol close to 100,000. Nicotine use doesn't generate many crimes or accidents, but alcohol does so in massive numbers, accounting for a third to a half of violent crimes and motor-vehicle deaths in the United States. Marijuana is, in many ways, less behaviorally risky than alcohol, primarily because it has no observable tendency to unleash aggression. Still, "less risky" isn't the same as safe.

And making a drug legal does not entirely eliminate the law-enforcement problem. Any regulation strict enough or any tax high enough to actually change behavior will face defiance and require enforcement. About two million arrests are made each year for public drunkenness, consumption in public, driving under the influence, sales to minors, possession by minors, or other violations of alcohol laws—nearly three times as many as for all marijuana violations combined. The laws against alcohol use by minors are massively evaded, creating both large numbers of arrests and contempt for laws that seem unreasonable to many. (At nineteen, someone can drive a car, vote, join the military, incur binding debts, get married, and be prosecuted as an adult, but not legally buy a drink.)

Even after legalization there will likely still be bans on stoned driving and on sales to minors; to date, there has been no serious proposal to legalize either activity. Therefore, legalization likely wouldn't entirely eliminate law enforcement from the picture.

The right comparison isn't between the burden of marijuana abuse under prohibition and the burden of prohibition itself; the right comparison is between the marijuana abuse and enforcement problems under some alternative policy and the combined damage from drug abuse, enforcement, and illicit markets under current policy—in both cases net of any benefits (e.g., pleasure and the treatment of illness) deriving from marijuana use.

But wasn't alcohol prohibition in the United States a complete failure?

Eventually the alcohol prohibition regime collapsed as the enforcement machinery failed to keep up with the growth of the illicit market. The growth of massive criminal enterprises created profound and lasting damage. But deaths from cirrhosis of the liver—a good measure of heavy drinking by long-term heavy drinkers—fell by about a third as prices approximately tripled. No one back then kept track of domestic assault rates, but everything we know about that phenomenon suggests that family violence probably fell along with heavy drinking.

And contrary to popular belief, the data do not neatly support the claim that Prohibition increased the murder rate overall; to some extent, the rise in beer-baron violence appears to have been compensated for by reductions in ordinary drunken murders.

As University of Pennsylvania economist Emily Owens observes, the Roaring Twenties were a period of urbanization, and big-city homicide rates tend to be higher than rural homicide rates, so the move to the cities was accompanied by an increase in murder. Furthermore, part of the purported "Prohibition effect" on homicide is a mere data artifact: the number of jurisdictions whose homicides were being counted by the federal government rose over the period.

How much of the increase in consumption after legalization would reflect increased heavy use rather than increased casual use?

For any newly legalized substance, most of the new users will be casual users. But most of the increased volume will reflect increased use by people who use frequently. The volume of drug consumption doesn't depend very strongly on the total number of users; what's crucial is the number of heavy users. One eight-joint-a-day smoker (and there are at least hundreds of thousands of such people in the U.S.) is more important to the marijuana industry—legal or illegal—than fifty people who smoke a joint a week.

This extreme skew in consumption rates is not unique to the drugs that are now banned, as statistics on alcohol consumption in the United States show. Research by Duke economist Philip J. Cook has categorized drinkers by their consumption, measured in average standard drinks per day (see chapter 1 for a discussion of the "standard drink"). The top tenth of American adults average three or more drinks a day each. That group puts away three-quarters of all the alcohol consumed. At the other end of the spectrum, about 40 percent of American adults report not having a single drink in the past month. So the top tenth of all people includes 15 percent of drinkers, and we can say that the top 15 percent of drinkers account for 75 percent of consumption. Consequently, except for the very few who drink expensive wine or very old Scotch, moderate drinkers make only a modest contribution to the revenues of brewers, vintners, distillers, and retail sellers.

The arithmetic for marijuana is similar. In household survey data, those who report consuming it more than twenty days in the past month (called "daily or near daily" users) account for 70 percent of all days of marijuana use. Broadening the definition slightly to include those reporting exactly twenty days of use increases that proportion to 80 percent. Since frequent users also consume more per day of use, those daily or near daily users account for more than four-fifths of the quantity consumed.

That has a frightening implication: if we create a licit commercial industry to grow and sell marijuana, the resulting businesses will have a strong financial incentive to create and sustain frequent and intensive consumption patterns, because the heaviest users consume so much of the product. So we should expect the industry's product design, pricing, and marketing to be devoted to creating as much heavy use as possible.

Assuming that marketing executives earn their large salaries, and TV networks earn their huge per-second rates for advertising time, by actually influencing consumer choices, the prospect of a marijuana industry dependent on consumers with cannabis use disorder ought to make a reasonable person nervous about legalizing along the commercial model we have for alcohol.

Can't the effects of marketing be reined in by regulations and taxes?

To some extent. In theory we could legalize marijuana and tax it back to its current illicit-market price, but then the financial reward for successfully selling untaxed marijuana would be as large as the current reward for selling illicit marijuana. The required excise tax could approach $10 per gram for high-potency marijuana. To put that in perspective, a pack of cigarettes weighs about twenty grams. So the tax on something as easy to conceal as a pack of cigarettes would need to be about $200. In the mid-1990s widespread tax evasion forced Canada to repeal a cigarette tax of under five dollars per pack.

Moreover, the taxation and regulation effort would have to contend with a licit industry, which would attempt to mobilize its employees, shareholders, and consumers to lobby against any effective restriction. Since the industry would be as dependent on problem users as the problem users are on their drug, we could expect all that lobbying effort to be devoted to preventing the adoption of policies that would effectively control addiction. The alcohol, tobacco, and gambling industries provide good examples.

True, tobacco companies in the United States have slowly been forced to rein in their marketing efforts—partly because cigarettes, unlike most other drugs, do not create a large number of happy, nonproblem users who are grateful to their suppliers. But that success is not universal: smoking rates continue to rise in many other countries. And even after that partial success, more than a thousand Americans a day die of smoking-related causes.

The alcoholic beverage industry, with its legion of not-very-profitable moderate users providing political cover for the relative handful of very profitable problem users, has had great success in thwarting effective policies to reduce problem drinking. Adjusted for inflation, alcohol taxes have fallen by four-fifths over the past sixty-five years, and it's still perfectly legal to sell alcohol to people who chronically get drunk and break the law.

What about legal availability without free trade? Couldn't that work?

Maybe. There could be a government monopoly, with the officials in charge being tasked with making drugs available but not promoting their use. Users could be allowed to produce their own drugs, or to form small consumer-owned cooperative groups, as they now do in Spain. In theory, physicians could be allowed to prescribe drugs for nonmedical use and given the responsibility for ensuring that their patients didn't slip into substance use disorder. (The record with opiate pain relievers, which have become a major abuse problem even though they are, by law, to be prescribed only for medical use, casts doubt on the healthcare system's capacity to do that job.) Users could be allowed to set monthly purchase quotas for themselves, with sellers required to enforce those limits.

Those are all options, at least in theory (see chapter 11). How well they would function in practice would have to be worked out in the real world rather than on paper. Implementation details can matter quite a bit, and there is no guarantee the political process would produce a scheme as well-crafted as the ones that can be drawn up as an academic exercise by scholars who can safely ignore the realities of politics and public administration.

Isn't it impossible to make someone better off by coercing behavioral change?

If you define well-being as getting what you want when you want it, then by definition restrictions make people worse off. If human beings were the perfectly rational actors depicted in elementary economics textbooks—Spock-like beings with perfect foresight and perfect self-command—that definition would make sense. In the actual world, with actual human beings, it is often false. That's the problem with John Stuart Mill's famous "harm principle," which holds:

> That the only purpose for which power can be rightfully exercised over any member of a civilized community, against his will, is to prevent harm to others. His own good, either physical or moral, is not sufficient warrant. He cannot rightfully be compelled to do or forbear because it will be better for him to do so, because it will make him happier, because, in the opinion of others, to do so would be wise, or even right.

When Mill wrote *On Liberty* in 1859 (partly as a protest against the recent enactment of alcohol prohibition in Maine), the harm principle represented a strikingly radical viewpoint. A century and a half later, it has come to seem like common sense. Countless people who have never read or even heard of Mill think that individuals should be free to choose their own lifestyles.

But the harm principle hides an important assumption: that every "member of a civilized community" is temptation-proof. For most of us, a moment of introspection suffices to refute that claim as it applies to ourselves. Few of us always act as we would like to act.

Drugs are a difficult policy problem precisely because drug taking is an activity more prone than most to escaping rational self-command. That being so, the case for protecting people from themselves—when it can be done at an acceptable cost—seems attractive, Mill's views to the contrary notwithstanding. As Mill himself says: "If anyone saw a person attempting to cross a bridge which had been ascertained to be unsafe, and there were no time to warn him of his danger, they might seize him and turn him back without any real infringement of his liberty; for liberty consists in doing what one desires, and he does not desire to fall into the river."

By the same token, while many people desire to use marijuana, no one desires to become addicted. This argument doesn't answer the practical question about how much drug control is enough, but the harm principle in the abstract does not answer that question either. Facts are needed.

*If people choose to harm themselves with drugs,
why is that anyone else's business?*

As a practical matter, those harming themselves often also harm others, at least when the behaviors involve losing control over the consumption of intoxicants. Nevertheless, imagining the pure case of someone who inflicts no tangible harms on anyone else can be a useful thought experiment for challenging the common propensity to constrain others' behavior merely because that behavior is different or unconventional.

That challenge encapsulates the central argument against any sort of paternalistic intervention in private behavior. To some libertarians and advocates of laissez-faire, it seems axiomatic. But it is subject to at least three substantive responses; how persuasive they seem will vary from case to case depending on facts, and from reader to reader depending on values.

First, by some reckonings, self-damage to a human being is still damage, and if it can be prevented at reasonable cost—including some restrictions on the freedom to engage in self-damaging behavior, as in Mill's bridge example—that's a good enough reason to interfere. We no longer criminalize attempted suicide, but police and emergency medical personnel routinely intervene to save the lives of people who have attempted to kill themselves, and that interference with the consequences of individual choice remains largely uncontroversial.

Second, only a hermit could ever truly engage in purely self-regarding behavior as Mill defines it. The rest of us have families, friends, neighbors, and coworkers, all of whom are likely to pay some sort of price if we get ourselves into profound trouble. If "any man's death diminishes me," then is self-destructive behavior ever fully self-regarding?

Obviously, these two claims could be carried to the extreme of requiring everyone to eat a healthy diet and get proper amounts of exercise and sleep. But the fact that a principle could be extended to the point of absurdity does not taint its less absurd applications. The practical claim that interventions in private consumption choices are likely to prove difficult to implement and often have damaging side effects is no doubt true, and it constitutes a good argument for moderation in drug control. But the sweeping assertion that self-damage should always be ignored is hard to justify, at least on the pragmatic, utilitarian grounds on which Mill in particular chose to take his stand. The claim that there is a "human right" to regulate one's own mental processes—chemically or otherwise—would, if accepted, be decisive. But Mill makes no such argument, and those who do have not offered very convincing reasons to support the claim.

The third answer to the question "Why is my drug habit anyone else's business?" is that people do not, in fact, make their decisions about drug consumption merely as individuals, without reference to the drug-consumption choices of others, any more than they decide how to dress without reference to how others dress. Fashion is a ferociously potent force, and a person's belief—true or false—about the drug-taking patterns of others turns out to have important causal power over his or her own drug taking, to the point where one technique for preventing drug abuse among adolescents is to correct their often inflated ideas about how many of their peers are using various drugs and how much they are using.

Abraham Lincoln, as a very young member of the Illinois legislature, laid out this argument in his remarkable Temperance Address, which may be the wisest, wittiest, and most eloquent set of reflections on drugs and drug abuse ever offered. (The sample below does not do full justice to Lincoln's argument; the full text, available online, repays close study.)

But it is said by some, that men will think and act for themselves; that none will disuse spirits or anything else, merely because his neighbors do; and that moral influence is not that powerful engine contended for. Let us examine this. Let me ask the man who could maintain this position most stiffly, what compensation he will accept to go to church some Sunday and sit during the sermon with his wife's bonnet upon his head? Not a trifle, I'll venture. And why not? There would be nothing irreligious in it: nothing immoral, nothing uncomfortable. Then why not? Is it not because there would be something egregiously *unfashionable* in it?

Then it is the influence of fashion; and what is the influence of fashion, but the influence that other people's actions have on our own actions, the strong inclination each of us feels to do as we see all our neighbors do? Nor is the influence of fashion confined to any particular thing or class of things. It is just as strong on one subject as another. Let us make it as unfashionable to withhold our names from the temperance cause as for husbands to wear their wives' bonnets to church, and instances will be just as rare in the one case as the other.

If Lincoln is right and drug taking is profoundly fashion-driven, the claim that it is "self-regarding behavior" cannot stand.

Again, the current state of the world concerning alcohol allows us to predict some of the likely consequences of legalizing marijuana. A nondrinker in a group of drinkers may not only feel uncomfortable, but may actually be unwelcome. (Part of the genius of the "designated driver" idea is that it provides a social role for the teetotaler.) And if that group of drinkers consists of workmates, teammates, schoolmates, neighbors, or kinsfolk, exclusion may carry a cost well beyond hurt feelings.

Today, there are relatively few social settings in which *not* smoking pot would single an adult out for unfavorable attention. But surely that fact results in part from the current prohibition. If marijuana were legal, some people who do not now use it, and would prefer not to use it, would find it more socially comfortable to go along with the crowd, possibly to their detriment.

None of that proves that any particular drug regulation is prudent. Nor does it justify the majority in quashing minority patterns of drug taking on mere whim. But the notion that there is a purely logical proof that all restrictions on drug taking must, in principle, be unjustified does not stand up to close inspection.

But isn't everyone with an addictive personality already addicted to something?

This argument for legalization is mere wishful thinking. While it's true that people with substance use disorders tend to have some personality traits in common, many of those traits (such as secretiveness) tend to develop and become entrenched only after addiction, not before. They are effects, not causes. Certainly there are differences across individuals and population groups in susceptibility to addictive behaviors, and some of those differences seem to have a genetic basis. But those are tendencies, not the irrevocable decrees of fate. When drugs are cheaper and more available, more people use more of them, and some of those people get caught up in bad habits, while others experience or cause harm from intoxicated behavior.

As will be discussed further in chapter 8 with reference to alcohol and marijuana in particular, while one drug can sometimes substitute for another, two drugs can also be mutually complementary—like printers and ink cartridges—so that making either one cheaper or more prevalent increases the desirability of the other. At present, there is simply no scientific basis for any confident assertion about how legalizing marijuana would affect heavy drinking, smoking, or dependence on other illegal drugs. There is a thin but encouraging literature suggesting that a legalization-induced increase in marijuana use might be accompanied by a reduction in abuse of prescription opiate pain killers. However, there is also a large and discouraging literature suggesting there may be a concomitant increase in tobacco use and addiction.

If the results of legalization are uncertain, why not just try it out, and go back to the current system if legalization doesn't work?

Some processes are reversible; some are not. If you melt an ice cube and then put it in the freezer, you get an ice cube back. But if you toast a piece of bread and put it in the freezer, you get cold toast, not fresh bread. Legalization is more like toasting bread than melting an ice cube.

If we tried out legalization just for a limited time or only in one area, we might not learn much about the effects of a permanent, national policy change. The number of problem users in the experimental area would likely go up, but how much of that would be "drug tourism" from elsewhere?

Yet "experimenting" with legalization nationally may be effectively impossible. If the result were little or no change in problem use—some would say anything up to a doubling—the experiment could be deemed a success, and there would be no reason to change back. But if the level of marijuana abuse quadrupled or quintupled, tobacco smoking rebounded, and problem drinking simultaneously increased rather than decreased—outcomes that cannot be ruled out—then there would be strong pressure to return to prohibition. But reinstituting a ban could create problems worse than those of the current situation. Those newly dependent marijuana users would not magically cease to be dependent if the law changed back. So restoring the original prohibition would lead to even larger illicit markets and market-related problems than there had been originally. Cold toast, not pretty ice cubes.

Additional Reading

Courtwright, David, "Mr. ATOD's Wild Ride."
Heyman, Gene M. *Addiction: A Disorder of Choice.*
Kleiman, Mark A. R. *Against Excess.*
Kleiman, Mark A. R., Jonathan P. Caulkins, and Angela Hawken. *Drugs and Drug Policy.*
Lincoln, Abraham. "Temperance Address."
MacCoun, Robert J., and Peter Reuter. "Assessing Drug Prohibition and Its Alternatives."
Rolles, Stephen, and Craig McClure. *After the War on Drugs.*
Schelling, Thomas C. "The Intimate Contest for Self-Command."

8

HOW IS LEGALIZATION OF MARIJUANA DIFFERENT FROM LEGALIZATION OF OTHER DRUGS?

How does legalizing marijuana compare to legalizing all drugs?

Legalizing marijuana involves both lower stakes and less uncertainty than legalizing any of the other major illicit drugs (cocaine/crack, heroin, and methamphetamine). Not that the consequences of marijuana legalization would be minor or easy to project; legalization would be a big change with unpredictable results. But the stakes are even higher and the uncertainties even greater when contemplating legalization of these other drugs.

A principal argument for legalizing all drugs is the anticipated reduction in crime, violence, corruption, and other problems associated with black markets. However, within the US borders, most of those problems stem from black markets associated with cocaine/crack, heroin, and methamphetamine, not marijuana, so legalizing marijuana would not do much to solve those problems.

Marijuana legalization also represents a smaller change from current policy than, for example, legalizing cocaine. Well before states began passing initiatives to legalize production of marijuana for recreational purposes, many jurisdictions had already decriminalized marijuana possession, allowed medical-marijuana, or both. Furthermore, even in the other states, enforcement against users has been gentle enough that survey respondents have only a vague idea whether they live in a state that has decriminalized or not.

Isn't marijuana known to be safe?

It's also argued that marijuana is natural, not addictive, and not toxic, and therefore shouldn't be prohibited. Indeed, on many dimensions marijuana is less risky than, say, methamphetamine.

However, there's nothing about a "natural" substance that guarantees it's safer than a synthetic. Nightshade, hemlock, monkshood, and castor beans are all natural, and all quite poisonous. Alcohol is a natural product; any fruit juice will ferment if left standing. Yet alcohol is still a dangerous drug.

It's true that refined chemicals can be more harmful than their natural sources (e.g., cocaine vs. coca leaves), and some processed forms of natural products (such as tobacco cigarettes) include harmful additives. But the health effects of marijuana have to be determined by evidence, not by assumption or assertion. Chapters 3 and 5 review that evidence. The basic finding is that using marijuana has adverse health effects, but the effects are generally not thought to be severe. Likewise, marijuana use can escalate to dependence. Indeed, about 4.1 million people in the United States self-report enough problems with their marijuana use to warrant a diagnosis of marijuana abuse or dependence.

If marijuana accounts for half of all drug arrests, would legalizing marijuana free up half of our prison cells?

No, not even close.

First of all, drug law violators account for only one-fifth of those in prison—though that is still a considerable number. One sometimes hears figures in the 50–60 percent range, but those pertain either to federal prisons or to the number of prisoners whose incarceration is linked in some way to their drug use (e.g., they committed a burglary to get money to buy drugs). The state prison systems collectively house roughly six times as many inmates as federal prisons, so the proportion in state facilities dominates the national (combined state and federal) figure.

The proportions are about the same in jails. Media accounts do not always differentiate between the two, but jails are not the same as prisons. To simplify, prisons are state and federal institutions that house people who have been convicted of a felony and received sentences of a year or longer. Jails are usually city or county facilities holding a mixture of people awaiting trial and those serving shorter sentences.

Would legalizing marijuana at least cut in half the number of drug law violators behind bars? Again, no; not even close. One of us, working along with Georgia State University criminologist Eric Sevigny, estimated that only about 8 percent of state and federal prison inmates serving time for drug law violations were marijuana-only offenders. (Some caught trafficking cocaine, methamphetamine, or heroin also possessed marijuana when arrested. But those individuals would still have been imprisoned if marijuana were legal.) Some other cases involve a mix of drug and nondrug violations. For example, there are convicted violent offenders who violated the terms of their probation or parole by getting caught with or testing positive for marijuana and are in prison. Their "controlling offense" would be the violent crime, but if marijuana were legal they might still be subject to community supervision. (Or not. Probationers and parolees are sometimes forbidden to use alcohol; such a rule could apply to marijuana after legalization.)

So the counting gets complicated, particularly for jails, but in round terms, drug violations account for about a fifth of incarceration, and marijuana-only violations account for less than 10 percent of that, or only about forty thousand people.

This might seem puzzling in light of claims that marijuana legalization would result in big criminal justice savings. For example, Harvard economist Jeff Miron has estimated that marijuana accounted for $13.7 billion of spending to enforce drug prohibition. But Miron did not break down inmates by drug. He assumed that the corrections budget for marijuana was the budget for all drug offenses multiplied by marijuana's share of arrests for drug sale or manufacture. This overestimates marijuana-related incarceration, because those arrested for marijuana are much less likely than those arrested for other drugs to be sentenced to long prison terms.

More recently, the American Civil Liberties Union estimated that the fiscal costs of marijuana possession enforcement in 2010 were about $3.6 billion, with low and high estimates ranging from $1.2 billion to $6 billion. However, the high estimate was largely based on Miron's methodology, and the middle estimate was simply the average of the low and high estimates. Even the lower estimate from

2010 may not be a lower bound for costs today, since there have been so many important changes in laws and enforcement since 2010 (including decriminalization in California and elsewhere, legalization in multiple states, and a 20 percent decline in the number of possession arrests).

Marijuana legalization would decrease the criminal justice costs associated with arresting and adjudicating adults for many marijuana offenses, and it will also reduce the collateral consequences of having a drug conviction; however, it will not eliminate marijuana-related police contacts. Marijuana will still likely be prohibited for those under 21 years old—about 20 percent of the current market—and in many places public consumption will still be an offense. There would also be the costs of developing a new regulatory system, pursuing tax evaders, and law enforcement to shut down the illicit market (which could be a significant cost in the early years).

How much drug-related crime, violence, and corruption would marijuana legalization eliminate?

Not much.

Arguably the greatest social cost of prohibiting most substances is the crime, violence, and corruption engendered by the resulting illicit markets. However, the great bulk of those problems stem from the markets for illegal stimulants (cocaine/crack and methamphetamine) and opiates (specifically heroin), not marijuana. There are not many drive-by shootings between rival marijuana gangs in the United States.

This is not an inevitable consequence of pharmacology. Rather, it is mostly a matter of economics. Marijuana production, distribution, and consumption in the United States usually do not involve transactions or penalties with stakes high enough to make it worth killing someone.

A cocaine shipment entering the United States might weigh 250 kilograms and be worth $10,000–$15,000 per kilogram, for a total value of $3 million; that shipment could be hidden in the trunk of a large sedan. Marijuana entering the United States from Mexico costs perhaps a few hundred dollars per pound, so $3 million worth would fill a five-ton truck. There is not much point trying to shoot one's way out of a traffic stop when the getaway vehicle is a semi.

Another big difference is that most (84 percent) household-survey respondents report obtaining the marijuana they used most recently from a friend or relative, and half (51 percent) say it was given to them for free. That stands in marked contrast to low-level distribution of heroin and crack, which often occurs in violent, localized markets controlled by armed gangs.

Would legalization increase marijuana use and dependence by as much as legalization of crack and other drugs would increase their markets?

Probably not.

It is very hard to predict how legalization of any substance will affect use and dependence. But legalization of marijuana would cause smaller changes in most of the key factors driving consumption—availability, price, social stigma, and enforcement risks for users—than would legalization of cocaine/crack, heroin, and methamphetamine.

Legalization, at least on the alcohol model, would generally increase availability. However, youth already report substantially greater availability for marijuana than for other illegal drugs, so there is less room for increase for marijuana. In 2015, four out of five twelfth graders describe marijuana as "fairly easy" or "very easy" to get. The corresponding proportions are only slightly higher for alcohol (87 percent) but much lower for cocaine (29 percent), crack (22 percent), heroin (20 percent), and meth (15 percent).

Likewise, legalization could reduce production costs dramatically for marijuana, but less than it would for the other major illegal drugs. Furthermore, at less than a dollar per stoned hour, today's marijuana prices are already pretty low.

And as argued above, current penalties may already be too low to deter much marijuana use—again, especially among juveniles. Likewise, marijuana is not widely perceived as harmful, so the endorsement implied by legalization may not much affect perceptions about how harmful it is to use marijuana. The same is probably true of the social stigma associated with use.

There is also the simple matter of numbers. About 45 percent of American adults say they have tried marijuana, compared with approximately 15 percent for cocaine. The ratio of unexposed to exposed potential customers is much lower for marijuana than for any other illegal drug.

Overall, then, it seems likely that legalizing marijuana would produce a smaller increase in prevalence and abuse than would legalizing other illicit drugs.

Would more marijuana use lead to more alcohol abuse, or less?

The scientific literature on this question is divided. Furthermore, the answer might be different for different groups of people, and might not remain the same over time.

It might seem intuitive that making marijuana more available would tend to decrease alcohol use; as competing means of altering one's mood, one drug can substitute for the other. No doubt if marijuana were legal, some of today's alcoholics would be daily pot smokers instead; that would, on balance, probably make them and those around them better off, in terms of physical health effects and the risks of accidental and deliberate injury to users and others.

But two drugs can also be mutually complementary. When two products are economic complements, making either one cheaper or more available increases demand for the other. That can be true because they are used together, like fishing reels and fishing lures, or because buying one good now (say, an automobile) leads to more consumption of a complement (gasoline or motor oil) later. Rum-and-cola, or a cup of coffee and a cigarette, illustrate the first type of complementarity. The effects of heavy drinking as a teenager on the risks of heroin addiction in adulthood illustrate the second type. Either or both sorts of complementarity could, in principle, apply to marijuana and any other drug. Most people with substance use disorders (except for those who are exclusively alcohol abusers) use at least two drugs; much of the folklore of drug use involves the effects of various drug combinations.

Economists have tried to estimate the effect that cheaper or more expensive marijuana has on alcohol use. Alas, different studies reach opposing conclusions, and some studies reach opposing conclusions for different population groups. Furthermore, these studies estimate contemporaneous effects through the price mechanism but miss any longer-term effects and those through other mechanisms (e.g., reputation and custom).

The uncertainties are amplified when considering legalization, because no country in the modern era had legalized marijuana before Uruguay did in 2013, so there are no historical data pertaining to its effects on alcohol use. We are just starting to get good science on how medical-marijuana laws affect the use of marijuana and other substances (see chapter 13), but those price drops are small compared with what we would expect under national legalization. Hence, there is no scientific basis for anyone to make confident assertions about what would happen to heavy drinking if marijuana were legalized.

This uncertainty matters enormously. Alcohol-related problems are much greater than those involving marijuana. The disparity varies by outcome; in the United States, three to four times as many people are dependent on alcohol as on marijuana (7.9 million vs. 2.8 million dependent users in 2013, by one measure), but alcohol causes more than ten times as much crime and violence. "Cost of illness" studies provide another relevant yardstick. The figure for excessive alcohol use (one estimate placed it at $224 billion in 2006) is comparable to that of all illicit drugs combined (estimated at $193 billion in 2007 by a similar methodology). Since marijuana accounts for a modest share of all illicit-drug damage, the cost of illness associated with alcohol could be perhaps five to ten times the corresponding figure for marijuana.

Hence, a small change in alcohol problems could outweigh a large change in marijuana problems. Imagine—and again, we don't know—that policy changes that led to doubling marijuana use disorder would cut alcohol use disorder by 10 percent. In cost-of-illness terms, those two effects could roughly cancel out; the losses from more potheads would be matched by the gains from fewer drunks. On the other hand, if legalization led to a 10 percent increase in alcohol use disorder, it's hard to see how any gains on the marijuana side could balance out the harms from increased heavy drinking. And yet, based on what is now known, it's not possible to rule out even bigger changes, in either direction.

Would more marijuana use lead to more or less abuse of other substances?

Similar concerns, and similar unpredictability, pertain to interactions with other drugs. Suppose legalization doubled marijuana use and marijuana-related substance use disorders. That would mean that millions of additional people would have a medically diagnosable problem controlling their substance use. If even a modest proportion of them subsequently started abusing cocaine, then that would be a sizable increase in cocaine abuse. By most measures, even complete elimination of all marijuana-related harms would not be enough to offset a 33 percent increase in cocaine-related harms. On the other hand, if cheaper marijuana prompted cocaine or meth abusers to "trade down" to a less disruptive dependence on marijuana, that would be a huge social gain.

Interactions with tobacco could matter even more. If a doubling in marijuana smoking led to even a 1 percent increase or decrease in tobacco smoking, that could be a swing of nearly five thousand more or fewer tobacco-related deaths per year; those are large numbers compared to the (quite small) number of deaths associated with marijuana.

The evidence concerning how lower prices and greater availability of marijuana affect use of other illegal drugs is just as divided as the evidence concerning effects on alcohol, and comes from a much thinner literature. The evidence concerning effects on tobacco use is stronger and is mostly bad news. Historically, marijuana and tobacco smoking have been complements, suggesting that legalization will increase tobacco smoking, although vaping and e-cigarettes might make the relationship going forward different than it has been in the past. A bright spot comes from a few studies suggesting that greater availability of marijuana may reduce problems associated with prescription pain killers.

This uncertainty makes it impossible at present to produce a solid benefit-cost analysis of marijuana legalization. Even if one could somehow pin down all the marijuana-related outcomes, there is no way to do so for indirect effects mediated through changes in the use of other substances.

If alcohol is more dangerous than marijuana, what's the logical justification for one being legal and the other illegal?

If we were making laws for a planet whose population had never experienced either marijuana or alcohol, and we had to choose one of the two drugs to make available, there would be a strong case for choosing marijuana, which has lower organic toxicity, lower addictive risk, and a much weaker link with accidents and violence.

But that's not the planet we live on. Here on Earth, alcohol has been an ingrained part of many cultures since the Neolithic Revolution. People have used cannabis products for thousands of years, but widespread use as an intoxicant in the United States is a phenomenon of the last hundred years. Even today only about one in thirteen Americans aged 18 and older currently uses marijuana (customarily defined as use within the last month); for alcohol, that figure is more than one in two.

History matters. Custom matters. Practicality matters. Even if there were public support for it, going back to alcohol prohibition wouldn't work—without a truly ferocious degree of law enforcement—precisely because centuries of tradition and decades of marketing have made alcohol a deeply ingrained feature of most social systems except where it is forbidden for religious reasons.

If alcohol had just been invented and no one was yet using it, it would go straight into Schedule I: high potential for abuse and no accepted medical value. And that ban might make sense. But once there is an established user base, prohibition becomes impractical. At least until recently, marijuana had not yet become similarly entrenched.

It's true that the arguments for maintaining marijuana prohibition also point strongly toward tighter controls on alcohol: higher taxes, limits on marketing, bans on sales to people convicted of driving drunk or other crimes committed under the influence. So it's fair to mock the "drug warriors" who worry about every intoxicant except the one that does the most damage. But, by the same token, advocates of marijuana legalization who point to the horrible damage alcohol does are actually making a strong argument for maintaining marijuana prohibition: the one intoxicating drug we legalized is the most harmful of all, despite many efforts at regulation.

Could it be reasonable to support legalizing marijuana while keeping some other drugs illegal?

Absolutely.

There is no logical reason to apply the same policies to all psychoactives. Most people support prohibiting crack but not caffeine, and that is an entirely defensible position.

A key reason someone might support legalizing marijuana but not the other major illicit drugs is that legalizing marijuana is less risky. Relative to cocaine, methamphetamine, and the opiates, marijuana enforcement is already lax, social stigma is rather modest, and dependence is easier to escape. So legalizing marijuana is less likely to produce problematic increases in dependence than legalizing any of those other substances.

Can two reasonable people sensibly disagree about marijuana legalization?

Certainly.

Even if we could accurately estimate all the gains and losses— which we can't—there's no reason two people holding different values couldn't reasonably disagree on whether those effects represented, on balance, progress or deterioration. One person might care enormously about reducing dependence; another might place greater emphasis on personal freedom and reducing criminal justice costs. Those two people could make the same predictions about the likely consequences of legalization but reach different conclusions about its desirability (see chapter 18).

Additional Reading

Blue Ribbon Commission on Marijuana Policy. *Pathways Report: Policy Options for Regulating Marijuana in California.*

Cook, Philip J. *Paying the Tab.*

Kaplan, John. *Marijuana: The New Prohibition.*

Kleiman, Mark A. R. *Against Excess.*

Kleiman, Mark A. R. *Marijuana: Costs of Abuse, Costs of Control.*

MacCoun, Robert J., and Peter Reuter. *Drug War Heresies.*

9

WHAT IF WE TREATED MARIJUANA LIKE ALCOHOL?

Marijuana-legalization advocates often say that we should "regulate marijuana like alcohol." What would that mean? US states vary in the way they handle alcohol, and some still allow sales only by state stores, but most apply more or less the following rules:

- Production, distribution, and sale are handled by private, for-profit businesses.
- Those commercial activities are subject to normal business regulations plus additional regulations specific to alcohol.
- The alcohol-specific regulations are largely designed to manage the market, not to minimize intoxication (other than behind the wheel, on the job, or by minors).
- Commercial producers and sellers need special licenses, and those licenses can be suspended or revoked for violations of the regulations.
- Laws restrict who may use, when and where they may use, and what they may do under the influence, but, for the most part, any adult not visibly under the influence can buy in unlimited quantities.
- Substance-specific taxes are added to the normal sales tax, but those taxes make up a modest portion of retail prices.

"Regulating marijuana like alcohol"—legalization on the alcohol model—would involve applying more or less the same rules to a legal marijuana market. That option might also be called "commercialization," to distinguish it from government monopoly, grow-your-own, or production and distribution limited to nonprofits or user co-ops (see chapter 11).

What special regulations could apply to legal marijuana?

Prohibition is a somewhat blunt instrument; legalization plus regulation and taxation allows for finer distinctions. Different localities might adopt different approaches according to local circumstances.

For example, municipalities might regulate where marijuana can be used. Drinking alcohol on the street, in parks, and in other outdoor public places is illegal in most of the United States, but drinking is allowed in restaurants and bars. In much of the country, the opposite holds true for tobacco: most indoor use in public spaces is banned to protect nonsmokers from secondhand smoke, but outdoor use is permitted.

Marijuana is both intoxicating (like alcohol) and often smoked (like tobacco), making secondhand exposure a risk, or at least an annoyance—some people find the odor of marijuana very hard to take. Marijuana regulations could combine approaches taken with alcohol and tobacco. Many jurisdictions already have special sanctions for smoking marijuana "in the public view" or ban indoor marijuana smoking in places where tobacco smoking is banned. What a user should do where smoking is banned both indoors and outdoors is a different question—is smoking allowed only in doorways?—as is deciding whether anti-smoking rules should apply to the use of vaporizers.

Using marijuana while driving would presumably still be illegal; most states ban having an open container of alcohol in a moving car. However, regulating marijuana-impaired driving faces a technical challenge: the most common marijuana tests do not reflect current intoxication or impairment even nearly as accurately as breath tests do for alcohol; instead, they detect use over the past several days, or—for frequent users—even weeks. Better testing methods could be developed; for example, blood-spot tests might become acceptable to perform at roadside even if blood draws are not. But there might be more fundamental limitations, as blood THC concentrations do not correlate well with impairment. Some Australian jurisdictions fall back on a saliva test that detects recent use (within hours), though not current impairment.

Marijuana products themselves could be regulated. For example, even if marijuana in its conventional form were legal, in theory one could still ban selling it in candy bars and brownies, paralleling efforts to limit the sale of "alcopops" that appeal to youth. In practice, state-level legalization of medical and recreational marijuana has been accompanied by an explosion of product forms and types. Washington State allows edibles but not candy; Colorado allows both but limits the THC dose per unit, largely in response to a wave of unintended overdoses from edibles that contained many doses within one pastry or candy bar.

Alcoholic beverages containing THC could be banned; there are currently restrictions on adding caffeine to alcoholic beverages on the grounds that it is an "unsafe food additive." Flavorings and other additives could likewise be banned or regulated, just as the Tobacco Control Act bans cigarettes containing fruit, candy, vanilla, or clove flavors. That wouldn't prevent users from doing their own blending. It isn't hard to combine THC-infused tinctures with conventional spirits, and companies sell hundreds of heat-resistant flavor options that do-it-yourself users can mix with THC and/or nicotine e-juice for their vaping pens.

Academic designs for ideal regulatory regimes often assume that potency is reliably measurable and discuss regulation of potency (typically measured by THC content), since more potent strains may create greater risks of adverse side effects. There is also emerging science concerning the interactions of THC with other cannabinoids; perhaps the seemingly dangerous very-high-THC, very-low-CBD varieties could be banned even if other high-THC forms were permitted—as absinthe has sometimes been banned over concerns about the toxin thujone even when other forms of alcohol are allowed. However, the trend to date in the United States has been only to require testing and accurate labeling—so users know what they are buying—not to limit what can be sold. In 2013, a bill was sent to the Dutch parliament to place cannabis with a THC concentration of 15 percent or more on Schedule I, thus banning it from the coffee shops, but it is unclear whether this will ever happen.

Observers' degree of optimism about regulations sometimes reflects broader habits of belief. Public-health-oriented advocates of legalization see great potential for careful regulation to mitigate the harms of marijuana use, while libertarian advocates are suspicious of regulation generally. Opponents of legalization see regulations as weak instruments in the face of the creative force of market innovation, particularly if the regulatory agencies get too cozy with marijuana-industry lobbyists.

Opinions likewise diverge with respect to the nature of products that will be offered. Optimists anticipate organically-grown, carefully-labeled labeled material that protects users from the risks of illicit-market products and allows informed customers to choose from an array of forms, varieties, and potencies to suit their personal reasons for using. Pessimists believe high-end products will exist but, like organic vegetables, will remain a niche market for the educated elite. They fear that the bulk of THC will be sold in forms more akin to "store brand" foods or mass-market beer—consistent quality sold at low cost without frills—and that such Walmart-like efficiency will relentlessly drive down the price of intoxication and thus increase the risks of substance use disorder. Likewise, pessimists worry that for-profit companies will promote blends designed to maximize frequent intoxication, perhaps by combining marijuana with nicotine. Some believe that in the natural course of events marijuana conglomerates will try to copy the tobacco companies' playbook, but have faith that wise government policies will save vulnerable consumers from the clutches of rapacious capitalists.

In any event, it is very hard to predict how the dance among producers' marketing strategies, consumers' tastes, and regulators' control efforts would play out. But a fair guess is that the commercial model would bring considerable variety and product proliferation, if for no other reason than that the producers might have a hard time making large profits if they sell only undifferentiated marijuana.

Could advertising be restricted in the United States?

Advertising restrictions are both important and controversial. Some public-health-oriented advocates of legalization argue that advertising and promotion would be banned; children's television shows couldn't be sponsored by sellers of marijuana lollipops. Uruguay's legalization law bans all forms of promotion and events. Skeptics warn, though, that such controls would be struck down in the United States after national legalization because the current judicial interpretation of First Amendment free-speech protections extends to "commercial free speech." (The experience to date is not informative; it is easier for states to restrict advertising of something that is still prohibited by federal law than it would be to maintain such restrictions on legal products.) And it is not only the US Constitution that matters; Washington State's lawyers told its marijuana regulators that any regulation of advertising that is not actively fraudulent or directed explicitly to children would violate sellers' free-speech rights under the state constitution.

The American rule applying free-speech doctrine to commercial advertising is virtually unparalleled elsewhere; many countries ban all forms of tobacco advertising, even requiring that cigarettes be sold in plain packages. Direct-to-consumer advertising of pharmaceuticals is also largely an American phenomenon. Even within the United States, application of the commercial free-speech doctrine is inconsistent, covering alcohol and pharmaceutical marketing but not, for example, securities promotion. So strong predictions about whether the courts would allow tight regulation of marijuana marketing ought to be taken with a grain of salt.

The nature and extent of advertising could depend in part on how much the industry came to be dominated by a few large corporations with national advertising budgets. In turn, industry structure would be influenced by advertising opportunities. The possibility of developing recognizable national brands might be exactly what drives the industry toward a small number of large firms, as happened in the beer industry.

The rise of digital and social media marketing methods complicates predictions. In the 1960s, broadcast television dominated advertising opportunities; today there are myriad other strategies, ranging from simple internet search engine optimization to social-media-based strategies, product placements, "adver-gaming," and viral-marketing strategies. It is much easier for regulators to monitor and control traditional advertising than to limit these newer promotional activities.

If production and distribution were restricted to nonprofit entities or government monopolies, that might remove the incentive for marketing. Or it might not; the aggressive marketing often associated with state lotteries is a warning in this regard.

A tempering option of denying state and federal tax deductions for advertising is, however, available. There is no constitutional right to advertising; indeed, a leading presidential candidate has proposed denying tax deductions for advertising prescription drugs to consumers.

How could marijuana be taxed?

Marijuana taxes could be assessed per unit weight, as with Alaska's tax of $50 per ounce on marijuana. However, taxing by weight gives an incentive to produce higher-potency products, because that would lower the tax per hour of intoxication.

Taxes could also or instead be based on value. For example, Colorado imposes a 10 percent tax on retail marijuana sales, in addition to standard sales taxes. (Colorado also notionally has a 15 percent tax on producers, but its implementation makes it operate as a tax on weight.)

These ad valorem (percentage-of-price) taxes are simple to collect, but they have two serious drawbacks. First, they amplify changes in price. When the pretax price goes down, so does the tax. Unless minimum price rules were enforced, in the long run, national legalization should drive down the price of no-frills, basic marijuana. That would undercut tax revenues and the prevention benefits of keeping prices high.

The second problem is gaming the tax with phony transfer payments or by bundling marijuana with another product or service. For example, a marijuana bar or buyers' club might use a high cover charge or membership fee (not taxed) to subsidize provision of cheap marijuana, particularly if it also sold food, not just marijuana. Colorado's Club 64 did this, deriving revenue from a $30 cover charge while giving marijuana (and alcohol) away for free. Likewise, if states retreated from the current rules restricting marijuana sales to stores that sell marijuana and nothing else, a convenience store might offer deeply discounted marijuana as a loss-leader to lure in customers who would then buy gas and snacks; the ad valorem tax on the discounted marijuana would be commensurately small.

So ad valorem taxes might work best in conjunction with minimum pricing rules, particularly if sales were limited to takeaway purchases from stand-alone stores.

Taxes could instead be based on potency, as with alcohol (distilled spirits are not only taxed more heavily than wine and beer, their taxes also rise with alcohol content). The THC content of marijuana—and thus its intoxicating power—varies enormously; 4–6 percent is typical now for commercial-grade, 10–20 percent for sinsemilla, and in excess of 40 percent for hashish and extracted concentrates. This parallels the range for alcohol, which varies from beer (commonly 2–6 percent alcohol by volume) to distilled spirits (typically 80–100 proof, which means 40–50 percent alcohol). However, taxing marijuana potency could be more complicated. Alcoholic drinks have just one type of psychoactive molecule (ethanol). Marijuana contains many, and their relative proportion can vary dramatically. (The "menu" of one marijuana dispensary advertises strains with THC/CBD ratios that vary from 1:2 to 100:1.)

A bill filed in the Massachusetts legislature in 2013 would have imposed a tax of $1,000 per ounce of THC (for example, $100 per ounce on marijuana that is 10 percent THC), but no jurisdiction has yet implemented such a policy.

It also matters where along the distribution chain taxes get collected. Marijuana is much more compact than alcohol. In terms of volume, a year's worth of marijuana for a two-joint-a-day user resembles a six-pack of beer, and by weight it is more like a single can. Whether a product is being concealed to evade outright prohibition or to dodge taxes, the more compact it is the easier it is to smuggle. There might be less tax evasion if taxes were collected at the point of production rather than (or in addition to) the point of sale, especially if production were limited to a small number of licensees.

Would regulations and taxes in practice approach the public health ideal?

Designing wise policies on the blackboard is easier than passing them through the legislature in the face of industry lobbying. The history of tobacco and alcohol regulation in the United States is hardly encouraging on this score, and the marijuana industry has rapidly insinuated itself into rulemaking processes in ways that pharmaceutical-industry executives can only daydream about. When the Oregon Liquor Control Commission named fifteen people to its marijuana rules advisory committee, they included the chief petitioner for the proposition legalizing marijuana, four entrepreneurs in the industry, and the founder of a company that tested marijuana for potency and contaminants. So, while it isn't hard to design a tax and regulatory system that looks good on paper, getting that system on the law books is harder.

Allowing a licit industry creates businesses with strong incentives to develop and sustain abusive consumption patterns, because people with the worst habits make the best customers, whether of marijuana, alcohol, cocaine, or slot machines. So one should expect a licit, for-profit marijuana industry to design its products, pricing, and marketing to promote as much frequent use and addiction as regulators allow.

Thus much will hinge on whether the regulatory agency views its job as thwarting such industry intentions, or as merely ensuring that companies obey the law. In caricature, those are the respective postures of the FDA vis-à-vis tobacco and of typical state alcohol control boards. The goal of the FDA's Center for Tobacco Products is to "reduce the harm from all regulated tobacco products . . . , including reducing the number of people who start to use tobacco products [and] encouraging more people to stop using." By contrast, the mission of the Washington State Liquor and Cannabis Board is to "promote public safety and trust through fair administration and enforcement of liquor, tobacco, and cannabis laws."

Even a regulator that wanted to tax and regulate in ways that promote public health over corporate profits would have to contend with an industry mobilizing its employees, shareholders, and consumers against any effective restriction. Since the industry profits from problem users, it will have an incentive to oppose policies that would effectively control addiction. Like alcohol but unlike tobacco, a licit marijuana industry would have millions of happy, nonproblem customers, and it would try to mobilize them against laws that would actually be disadvantageous to the industry but could be made to seem threatening to consumers.

How much enforcement would regulation and taxation require?

That depends entirely on how much regulation and taxation gets imposed. If marijuana were legalized on a completely free-market basis, the minimal regulations would generate minimal regulatory costs. If the only tax on marijuana were the general sales tax, there would be no more reason to evade that tax than the sales tax on soap. The more regulations and the higher the taxes, the more expensive they would be to enforce. So it's not possible to predict the cost of regulation and tax collection in advance, without specifying the rules to be enforced and the taxes to be collected.

There is the option of having a lot of taxes and regulations but not bothering to enforce them. But then you shouldn't expect them to have much effect. Any regulation tight enough and any tax high enough to actually change behavior is worth evading, and therefore needs to be enforced if it is to work.

Federal, state, and local governments spend hundreds of millions of dollars each year enforcing the rules about, and collecting the taxes on, alcohol and tobacco. By some standards, that effort is woefully inadequate. Billions of dollars in alcohol and especially tobacco taxes go uncollected, and minors continue to have easy access to goods nominally forbidden to them. States and localities with high tobacco taxes face massive smuggling of cigarettes from low-tax states. So enforcing marijuana taxes and regulations stringently enough to ensure compliance would be a significant task.

Consider, for example, the seemingly straightforward proposition that legal marijuana should be assayed and labeled with the content of its main psychoactives and tested for dangerous contaminants such as pesticides, molds, and fungi. If regulations required every package to be tested individually, the cost of testing would be prohibitive. The less frequent the sampling, the greater the risk of quality variations or contamination: consider the repeated outbreaks of salmonella in fresh eggs. States could delegate the testing task to the industry, and do spot audits to ensure the testing was being done honestly, but the cost of that system would rise with the extent of the auditing. The "no free lunch" rule applies everywhere.

How many marijuana-related arrests would there be after legalization?

Legalization will not free police from all marijuana-related responsibilities. They would still have to enforce rules about underage possession, distribution to minors, impaired driving, and consumption where use is banned, just as they now do for alcohol.

According to the 2013 national household survey, 7.9 million people self-reported enough problems with alcohol to meet the criteria for dependence. For marijuana the corresponding number was 2.8 million. Alcohol generated two million arrests in 2013 (drunk and disorderly, DUI, open container, underage drinking, sales to minors)—about one per year for every four dependent users. Marijuana generated 700,000 arrests (possession and sale), also about one per year for every four dependent users. So legality does not automatically generate very low rates of arrest.

Nevertheless, legalization may replace some custodial arrests with citations, just as decriminalization does. In 2014, after legalization in Colorado, there were 770 instances of the Denver police citing (or in some cases arresting) people for unlawful public display or consumption of marijuana, and hundreds more for possession and use in parks. (In 2015, Denver police gave 196 citations over the weekend preceding April 20 alone.) In per capita terms, the 2014 rate is within a factor of two of the national arrest rate for marijuana offenses. Citations are much less costly than arrests, but the number of police contacts will not go to zero.

What would happen to marijuana prices after national legalization?

Prices in Dutch coffee shops and California medical dispensaries are not a good indicator of what prices would be after national legalization, because neither place has large-scale, open, commercial production. In the Netherlands, retail selling is tolerated, but growers and wholesale dealers still face potential prison time and therefore still have to hide. The situation in California is murkier, but even there growing isn't entirely safe from enforcement, as one hapless entrepreneur who thought he was complying with state law discovered when he was indicted on federal charges carrying a five-year mandatory prison term.

Current prices in Colorado and Washington State aren't good indicators either, for three reasons. First, the Obama administration's semiformal toleration of the marijuana industry in those places is not the same as national legalization. It leaves the tolerated industry with problems not faced by legal industries, including a ban on interstate marketing and sales, limitations on access to financial services, and rules that in effect impose higher business income taxes on sellers of illicit drugs. Second, the policy of toleration could be changed at any moment—say, under a new administration in 2017—with retroactive effect; people could go to prison then for activity they engage in now. Third, it will take time—perhaps five to ten years after national legalization—for the industry to ramp up, achieve economies of scale, and fully develop and exploit more efficient production and distribution methods. To give a simple example, most production in Colorado and Washington is still done indoors under artificial lights; the resulting electricity bills alone may exceed the total cost of growing in greenhouses in the long run. And so far Uruguay has implemented legalization of production only at home and in small co-ops.

Since no industrialized nation in the modern era has yet implemented large-scale commercial production nationally, there are no solid historical analogies one can draw on to estimate what production costs or prices would be under those conditions. Instead, one has to work through the numbers, the same way a farmer would when considering the possibility of growing any other new crop.

Thinking about the problem that way suggests that legalization might dramatically reduce production costs in the long run. The size of the potential decline is not widely appreciated.

Herbal marijuana is just dried plant material. A joint has about as much of that plant material as a teabag. Yet the marijuana in a joint currently costs ten to one hundred times as much as a comparable amount of tea sold as a box of teabags in a supermarket. That is primarily because prohibition has forced producers to operate in inefficient ways, not because of any intrinsic difficulties with growing the cannabis plant.

Most plant products are really cheap per gram, but serving sizes are much larger for fruits and vegetables than they are for marijuana. A gram a day of marijuana suffices for all but the heaviest users. A gram of apple a day wouldn't keep the doctor or hunger pangs away; it would amount to just one apple every three months.

Sinsemilla prices in the United States have already fallen as policies have liberalized; in California, prices have fallen (on an inflation-adjusted basis) from well over five thousand dollars per pound to the producer (what is called the "farm gate price") in the mid- to late 1990s to roughly two thousand per pound in 2010. Since then pound prices have been falling by roughly 10–15 percent a year; retail prices have also fallen, but not as quickly.

Those prices are still greatly inflated by the fact that marijuana growing is illegal (or, in California, quasi-legal). The United Nations reports that wholesale prices of commercial grade marijuana in Mexico are just $80 per pound, and prices of $30–$50 per pound are reported anecdotally. Granted, that is typically an inferior product with perhaps one-third the THC of California-grown sinsemilla, but the price per unit of THC is still just one-tenth that of the California product at wholesale.

Another sign of the effects of prohibition is that the price of that pound jumps from $80 to $400 on the US side of the border. And wholesale prices within the United States increase by an additional roughly $400 per pound per thousand miles as one moves north and east, e.g., to $800 per pound in cities one thousand miles from the border. Needless to say, trucking Mexican cucumbers costs much less. (As this was written, the USDA was quoting truckload prices for transporting Mexican produce to northern US cities that worked out to almost exactly 4 cents per pound per thousand miles, or one ten-thousandth the cost gradient of marijuana under prohibition.)

The key question is how cheaply professional farmers in the United States could produce THC after legalization, when the threat of enforcement is even lower than it is now in Mexico.

Agricultural experiments show that outdoor farming can achieve yields of two to three thousand pounds of (dry) usable marijuana per acre per year, with roughly six hundred pounds of that being flowers and the rest leaves and other lower-quality material that could be used to produce extracts.

In the United States marijuana is often grown from transplanted cuttings rather than seeds. Production costs for transplanted crops, such as cherry tomatoes and asparagus, are generally in the range of $5,000–$20,000 per acre. This suggests production costs for outdoor growing might be under $20 per pound for the flowers ($10,000 per acre divided by six hundred pounds per acre). The two thousand or so additional pounds of lower quality material might in total contain nearly as much THC suitable for extraction as do the six hundred pounds of flowers, with the lower potency being offset by the greater mass. So, on a "bud-equivalent" basis the cost per pound might fall further, perhaps to around $10, as compared to the current figure of more than $1,000.

Production costs could be even lower if the crop were grown solely for extracts. The cannabis plant is already farmed in Canada for industrial hemp, with costs generally under $500 per acre. If similar costs applied to cannabis plants grown in a similar manner but for THC extraction, production costs could be about twenty cents a pound of material harvested. Even if that material's extractable THC content were only 1 percent, the cost per unit of THC would be comparable to the cost estimated above for growing higher-potency cannabis from transplanted cuttings. Professional farmers growing in black dirt might coax out greater concentrations than can be achieved by backyard hobbyists or illicit growers working marginal hillsides in national forests.

Under conditions of illegality, marijuana processing—manicuring, drying, curing, resin production, etc.—is as burdensome as growing. However, legalization, and the consequent mechanization, could change this dramatically; tobacco costs less than a dollar a pound to receive, grade, stem, and cure.

So in the long run, after the industry has had time to mature, achieve economies of scale, and figure out ways to mechanize steps that are now done by hand, we could see production costs under national legalization as low as $10 or $20 per pound of flowers, or the equivalent of that in terms of THC content. Actual experience may be different; once production costs fall substantially, squeezing them down further may be less important than other considerations; just as some manufacturers have brought production back into the United States despite modestly higher costs because of other advantages. The key point is that national legalization may make it technically possible to achieve very low production costs per unit of THC.

Production costs anywhere near these figures could upend the traditional industry structure. Since a competitive market tends to drive prices down toward costs, the effect on patterns of use could be profound. The typical marijuana user who consumes once a week and so uses about an ounce a year isn't spending enough even at today's prices for price to matter much. But the heavy daily users who dominate consumption now spend a few thousand dollars per year each. In the long run, after national legalization, it might cost as little as $25 to produce that amount of intoxicant.

Legal marijuana could become far and away the cheapest intoxicant on a per-hour basis. At current supermarket beer prices, getting drunk costs something like $5–$10—call it a dollar or two per drunken hour. The price of marijuana intoxication today is roughly comparable. But unless regulators impose very heavy taxes or price floors, commercial legalization at the national level might allow a user to buy an hour's marijuana intoxication for dimes rather than dollars. It's hard to imagine that such a dramatic price drop wouldn't affect patterns of use. (A market in very cheap generic marijuana could co-exist with a higher-priced market for artisanal products.)

Note: These calculations are for outdoor production. Parallel calculations for greenhouse-based growing in warmer states suggest production costs that are higher, but only by a modest multiple, leaving the overall conclusion intact. Under national legalization, production will migrate to wherever costs are lowest.

How many people would be employed in marijuana growing?

Probably not many, once mechanization takes hold.

Marijuana is not nearly as potent per gram as cocaine or heroin, but its production is far more efficient per square foot. The UN estimates that the world's twenty million opiate users are supplied by about 200,000 hectares of poppy cultivation, or just a little over 1,000 square feet per user. It would take fifty very determined smokers to consume the fifty pounds of marijuana that could be produced on that amount of farmland. So production to supply today's THC consumption for the entire United States could take less than 10,000 acres—about the size of five or ten good-sized Iowa corn farms—out of the country's 400 million acres of cropland.

Even if legalization were to triple consumption, the number of American farmworkers employed in marijuana production could well be modest, perhaps under 25,000. (Production under less mechanized conditions in other countries could require more labor.) Hence, for the US farm sector, legal marijuana would be a minor specialty crop, and growing it would not have great economic significance outside of the handful of counties where that farming might concentrate.

It is harder to guess how many jobs would be created in ancillary production activities. Vaping pens might be manufactured mostly abroad, but production of edibles and THC-infused alcoholic drinks might generate jobs in the United States.

The greatest number of jobs might be in retail sales. If sales were restricted to marijuana-only stores, the retail sector might create tens of thousands of jobs. (Washington State's state-operated liquor stores employed a little over one full time employee per million dollars in liquor sold before they were privatized.) If marijuana were folded into general retailing, the number might be smaller. Whether those jobs would be well-paid partly depends on whether states require professional certification for "budtenders." The number of retail jobs might also depend on whether most marijuana is sold in a basic, unbranded form (as most vegetables are today), or whether premium brands predominate (compare store-clerk hours per pound of chocolate sold at Godiva shops with that for Hershey bars sold in convenience stores). On the other hand, if producers were allowed to sell by mail-order, distribution costs and related employment would be negligible; neither Amazon nor the Postal Service would have to add many employees to handle marijuana along with everything else.

If sale for on-premises use were allowed, there might be new jobs in marijuana "coffee shops" or marijuana-oriented music venues. Those might or might not replace jobs in bars and clubs that serve alcohol. Some additional jobs will be created in regulatory and compliance agencies.

What would the pretax retail price be for unbranded marijuana?

Nothing about marijuana production makes it a natural monopoly; the technical barriers to entry are low. So "regulate like alcohol" might create a competitive market with many producers. The other possibility is that a few big producers might convince consumers to place a high value on specific brands, as brewers and cigarette companies have done with similarly easy-to-produce commodities.

If the market remained fragmented and there were no minimum pricing rules, the pretax retail price of standard (generic, unbranded) marijuana might be bid down close to what it costs to produce and distribute the marijuana, including a competitive rate of profit.

Suppose the wholesale price (including producer taxes) were $40 per pound ($2.50 per ounce). That value-to-weight ratio would be within the range of typical consumer goods: higher than most fruits and vegetables but not as high as clothing or cigarettes. So retail markups for familiar goods may be relevant for thinking about marijuana after national legalization if it were sold in typical stores, not standalone marijuana-only shops.

For example, a supermarket sells meat from a three-hundred-pound side of beef whose wholesale price is $2–$2.50 per pound (adjusting for fat and bone) for $5–$15 per pound. If the markup on an ounce of legal marijuana were similar to that on a pound of meat, then $5–$15 per ounce (plus taxes) might be one guess of the retail price of no-frills marijuana.

On the other hand, a pack of cigarettes with a wholesale price of $2–$2.50 sells at retail for only $3–$4 (before the considerable taxes), substantially lower than the estimate based on meat. Either figure would be only a few percent of today's prices of about $300 per ounce for medium-grade marijuana. (Again, margins might be even lower by mail-order, if that were allowed.)

Reasoning by analogy is tricky, and these figures are only very rough guides. They are, however, consistent with independent estimates offered by Dale Gieringer, director of the California chapter of NORML, a group that advocates legalization. Gieringer testified before the California Assembly that if marijuana were unregulated, the price "would presumably drop as low as that of other legal herbs such as tea or tobacco—on the order of a few dollars per ounce . . . or a few cents per joint."

So after national legalization under a competitive industry model in which regulations sought only to manage the market and not to constrain its size, the price of basic, unbranded, no-frills marijuana could in theory fall to a very small fraction of current prices. Various things, including taxes and onerous regulations, might cushion the fall, but not prevent it. And it would be a surprise if such low prices failed to increase substantially the quantity consumed and the number of people with cannabis use disorder.

What would the after-tax retail price be for unbranded marijuana?

In Colorado and Washington at present the taxed price is anywhere from 33 percent to 100 percent higher than the untaxed price. Even if taxes doubled a $3.50-per-ounce before-tax price for unbranded marijuana to $7 per ounce, the monetary cost to consumers would still be almost inconsequential. The figure of $7 per ounce equals twenty-five cents a gram, or a dime for a 0.4-gram joint. Even a heavy, two-gram-per-day user would still be spending only fifty cents a day on marijuana—which is closer to the cost of a chewing gum habit than the cost of a coffee habit.

On the other hand, the potential for generating tax revenues motivates much of the interest in marijuana legalization. So it is worth asking how high a tax could be assessed without being undercut by tax evasion.

In percentage terms, the highest excise taxes collected in the United States today on consumer goods are those on cigarettes. The combined federal and state excise taxes on cigarettes average $2.60 and approach $5.50 per pack in New York State. (Some local city taxes push the total even higher, but those are frequently evaded; University of Illinois at Chicago economist David Merriman found that only one-third of cigarette packs discarded in Chicago bore a tax stamp indicating payment of Cook County's $2-per-pack tax.)

These tobacco excise taxes produce substantial evasion, with cigarettes being smuggled from low-tax states or bought on Native American reservations. That is sobering, because a $5.50-per-pack tax on a twenty-gram pack of cigarettes is only about $7.50 per ounce, far below Alaska's $50-per-ounce marijuana tax, let alone the gap between current prices and possible future production costs.

Another relevant benchmark is the markup when marijuana is smuggled into the United States from Mexico. People who evade taxes have to balance the money saved against the risk of arrest, just as smugglers do. The intensity of prosecution of tax cheats might not support price gaps between taxed and untaxed marijuana greater than the price gap observed today across the US-Mexico border. That price gap is about $300–$350 per pound, or about $20 per ounce.

Another piece of evidence: the effective tax in Colorado on $200-per-ounce retail (i.e., nonmedical) marijuana works out to about $45 per ounce, and many Colorado residents avoid (most of) this tax by purchasing through the medical rather than the recreational market.

On the other hand, because people use so little (by weight), the tax burden might not motivate much evasion. The average pack-a-day tobacco smoker in the United States would pay about $1,000 per year in state and federal taxes if all taxes were paid. In contrast, a

$20-per-ounce tax would only amount to $250 per year in taxes for a gram-a-day marijuana user.

So a guess, and it is only a guess, is that state-specific taxes up to $5 per ounce could be collected without difficulty; taxes of $5–$35 per ounce might induce some tax evasion; and taxes above $50 per ounce might be widely evaded unless the regulatory regime were carefully designed to make tax evasion difficult. (A uniform national tax would be easier to collect because it would eliminate interstate smuggling.)

This has two important implications. First, the retail price of no-frills marijuana might be driven more by taxation than by production costs. Second, state tax revenues from no-frills marijuana may be limited. Even if a $20-per-ounce tax could be imposed in a way that generated no evasion, and legalization tripled the amount of THC consumed, a market that adjusted to these taxes by shifting to high-potency forms might produce tax revenues of only a few billions of dollars per year nationwide. There might be greater potential for tax revenue from more expensive, branded forms, or from uniform national taxes.

What would the retail price be for branded and other forms of marijuana?

In the long run, after national legalization, marijuana may cost very little to produce. But people value marijuana highly; most marijuana is consumed by heavy users who are now spending well over $1,000 per year on it. Producers could make more money by convincing users to pay what the marijuana is worth to them, not just the generic competitive market price. So producers may try very hard to make their marijuana appear different or better or more appealing than the no-frills versions of the product.

There are myriad ways of doing this. High-end bottled water brands sell for more than common brands, and for vastly more than tap water, mostly because of the convenient package and advertising-induced associations with health, fitness, and sophistication. Mass-market beer, tobacco, and soft drink companies invest billions in advertising campaigns to keep customers from defecting to cheaper generic or store-brand products. Purveyors of fine chocolates package their candies in elaborate golden boxes that come with guidebooks describing each individual piece. In some cases, of course, brand cachet reflects genuine performance differences, and the chemical complexity of marijuana might create room for potentially profitable product differentiation.

From a public-health perspective, branding would be a mixed blessing. On the one hand, it would moderate the price collapse and associated increase in use among those who can be persuaded to prefer expensive brands. On the other hand, branding via multi-million-dollar marketing campaigns designed to associate specific marijuana brands with youth, pleasure, and glamour could also end up promoting marijuana use generally. (The public-health community, with some justification, distrusts tobacco-industry assurances that advertising merely shifts shares of a fixed market among brands without increasing smoking overall.) We should also expect the creativity unleashed by market competition to generate product innovation. Even the portents already visible are enough to shatter notions that legalized marijuana will be just like the old illegal market, only without the arrests. Medical-marijuana dispensaries and legal marijuana stores already sell a range of edibles, including gummy candies, chocolate bars, gingerbread, peanut butter, and cooking oils, largely unknown to the illicit market before the emergence of medical-marijuana sales after 1996.

If regulators allow it, innovation may also come from producers of conventional products, not just from marijuana producers. A chef, baker, confectioner, vintner, or brewer might jump at the chance to add such a cheap ingredient, in either trace or meaningful amounts, to dramatically distinguish his or her dish, cookie, candy, or beer from the competition. To give one example, Godiva sells top-of-the-line brownies for a dollar each (in packages of sixteen). After legalization it would cost a competitor pennies to add to its brownies as much marijuana as there is in a brownie that dispensaries now sell for ten dollars.

Such bundling could also occur at the service or experience level. Cafes with just the right atmosphere can charge far more for coffee and baguettes than soulless chains do, and both Napa Valley's wineries and Lancaster County's Amish farms support tourism that generates revenues that substantially supplement conventional product sales. It is easy to imagine marijuana-based analogues. Indeed, the *New York Times* reports that the Colorado Cannabis

Ranch and Amphitheater has invested $35 million in what it calls "the world's first weedery" and is raising $100 million in additional financing to expand to other states.

The revenue potential from branded or bundled marijuana sales is impossible to predict. But it's easy to imagine that much of the industry's profits would come from specialty products, even if the majority of the intoxication comes from forms that provide more bhang for the buck. Indeed, it is precisely because generic marijuana intoxication could be so cheap that the sizable profits might be made by branding or by bundling the intoxicant with some other product or service.

Would some businesses give legal marijuana away free?

They might well, if regulators allow it. The cost numbers make it seem possible.

After legalization, producing a pound of high-quality marijuana might cost $20. Suppose, for the sake of argument, that after (machine) rolling into joints, modest taxes, producer margin, and delivery charges, a bar or restaurant could order a pound of sinsemilla joints from wholesale suppliers for $45. That would be $0.10 a gram, or four or five cents per joint.

A nickel a joint would put marijuana within the range of various things that restaurants and bars give away. Packets of artificial sweeteners can be purchased for $60 for a box of two thousand packets (three cents per packet). Ketchup packets are about the same, while bulk prices for fortune cookies and packets of crayons that restaurants give kids are closer to five cents apiece. Unit costs for after-dinner mints range from two to seven cents, and a one-ounce handful of salted nuts can cost between a dime (peanuts) and a quarter or more (cashews).

If smoking a joint made restaurant patrons hungrier or casino patrons more reckless, would establishments give marijuana away as a loss leader? That seems hard to imagine, but it is also hard to argue that cost considerations would preclude it. (Restaurant operators might worry more about slowing the turnover of tables than about the cost of marijuana.)

Thus, there are at least three pricing scenarios: users paying very low prices at stores for generic marijuana, users paying much higher prices for branded marijuana made alluring through expensive marketing campaigns, and users being comped free marijuana by companies trying to woo them into other purchases.

All three could occur together. Anyone can get cheap water from the tap, but some still pay about five thousand times as much per unit for bottled water, while restaurants give you a glass for free. Likewise, grocery stores sell bags of bite-sized chocolate morsels at a nickel each, Godiva sells slightly larger morsels for more than $2 per piece, and fancy hotels leave them on your pillow.

How much would consumption increase?

No one knows how much nationwide legalization would increase consumption; we're in the realm of guessing, not forecasting.

Reasoning by historical analogy is tempting: "Lifting alcohol prohibition did this, so lifting marijuana prohibition will do that." Or "Consumption in the Netherlands is such-and-such a percentage of consumption in California, therefore . . ."

Fifteen years ago Rob MacCoun and Peter Reuter, two of the most respected scholars in drug policy, wrote a book called *Drug War Heresies*, the culmination of a decade-long systematic attempt to learn about legalization from comparisons with other times, places, and vices (such as prostitution and gambling). It still stands today as one of the five most important books ever written in the field, and we urge everyone to read it. Yet its ultimate stance is agnostic about the consequences of marijuana legalization; such comparisons simply do not provide definitive guidance. The RAND marijuana modeling project—in which two of us have been deeply involved—tried to generate estimates from quantitative modeling, and reached no clearer answer. Legalized commercial production is so unlike what has been done in the Netherlands, Australia, Portugal, California, or anywhere else for which reliable data exist that predictions cannot be made with any precision.

It can be instructive, though, to identify some of the mechanisms through which legalization might influence use.

The most tangible mechanism is price. A compelling body of empirical literature shows that drug consumption, like consumption of (almost) every other commodity, tends to rise when prices fall. Lower prices contribute to higher rates of initiation, greater consumption per year by those who consume, and lower rates of quitting. The effects measured so far are not small, but they are all estimated from observed data—that is, from relatively modest price changes. There is simply no scientific way to extrapolate from that historical experience to project the consequences of the declines that could accompany commercial legalization at the national level.

Different and equally plausible assumptions—all fully consistent with available data—can produce dramatically different predictions of the consequences of very large declines in price. Once the cost of intoxication falls to ten cents per hour, it may not matter much if it falls still further to a nickel rather than a dime. The value of the user's time (even the cost of the snack foods consumed while stoned) would outstrip the cost of the marijuana itself.

Legalization would also create nonprice effects. Users would be subject to no legal risk and reduced social disapproval (perhaps reflected in the omission of marijuana from workplace drug testing). Better labeling and quality control—and a shift away from smoking—might reduce health risks. And there could be advertising and promotion encouraging use. In addition to the direct effects of advertising, journalistic coverage of marijuana might become more positive if marijuana vendors become important sources of advertising revenue. (Before the first surgeon general's report on smoking and health, the only mass-market magazine in the United States that reported aggressively on the health effects of tobacco was *Reader's Digest*, whose revenues relied on subscriptions rather than advertising.)

Based on comparison of a wide range of Dutch and US indicators, and also drawing on other jurisdictions, MacCoun estimated that such effects might increase consumption by 5–50 percent over and above the increase caused by a fall in prices.

All things considered, commercial legalization on the national level could well increase consumption substantially, but there's no good reason to expect the increases to be catastrophic. A doubling or a tripling in the (potency-adjusted) quantity consumed is not an unreasonable guess, but that's all it is; if twenty years after national legalization the ultimate change in consumption were greater or smaller, that wouldn't be a big surprise.

Would legalization reduce drug violence in Mexico?

Mexican drug policy researcher Alejandro Hope reports that marijuana accounts for about 30 percent of the drug-export revenues of the major Mexican drug trafficking organizations (DTOs). Those outfits are responsible in large part for the appalling upsurge in violence in Mexico since the mid-2000s. National marijuana legalization in the United States would reduce those sales to nearly zero (unless taxes were high enough to support continued smuggling for tax evasion). If taking money away from the so-called cartels (not an accurate term, but the one in current use) reduced their violence, that would be a substantial advantage of legalization.

However, cartel violence might not drop by anything like 30 percent. First, a 30 percent reduction in drug-export revenue does not imply a 30 percent reduction in total revenue. Despite the D in the acronym, DTOs are diversified criminal enterprises that parlay their capacity for violence into a variety of revenue streams including kidnapping, extortion, carjacking, and other activities.

It is not even clear that a 30 percent reduction in total revenue would cut violence by 30 percent. It might. Or it might prompt reallocation of DTOs' resources from drug trafficking into other activities, some of which might generate as much violence as drug trafficking does. And even if the DTOs laid off some of their violent workers, the alternative employment those workers sought might or might not be peaceful.

So there are many caveats. However, the basic point presumably holds: legalization might make a meaningful, but not decisive, contribution to reducing the flow of funds to violent Mexican DTOs and thus make the Mexican government's task of restoring public safety that much easier.

Does legalization pass the benefit-cost test?

At one level, benefit-cost analysis is no more than common sense. If the sum of the advantages (benefits) of some proposed policy exceeds the sum of its disadvantages (costs), then making the change is better than preserving the status quo. This sounds simple, but there are serious debates about what to count as benefits and costs, especially whether and how the analysis counts the damage people who use marijuana do to themselves.

Economists doing benefit-cost analysis typically ignore those costs, relying on the principle of "consumer sovereignty," which asserts that consumers know what they want and want what they buy. From consumer sovereignty there follows "revealed preference," the principle that preferences can be inferred from actions. If someone pays $10 for a dose of some drug, that action is presumed to reveal that the consumer values the resulting experience at no less than $10; a rationally selfish consumer wouldn't choose to do something that didn't create a net personal gain. Thus consumer sovereignty implies that consumers are never harmed by their voluntary choices.

Conventional benefit-cost analyses, done on these principles, favor marijuana legalization. Once it is accepted as axiomatic that all voluntary purchases improve consumers' welfare, then almost all government efforts to prevent people from using something they want—in this case, marijuana—stand condemned.

Those with less faith in the flawless wisdom of shoppers may remain unconvinced. Some people, perhaps thinking of pet rocks, timeshares, and candy bought on impulse in the checkout line, are skeptical about consumer choice and the benefits of competitive markets generally. But an intermediate position accepts consumer sovereignty for most goods, yet still carves out an exception for intoxicating substances that induce substance use disorders, especially for consumers who initiate as adolescents. (Three-quarters of current marijuana users initiated before age 18; more than 90 percent initiated before turning 21.)

On this intermediate view, if someone finds his or her drug-taking behavior slipping out of voluntary control, then the axiom of revealed preference may not apply. (The criteria for judging that someone has a substance use disorder include trying but failing to cut back use.) Conventional benefit-cost analysis simply doesn't know what to make of the phenomenon of temptation.

Some writers in the research tradition of behavioral economics propose extending benefit-cost analysis to incorporate the idea of "internalities": losses to an individual from his or her own ill-judged behavior. That would allow for the possibility of a "consumer deficit" as well as the more usual consumer surplus. Thomas Schelling has written of the "divided self;" for example, someone who both wants to use marijuana and wishes not to have that desire. Such conflicting urges can lead to behavior that befuddles economic logic, such as flushing already-purchased drugs down the drain and then going out later to replace them. Other economists and psychologists, such as Daniel Kahneman and George Lowenstein, have shown that time-inconsistent preferences and inconsistencies between "hot" and "cold" emotional states also undermine the rationale underlying consumer sovereignty. Richard Thaler and Cass Sunstein highlight how much choices can be influenced by the way they are presented and even by the order they are presented in; when that is true, which of two opposite choices should we take to represent the consumer's true preference?

Once an exception has been made to the principle of consumer sovereignty, the clear affirmative answer to the question of whether legalization passes a benefit-cost test has to be replaced by a more cautious "It depends."

It depends crucially on how legalization would affect heavy or dependent use. Those who believe use would go up only modestly (say 50 percent or less) will probably conclude that legalization would do more good than harm. Prohibition tends to reduce use and use-related problems relative to legalization, including substance use disorder, but creates black markets and problems related to these markets. If the prohibition isn't delivering much in the way of reduced use and dependence, then it doesn't have much to say for itself in a benefit-cost analysis.

But it seems more reasonable to think of commercial legalization in particular—as opposed to the middle-path options discussed in chapter 11—as having a fairly high likelihood of doubling or tripling use; the impact might be even more profound than that. There is great uncertainty, and much depends on implementation details, but expecting only minimal increases in use and dependence seems unrealistic if for-profit production and promotion are permitted.

Many analyses that dismiss out of hand the possibility that marijuana consumption can be a net harm for the user focus instead on quantifying and comparing the more tangible costs resulting from legalization and prohibition, such as enforcement expenditures, in great detail. However, tangible costs would end up playing a modest role in more comprehensive analysis. Yes, legalization will increase the number of users in need of treatment but decrease the workload of police and courts. But the monetary costs associated with those activities are not their most important effects. (These costs are in the low billions of dollars per year nationally, rather than in the tens of billions.)

The more important outcomes are so difficult to monetize that they tend to get left out. For example, some tens of thousands of marijuana distributors are in prison, and some hundreds of thousands of people are arrested for marijuana violations each year. Quite apart from the budgetary costs to enforcement agencies, there is a real, though hard-to-quantify, cost to those individuals and their families, in terms of direct suffering, reduced job prospects, health damage, and other effects. What would you pay to keep your parent, sibling, spouse, or child from serving a year in prison, or even a night in jail? And if you were the prisoner, how much per day would you pay to get out?

On the other side, there are currently about one million children living with a parent who meets clinical criteria for marijuana abuse or dependence. Legalization would presumably increase that number. There is no good way to quantify how a parent's substance abuse or dependence affects his or her children, but it's hard to imagine that it improves parenting (unless the marijuana dependence is substituting for dependence on alcohol or other drugs).

Most people would at least agree that reduced criminal punishment would be a benefit of legalization, while increased exposure of children to dependent parents would be a cost. However, for what is arguably the most salient consequence of legalization—the increase in marijuana intoxication—there is not even agreement as to whether it is a net benefit or a cost.

Currently, marijuana consumption in the United States produces (very roughly) twenty billion hours of intoxication every year. Commercial legalization could easily add another 15–40 billion hours. It is not clear how that outcome scores in a benefit-cost analysis: some of those hours are intensely pleasurable and cause no harm to the user or anyone else; others contribute to dysfunction and personal failure. Either way, at a valuation—positive or negative—of even $1 per hour, the change in use would swamp all other gains and losses pertaining directly to marijuana. (Indirect effects on problem drinking, tobacco smoking, and use of other drugs could be just as important.)

As noted previously, standard economic reasoning holds that consumption necessarily makes consumers better off. A precise estimate would require some heroic assumptions, but people routinely pay several dollars per hour for various forms of entertainment ($10, for example, to watch a movie that lasts two hours), and prices after legalization would be low. So it is easy to imagine an average surplus of several dollars per hour, suggesting that legalization will bring new happiness to users measured in the many tens of billions of dollars.

But this rosy picture darkens once we consider the possibility of consumer deficits. When people make poor choices and pay more than something is worth to them, they end up regretting the purchase. Indeed, it's possible to regret consuming things received for free—a phenomenon familiar to anyone who has overeaten at a banquet or overindulged at a party. That the canons of standard economic analysis—including consumer sovereignty and revealed preference—rule out the very idea that people might ever make poor consumption decisions simply shows the limitations of that form of analysis.

Forty percent of days of marijuana use involve people who self-report enough problems to meet the clinical definition of substance abuse or dependence, and, inasmuch as denial is a hallmark of addiction, there are likely others who suffer such problems but do not report them. Furthermore, problem users probably consume more per day of use than controlled users.

The problem from an analyst's perspective is that we simply do not know how to score or value those hours of intoxication for either nondependent or dependent users. Those are questions of personal values as much as they are matters for laboratory measurement; if you think—as some of the world's major spiritual traditions do—that intoxication is a violation of the natural order, then you're going to have a hard time ascribing benefit to it even if you understand that some people enjoy it.

But even if you accept that drug use can be beneficial, the question of whether some particular individual's drug use is enriching his or her life, rather than narrowing and impoverishing it, is not a question with a simple answer. Indeed, it may not even be a question on which the individual consumer has a consistent view. Someone might regret his or her last experience and fear the weakness that might lead to the next, but in the moment have a strong desire to light up. Under those circumstances, it's hard to justify any strong assertion about the net benefits or costs of legalization.

Additional Reading

Caulkins, Jonathan P., Beau Kilmer, Mark A. R. Kleiman, et al. "Considering Marijuana Legalization."

Kilmer, Beau, Jonathan P. Caulkins, Rosalie L. Pacula, et al. *Altered State?*

Kleiman, Mark A. R. *Against Excess.*

MacCoun, Robert J., and Peter Reuter. *Drug War Heresies.*

Oglesby, Pat. "Marijuana Advertising: The Federal Tax Stalemate."

10

HOW WOULD ALCOHOL-STYLE LEGALIZATION AFFECT ME PERSONALLY?

Policy analysis, in keeping with Jeremy Bentham's principle of seeking "the greatest good for the greatest number," tends to focus on aggregate or average effects, with an occasional glance at distributional issues: in particular, the effects of a policy on those currently disadvantaged. Politics, by contrast, has to pay attention to how a proposal would affect the members of identified groups with various situations and interests. So the debate about marijuana legalization needs to consider group-specific impacts.

How would legalization affect me if I'm a typical regular adult user?

Legalization would let you walk the streets with an eighth in your pocket, or drive with an ounce in your glove compartment, and never worry about getting arrested for possession. You could still be arrested for smoking and driving, using in public, or sharing a joint with—or, worse, selling a joint to—someone who is under 21, and you might run afoul of laws about indoor smoking aimed primarily at cigarette users, but the police would not bother you for smoking in your living room or at a neighbor's barbeque.

Commercial legalization would greatly increase the variety of products available to you. There are reportedly 350 distinct types and sizes of toothpaste in American drugstores, and more than three thousand (mostly micro-) breweries in the United States, many selling multiple varieties of beer. The range of marijuana products available in legal retailers in Colorado and Washington suggests that commercial forces are sending marijuana down the same path. Not only are there dozens of strains and varieties of "flowers," there are myriad other ways to use, from vape pens loaded with "hash oil" to edibles and beverages and dabs and lotions.

With required chemical testing and labeling, you might find it as easy to monitor your THC intake as it is for a drinker to keep track of alcohol intake. And to the extent that chemicals other than THC importantly influence your subjective experience and risks of running into problems, testing and labeling might help you find the right mix (or mixes) of chemicals, in addition to the right THC level. All of that would be a far cry from asking your illicit pot dealer where the product comes from, or even from listening to a stoned budtender's deeply held but not necessarily accurate opinions about what sort of marijuana goes best with work, study, meditation, or music.

Legalization can also save you money—at least it could if you eschew sampling all that product variety and stick with the basic products you were buying before legalization. If you're a near-daily user, you could save hundreds of dollars a year. But if you think you need to color-coordinate your vape pen with your clothes, or pair the proper THC-infused premium elixir with the main course at dinner, your overall spending on marijuana-related products might rise.

If the high price of illegal marijuana has been limiting how often or how much you use, the dramatically lower prices resulting from legalization will give you the option of spending more time under the influence. That will increase the risk that your marijuana use will escalate to the problem level, and you may find that your mother was right: bad habits are easier to acquire than to lose.

Legalization would reduce the stigma associated with illegal smoking. With a decrease in stigma, increased availability, and the likely barrage of advertising, you might find it more acceptable to use in the presence of non-users, but also harder to get away from marijuana if you wanted or needed to quit. After legalization, simply avoiding your pot-smoking friends would not insulate you from easy access and tempting pro-marijuana messages.

Further, we still have a lot to learn about the health effects of the high-potency products that will be part of the full range of potencies available. Most of what we know about health risks is based on people who smoked marijuana when THC levels were much lower. Using high-potency sinsemilla or regularly dabbing (flash-vaporizing concentrated extracts) might turn out to be riskier.

So legalization could improve your quality of life and reduce your cost of living, if you don't abuse pot or become dependent on it.

How would legalization affect me if I'm already dependent on marijuana?

It could save you a bunch of money and free you from legal risk. Depending on how employers' policies change, it might reduce your risk of getting fired. You might (or might not) find that having products labeled with their chemical content helps you bring your consumption under better control.

But increased marketing and availability might make it harder to moderate your use or quit entirely. You'd be in the same position as an alcoholic trying to quit while walking by liquor stores every day, watching beer commercials during the game, and finding alcohol for sale in grocery stores.

If you've been doing a little marijuana dealing on the side, that source of income will largely disappear, because your customers will be able to buy directly from legal retailers.

Many legalization proposals plan to set aside some tax revenue to fund more and better treatment programs, but those dedicated lines of funding have not always materialized at promised levels. However, legal changes unrelated to marijuana (including mental health parity laws and the Affordable Care Act) should improve treatment funding over time, whatever happens to marijuana laws.

How would legalization affect me if I'm an occasional marijuana user?

Legalization might not affect you dramatically. If your conscience was bothered by breaking the law or by patronizing an illicit market, you'll sleep easier. The risk of arrest would disappear (if you are an adult) and the marijuana might be cheaper, but your arrest risk was already low and you weren't spending much on pot anyhow. Perhaps your biggest gain, other than not having to hide your use, would be possibly decreased risk of workplace consequences.

On the other hand, if the illegality of marijuana was holding you back from moving on to regular use, then your life could change a lot. If you were careful and fortunate, the result might be many hours spent enjoying all of the options that legalization creates, including the candies, packaged foods, and baked goods infused with marijuana, without that use spilling over to interfere with work and other life responsibilities.

But legalization would also mean there are marketing professionals working hard to turn you into a heavy user, because heavy users are great customers. The alcohol and tobacco companies operate that way, and there is no reason to believe marijuana companies would be any different. State and federal officials might try to regulate these advertisements, but the free speech clause of the First Amendment, and analogous state constitutional rules, as extended to "commercial speech" by the courts, would limit their efforts.

There would also be short-run consequences of ramping up your marijuana use if you aren't careful about times, places, and associated activities, including drinking alcohol.

For you, as for more frequent users, legalization could be a win—but only if you kept your pot use under control. That may be harder than it sounds. Consumption patterns, especially around drug use, are dictated by fashion as well as by personal choice, and legalization and the resulting marketing effort is likely to make marijuana use, including heavy use, more fashionable.

How would legalization affect me if I'm not currently a marijuana user?

If you're not currently using because you think marijuana is morally wrong, or because you're worried about its effects on your health or your abilities, you presumably would continue to abstain, but would do so amid daily reminders of normalized marijuana use, everywhere from newspaper ads and product placements in television shows to national cannabis industry trade shows coming to the local convention center. That might make you uncomfortable, especially at first.

If you have no qualms about marijuana use but are simply not interested in using, perhaps because you think it is unhealthy, then not much would change for you, unless marketing or changing social customs led you to change your behavior. Other people will be paying marijuana taxes, but don't expect that to reduce your property or income tax bills noticeably; the marijuana tax revenues won't be that large.

But if you're not currently using out of respect for the law or fear of legal or social consequences, then legalization will present you with additional opportunities, which you could use well or badly. In some settings, you might feel social pressure to smoke, just as some nondrinkers now feel social pressure to drink.

There is debate about whether legalization will make our roads less safe. As discussed in chapter 3, drunk drivers are more dangerous than drivers who are merely stoned, but some of those stoned drivers will also have been drinking, and of course driving under the influence of marijuana is more dangerous than driving sober.

The overall effect on your probability of getting in a crash may depend largely on how legalization affects the number of miles driven under the influence of alcohol, and no one yet knows how that will turn out.

How would legalization affect me if I'm a medical-marijuana patient?

There are two kinds of medical-marijuana patients. The larger group buys medical-marijuana for nonmedical purposes. If you're in that group, full legalization will spare you from having to get a recommendation from a doctor. You may wind up paying higher taxes, but that is likely to be more than made up for by falling prices.

If you're in the smaller group of people who actually have serious medical conditions, legalization will make it easier for scientists to conduct research on the medical uses of marijuana and learn which components and amounts are best for specific ailments. You'll also see greater availability at lower prices, and more accurate labeling. But don't expect conventional marijuana—as opposed to pharmaceutical cannabinoids—to be covered by your health insurance, unless and until someone gets FDA approval for an herbal cannabis product. (Our best estimate of that date is the twelfth of Never, but surprises do happen.)

If you live in a state that does not allow medical dispensaries, legalization will provide access to a wide variety of products. If you already had access to dispensaries, the incremental effect will be smaller. In either case, don't forget that even medical use carries health risks (see chapter 3). This is why you need to discuss your treatment plan with a genuine healthcare provider who will monitor your progress (as opposed to a kush doc who just writes recommendations for a fee).

How would legalization affect me if I'm a marijuana grower?

At first glance, legalization might seem like a great opportunity because it would free you from the fear of arrest. Moreover, you would be able to use the court system to enforce contracts and resolve disputes with employees and customers, and work with the fire department and security companies to make sure that you are protected against fires and intruders. The days of paying trimmers $20–$25 an hour would be over. You could now hire farm laborers at close to minimum wage, employ technologies that make harvesting more efficient, and freely relocate to whichever jurisdiction has the least onerous taxes and regulations.

Or, more accurately, you may have to do all of this; those cost-saving efficiencies will also be available to your competitors. The one certainty about legalization is that production costs for basic marijuana will fall, and fall substantially; that's the nature of competitive enterprise.

Large commercial farms will be able to produce at prices small-scale producers couldn't possibly match. So legalization would put you out of business, or at least out of your current business. Perhaps you would be among the lucky few who prosper by creating larger firms that replace the rest. Or perhaps you would survive in a niche market producing organic or specialty strains. Otherwise you are going to be looking for a new line of work, because the skills that made you successful at cultivating illegal crops will not have much value. Growing in greenhouses or on farms may render skill at growing under artificial lights or in guerrilla grows obsolete, and skill at managing national consumer brands may be more important than horticultural skills of any sort.

Total earnings by growers of legal marijuana would be a small fraction of the billions now earned in illegal production. When a joint can be produced for what a teabag costs, much of the imaginary wealth now spurring the ambitions of "potrepreneurs" will disappear like fairy gold.

How would legalization affect me if I lead a Mexican drug trafficking organization (DTO)?

You would lose some money, but, as you know, the oft-repeated claim that DTOs earn 60 percent of their revenues from moving marijuana to the United States is wildly inflated.

However, the revenues that you do derive from transporting marijuana to the United States would be curtailed. You and your colleagues are experts at smuggling, corruption, and violence, but you can't match farmers at farming. Even the still-illegal sales to minors would largely be made by friends and older siblings buying from legal suppliers.

The role of organized criminal groups in the post-legalization market will dwindle to smuggling to evade state taxes, as is now the case with tobacco. And it is not clear that Mexican DTOs in particular will dominate even that smaller activity.

So if the federal government legalizes, you can forget about supplying the US marijuana market. Still, you won't be put out of business.

How would legalization affect me if I'm a taxpayer?

Not much, either way. Legalization would eliminate some enforcement costs while potentially increasing others (e.g., stoned driving) and creating costs of running the regulatory system. It would also bring in some tax revenue, but so far no state has been willing to impose a level of taxes sufficient to materially change the state budget picture.

How would legalization affect me if I'm an employer?

Obviously, you do not want your employees coming to work intoxicated; that can hamper productivity and be both a safety risk and a source of legal liability for you. If your state recognizes the legal doctrine of "employment at will" and if you don't have a union contract, you can fire employees who fail to meet performance standards regardless of whether the failure is attributable to alcohol, marijuana, cocaine, or something else entirely. That will not change with legalization.

But if laws or contracts require you to show cause for firing someone, legalization will make that harder. Standard drug tests detect past marijuana use, not impairment or even just recent use. When the drug is illegal, mere use can be grounds for dismissal. If the substance is legal, then off-premise use that does not impair job performance may be protected. Or maybe not; some states allow employers to require employees to abstain from tobacco even outside of work hours—although that has to do in part with increases in healthcare costs, which may not pertain to marijuana.

The use of marijuana as medicine—albeit not FDA-approved medicine—to treat conditions that are protected by the Americans with Disabilities Act would be a further complication, especially if those employees' work takes them overseas to places where marijuana is still strictly prohibited.

Some of the new state-level legalization laws forbid you from testing applicants for marijuana; others make it explicit that they do not restrict the freedom of action of employers. It remains to be seen how national legalization would balance user rights against employers' interests, and whether the national law will improve consistency across states.

Some employers now test for alcohol, so there is precedent for testing for legal substances. However, legalization would not by itself improve drug-testing technology.

Ultimately, the effect of marijuana legalization on your business will depend on the particulars of what is allowed and who allows it (i.e., the federal government or just individual states). In most industries marijuana use by employees will pose less of a problem than alcohol use now does. However, in the first decade after legalization, marijuana-related employment law will be a growth industry, spawning a plethora of lawyers and consultants specialized in assisting employers like you with the transition—at a price.

How would legalization affect me if I'm a parent of a teenager?

Your teenagers already have access to marijuana. Nationally, 80 percent of high-school seniors report that it is "fairly easy" or "very easy" to get marijuana; the comparable figure for alcohol—87 percent—isn't much higher. Perceived marijuana availability hasn't changed much since you were in high school; between 1975 and 2015, the share of high-school seniors reporting that it was easy to get marijuana always fluctuated between 80 percent and 90 percent.

Some advocates claim that legalization will make it harder for kids to get marijuana because drug dealers don't check IDs. Be skeptical. The fact that it is easier for high-school seniors to obtain alcohol suggests that marijuana will still be readily available after legalization. Older siblings and friends, unscrupulous and naive cashiers, fake IDs, straw purchasers, theft, and home cultivation will feed the under-21 market.

You would still have to worry about your kids getting intoxicated and ending up in a bad situation, and maybe more than you do today. Much depends on how legalization influences teen alcohol and tobacco use, and how often your kids and their friends get stoned and drunk at the same time.

On the other hand, you wouldn't have to worry as much about the risk that your teenager will be arrested and acquire the sort of criminal record that could seriously damage his or her life chances. While most legalization proposals would keep marijuana illegal for those under 21, the sanctions for underage use might be gentler, making arrest both less damaging and less of a deterrent to use. For tobacco, sanctions are directed primarily at the vendors who supply minors; "possession, use, and purchase" (PUP) laws exist but are often not aggressively enforced against minors. That's the good news. The bad news is that, insofar as the threat of arrest has been keeping your teen away from pot, getting rid of that threat might increase his or her chance of deciding to start or continue marijuana use.

Falling prices are a threat. Teenagers tend to have less disposable income than adults, so the artificially high marijuana prices created by prohibition help discourage them from using, and in particular from using heavily. Some of the drop in adult prices will filter through to minors. That suggests—though we don't yet have direct evidence—that legalization will increase the rate at which adolescents develop marijuana use disorder.

In addition, legalization may well make it much easier for your kids to get access to the really strong stuff, as falling prices bring high-potency material within their financial reach. There is reason to think that highly potent marijuana carries with it higher risks of anxiety attacks, reduced academic performance, and substance use disorder (see chapter 3). Unfortunately, much of the reassuring research about the relative safety of marijuana was conducted when the material was far less potent than it is today, and when marijuana use typically started among college freshmen instead of high-school freshmen.

Expect commercial legalization to increase the availability of pot-infused candy bars, beverages, and baked goods along with aggressive advertising, notionally directed at 21-year-olds but intentionally appealing also to your teens. Growing use of edibles, and of vaping rather than smoking, would make it much easier for your kids to use at school, in the car, and even at home, without being detected.

THC-infused candy bars are an even bigger worry for parents with younger children, who can't distinguish them from regular candy.

Perhaps your biggest concern, other than the risk that your child will develop a cannabis use disorder, is the effect of frequent consumption on emotional maturation and on academic performance. There is still no evidence that occasional (less-than-weekly) pot use is harmful, but there is increasing evidence that daily or near-daily use of high-potency marijuana by adolescents poses substantial risks (see chapter 3 for a description of the risks of using marijuana). So far, there is no clear evidence that liberalizing marijuana laws has increased underage use. But that fact is only moderately reassuring; so far, there's not much evidence at all on either side of the question.

11

BETWEEN MARIJUANA PROHIBITION AND COMMERCIAL LEGALIZATION

IS THERE ANY MIDDLE GROUND?

Are there options in between prohibition and commercial legalization?

Yes. It's possible to move a meaningful distance away from prohibition without jumping all the way to the sort of alcohol-style commercial availability described in chapter 9.

Discussions of marijuana policy in the United States often distinguish among only three positions: prohibition, decriminalization, and legalization. That trichotomy is terribly misleading: it suggests that "legalization" is a single, well-defined option, while in fact many different options fit that label. The trichotomy also misleadingly suggests that the middle ground is limited to decriminalization.

In the United States most of the debate and policy innovation focuses on the commercial, or alcohol, model, but commercialization may not be the most desirable version of legalization. Indeed, some years ago two of us attended a meeting in the Netherlands with academics who generally supported legalization, as they understood the idea. We described California's Proposition 19, which was narrowly voted down in 2010; had it passed, it would have made marijuana available on the alcohol model. These reform-minded academics looked appalled. They said, "But surely no one would be stupid enough to do *that*!" It seemed obvious to them that citizens should have a right to use marijuana, and equally obvious that consumers needed protection from exploitation by entrepreneurs seeking to profit from drug abuse and dependence. So they assumed that "legalization" meant some sort of government monopoly or a co-op model such as in Spain or Belgium. This reflects a gap in political culture between the enthusiasm for free markets (and distrust of governments) now typical of the United States and the more paternalistic traditions of Europe.

We were among the eight authors of a RAND report for the state of Vermont that describes many different "architectures" for legalization. These fall into two general categories: those that do and those that do not allow large-scale production, with all that implies in terms of production efficiency and product innovation. Small-scale production options include allowing *limited* home production or allowing *small* marijuana co-operatives within which members grow and share their marijuana but never sell to the public. We emphasize "limited" because it takes very little space to supply one person and "small" because experience in Spain shows that cannabis clubs have a tendency to morph into larger, profit-oriented enterprises.

While these options might not generate the aggressive advertising and lobbying that are associated with American-style commercialization, they would also not bring in much tax revenue. Nor should one expect them to displace as much of the black market as would options allowing large-scale production.

The commercial model appeals to many people because of its potential for generating tax revenue, but other "large-scale" options for legalization we describe below are just as capable of bringing money into the public purse. Even alcohol-style commercial legalization is not the most extreme option. A jurisdiction could simply delete marijuana from its list of controlled substances and not impose any new product-specific taxes, rules, or regulations. That would be a dream scenario for strict libertarians and a nightmare for those concerned about the risks of substance use disorder.

What has been learned from decriminalization?

Decriminalization typically refers to removing criminal penalties for possession of amounts suitable for personal consumption, at least for first-time offenders. That does not require that possession of a small amount be made legal; it could still be punished with fines, treatment mandates, or other civil sanctions, just not criminal conviction or criminal penalties. Curiously, the full legalization of possession, while still banning production and sale—the system in effect during alcohol prohibition—has not attracted much attention. Eliminating penalties on users entirely is an understudied alternative to merely reducing them.

About a dozen US states sharply reduced their statutory penalties for marijuana possession in the 1970s, beginning with Oregon in 1973 (see chapter 6). After a hiatus, that trend is continuing. Now the number that have decriminalized possession or legalized sale is closer to twenty, covering about 40 percent of the US population.

This experience shows that one can decriminalize marijuana without making the sky fall. Indeed, Stanford law professor Rob MacCoun observes that the average citizen's grasp of marijuana laws is pretty tenuous; in both decriminalized and non-decriminalized states, about the same proportion of survey respondents believe that marijuana possession can lead to a jail sentence in their state.

A considerable literature tries to estimate the effects of decriminalization on marijuana use. One approach examines a panel of states over time to see if use is higher in those states after decriminalization than in other states or in earlier years. There is some evidence of increased use. For example, former RAND economist Karyn Model observed that emergency-room mentions for marijuana increased after decriminalization while mentions for other drugs fell, suggesting both some impact on marijuana use and some substitution of marijuana for other drugs. However, the majority of the early studies found little if any effect.

More recently, Rosalie Pacula—another RAND economist—and her colleagues found that some of the earlier studies had erred by treating all of the early changes as equivalent, even though some states had merely reduced the severity of sanctions, leaving possession a criminal offense, while others had truly decriminalized. Some recent studies that use more nuanced categorizations of control regimes find that the lower penalties are linked to increases in consumption, though not large increases.

One challenge to all such before-and-after comparisons is that enforcement risk in practice may not correspond closely to the policy proclaimed in the law. Sometimes formal decriminalization simply ratifies practices already in place; in those cases, changing the law has little impact on actual arrest patterns. Moreover, Pacula and colleagues found that, by 2000, marijuana arrest rates were about the same in the states that had eliminated criminal penalties as in other states.

More than twenty other countries have decriminalized marijuana, and some have decriminalized possession of small quantities of other drugs. These examples teach interesting lessons. For example, some jurisdictions in Australia implemented "infringement" schemes, substituting fines or education programs for criminal sanctions. In South Australia, police responded by taking action against individuals they would previously have ignored altogether. (This effect is called "net widening.") Since many of those cited never paid their fines and some subsequently went to jail for nonpayment, the "expiation notice" policy actually increased the number of people going to jail.

Whether decriminalization in Australia increased consumption is debated; some studies say no (consumption went up everywhere, not just in places that decriminalized), while others find effects in some subpopulations—more for older than for younger users, for example. A study by economists Anne-Line Bretteville Jensen and Jenny Williams suggests that Australian decriminalization shifted initiation to earlier ages without affecting the number who initiate at some point.

Thus decriminalization may or may not increase use; where it does, it doesn't do so by much. Likewise, it can reduce enforcement costs dramatically, as it did in Vermont, but does not always do so. In the United States, given the strong concentration of marijuana-possession arrests in poor and minority communities and the large number of those arrests, the strongest case for decriminalization may be its potential for easing police/community tensions.

What about legalizing marijuana the way Portugal did (not)?

Along with the Netherlands, Portugal is often held up in the United States as the poster child for successful legalization. What actually happened there was the complete decriminalization of possession for personal use for all drugs, not just marijuana. Indeed, the policy change was motivated primarily by problems with injection drug use, and its (sharply debated) effects on drug-related deaths, crime, HIV/AIDS, and incarceration came mostly from effects on heroin users. So the main reason the United States can't "just legalize marijuana the way Portugal did" is that Portugal's policy wasn't about marijuana and wasn't legalization.

The Portuguese reform was passed in 2001, building on a series of policy changes going back to the 1980s. The new law makes acquisition, use, and possession of up to ten days' supply of any controlled drug an administrative offense rather than a crime. Decriminalization of use is not unique to Portugal; Spain, Italy, and the Czech Republic all have it in one form or another. Portugal's approach differs because, in addition to reducing punitiveness, the country expanded efforts to dissuade, treat, and reintegrate users. The reform was introduced alongside a large investment in treatment, prevention, harm reduction, and social reintegration services. And while Portuguese police cannot arrest users for possessing small quantities, they are still expected to issue citations to those they see using or possessing drugs. Those cited appear before "commissions for the dissuasion of drug addiction" (CDTs, in the Portuguese acronym). The CDTs, which typically include a clinician, a lawyer, and a social worker, have great latitude to impose a variety of sanctions, including fines, community service, revocation of professional licenses, and what are essentially injunctions (e.g., against going to particular places). However, the CDTs' objective is behavior change, not punishment, and in some cases, after a hearing the commission decides that the consumer doesn't have a drug problem and lets the matter drop.

Clearly, Portugal pioneered an innovative middle path, but Portugal's experience cannot support confident projections about what would happen if another country were to do the same. The main target of Portugal's reform was heroin, not cannabis, and the new policy demanded a significant investment in resources to achieve its public health gains. Current US policies are not much like those of Portugal before the reform, and programs and policies developed in one country or culture can play out dramatically differently if transplanted to another culture. On the other hand, the Portuguese experience demonstrates that arresting users is not essential to drug prohibition.

What about imitating the Dutch approach?

The Netherlands has never legalized marijuana. Dutch law—in keeping with international agreements—criminalizes production and sale of the same drugs that are illegal elsewhere. However, an explicit, formal exception was created in 1976 for sale of limited quantities of marijuana. That activity, while nominally illegal, is not subject to enforcement, and about six hundred "coffee shops" openly sell marijuana. The purchase limit was formerly thirty grams, a bit more than an ounce, but was reduced to five grams (enough for about ten joints) in 1996.

In 2012, even as Colorado and Washington voted to legalize marijuana, the Dutch attempted to tighten up their coffee shop system. The irony was noted by pundits across the globe, but the Dutch crackdown didn't last long. Beginning in three southern provinces in May 2012, coffee shops could only sell to users that registered with the club (the private club criterion), and only Dutch residents could register (the residency criterion). According to Dutch researcher Marianne van Ooyen-Houben and her colleagues, this decreased drug tourism from foreigners, but also created illicit market demand, since many Dutch users did not want to register with a club, and the registration criterion was soon abolished. Implementation of the residency requirement is now left to the discretion of local authorities, and most jurisdictions—including Amsterdam—have decided not to enforce it. A bill was also submitted to parliament that would have made any product containing more than 15 percent THC a Schedule I substance, but it is unclear whether this will be implemented.

This waffling reflects tensions across levels of government, with the national government turning more conservative and some localities welcoming restrictions on coffee shops while others resist change. Growing cannabis is still a crime in the Netherlands (though growing one or two plants for personal use is generally tolerated in practice), as is importing it. Sanctions vary sharply with quantities, but supplying large quantities still lands people in prison. As the Dutch say, the front door of the coffee shops (where the customers enter) is (almost) legal, but the back door (where the product comes in) is entirely illegal. As a result, coffee-shop cannabis costs about what fully illicit cannabis costs elsewhere in Europe or in the United

States: about $10 a gram for material of moderately high potency. By keeping production and wholesale distribution illegal, the Dutch have kept cannabis prices high and marketing to a minimum. That situation is a far cry from alcohol-style legalization.

Nonetheless, marijuana prevalence in the Netherlands roughly doubled—from a fairly low base—not when the policy was first passed but later, as coffee shops began to proliferate (roughly between 1984 and 1996). As Rob MacCoun of Stanford has noted, Dutch prevalence subsequently fell back by about 20 percent between 1997 and 2005, a period during which the number of coffee shops was cut back by 40 percent (and when some other European countries were seeing continued increases). So it is plausible that the Dutch have a somewhat higher prevalence than they would have if they had merely legalized possession but not allowed commercial retailing.

Until recently the conventional wisdom was that the Dutch approach was successful in achieving its objectives, including making it possible for people to obtain marijuana without encountering purveyors of more dangerous drugs. There seems, though, to be increasing frustration with the inherent tensions in official approval of businesses that sell goods whose production the government seeks to suppress. This front-door/back-door inconsistency might be a workable compromise during a transition, but it is an awkward situation to face indefinitely.

What about just allowing home production?

The Dutch approach allows people to buy something that cannot be produced legally. Coffee shops paper over the paradox, because users themselves do not interact with criminals. But shop owners must.

The gentlest way to provide a legal source of supply would be to allow individual users to grow their own and perhaps give to (but not sell to) friends. Marijuana is not particularly difficult to grow. One has to be a little conscientious, but almost anyone with adequate space can develop the knack. Indeed, it is becoming increasingly common in many countries, although grow-your-own still accounts for a modest share of the market in the United States. The household survey asks marijuana users how they obtained the marijuana they used most recently. The majority say they bought it (56 percent) or got it for free or shared (39 percent), but 3.5 percent report growing their own—a proportion that rises to 6.6 percent among those who use daily or near-daily.

Allowing grow-your-own marijuana has clear appeal. It siphons some demand away from the black market, reducing criminals' incomes. Yet, since grow-your-own activities are necessarily small, they do not enjoy the economies of scale that would accompany commercial production. So the effective cost of production—in terms of time and effort—is much higher than it would be if commercial production were legal. And of course without legal sale there can be no advertising.

That approach appeals to those who desire to limit the increase in consumption and dependence that will follow legalization, but appalls the free-market devotees who want to maximize efficiency and offer consumers the widest possible variety of marijuana at the lowest possible cost. (Concentrates for vaporization are harder to produce safely at home; that is a bug from the libertarian perspective but might be a feature from the public-health perspective.) There are also complications. It is not easy to set quantity limits. If the law limits the number of plants, people can grow very large plants. If the law limits growing area, people can grow very densely. If the law limits weight, it might be hard for even well-meaning users to comply; one full-size outdoor plant can yield a pound of marijuana, which is more than three times the average annual per capita consumption. And it is not clear how police are supposed to enforce any limits on activity undertaken inside private residences. On the other hand, a quantity limit does make it easier for police to enforce the rules against home production for sale.

Alaska pioneered legal home growing in the United States. A 1975 Alaska State Supreme Court ruling effectively legalized growing amounts suitable for personal consumption at home by determining that it was covered by the right of privacy guaranteed by the state constitution. The threshold quantity was set at four ounces or twenty-five plants. Those (relatively high) limits and the entire constitutional premise were later challenged, starting with a 1990 voter initiative that sought to reverse the original case. There was a period of legal limbo, but a 2003 case reaffirming the 1975 ruling settled the issue.

A number of states' medical-marijuana laws allow registered patients or their care givers to grow their own, up to some limit (e.g., in California the limit is eight ounces plus up to six mature or twelve immature plants). Colorado, Jamaica, Oregon, and Uruguay legalized home production through the same measures that legalized marijuana more generally; for the time being, Washington, DC, only allows "grow and give," while Washington State allows commercial sale but bans home growing except for medical use.

It is not clear whether grow-your-own policies affect use appreciably, perhaps in part because illicit-market supply is so readily available that only true devotees bother to grow their own. The most recent state-specific estimates report that Alaska has the eighth highest rate of past-month use, trailing only the other jurisdictions that passed propositions liberalizing their marijuana policies (Colorado, Oregon, Washington State, and Washington, DC) and three states in the northeast: Maine, Rhode Island, and Vermont. However, there was no obvious jump associated with the 2003 ruling. Likewise, use rates in South Australia, which had at one point decriminalized growing as many as ten plants (later cut to three plants and now to one plant), paralleled those elsewhere in Australia, although that may be in part because South Australian home-growers exported some of their crop to other Australian states.

Compared to other forms of legalization, allowing home production is a fairly low-stakes move. It solves the problem of providing law-abiding adults with a legal source of supply, but might have only limited impact on the volume of illicit-market activity or law enforcement.

What about user co-ops and collectives?

A step beyond grow-your-own is allowing growing, sharing, and trading among members of cooperative groups. Spain pioneered this approach, with smaller numbers of such collectives now operating in Belgium, the Netherlands, and Slovenia. Spain criminalizes only sale, not possession or cultivation for one's own use; drug-sharing clubs inhabit a legal gray area. Belgium's story is complicated, but, like Spain, whatever legal protection the clubs have comes more from absence of enforcement than proactive legislation. Uruguay has gone further, explicitly legalizing co-ops with up to forty-five members.

Cannabis-sharing clubs solve a problem familiar to anyone who has grown zucchini; it is hard not to overproduce. A good grower can produce 300–400 grams per (outdoor) plant, so the exceptions for "amounts suitable for personal consumption" (usually defined as an ounce, or about 28 grams) do not protect people growing their own. Furthermore, if that one plant were to die—which happens—the user would have no recourse but the illegal market. In addition, there are many strains of marijuana. One person growing for personal consumption would not have access to a variety of strains. By contrast, one Spanish club manager we talked to said his club grows fewer than three hundred (outdoor) plants per year for its three hundred members—i.e., less than one plant per person per year—but can still offer members choices from a variety of strains; some also offer concentrates for vaporizing, whose manufacture requires more production equipment and skill than a home-grower is likely to have available.

The clubs are supposed to operate on a nonprofit basis. That same manager estimated a production cost of two to three euros per gram, and the club sells to members at about twice that amount, which is still below black-market prices. The net revenues are used to fund social activities and activism (e.g., renting buses to take members to protests in the capital).

An ideal club would self-manage to control diversion. For example, a club might limit acquisitions to two grams per day, require participants to be 18, or have members sign a statement certifying they had already been using marijuana before joining the club and do not simultaneously belong to a second club. Pledges are hard to enforce without a central registry, but apparently there is a case in Belgium of a club expelling someone after he registered his father as a member in order to effectively have two simultaneous memberships.

If all clubs stayed small and served only their own members, clubs would offer the appealing prospect of displacing a significant share of illicit-market demand (more than own-growing could) without promoting greater demand, the way profit-oriented companies in a free enterprise model might be expected to.

Unfortunately, not all clubs in Spain have been so well-behaved. Each club has its own rules. Some serve as fronts for professional dealers. Others have simply grown so large and entrepreneurial in product offerings that they violate the spirit of the club model. In

July 2015 the Spanish Supreme Court ruled that the structure and functioning of a club in Bilbao with 290 members exceeded what was allowed under the concept of shared consumption.

So it is not clear whether the co-op model will be sustainable. The Federation of Cannabis Associations is trying to find ways to certify the good behavior of responsible clubs before shady operations undermine the overall concept. Others argue that the key is formal legalization and regulation, as in Uruguay. Time will tell. As with any other policy, the reality on the ground may turn out to have only a distant resemblance to the theory on paper.

What about a very liberal medical-marijuana system?

Some states provide medical-marijuana only to people with cancer, HIV/AIDS, multiple sclerosis, and other serious conditions; others, such as California, allow more or less anyone to claim a need for medical-marijuana (see chapter 13). When well implemented, strict medical-marijuana laws should have little impact on the black market, supply, or the overall prevalence of use. That approach isn't as much a form of legalization as it is a workaround bypassing the regulatory process for medications.

However, a medical-marijuana program with very liberal criteria for determining who is eligible can serve a substantial share of the market. Combining that with strict regulations to ensure dispensaries look more like genuine user co-ops than commercial enterprises or drug dealers with storefronts could create a form of quasi-legalization that provides serious competition for black market activities without tipping over into commercial legalization. However, many if not most dispensaries in California effectively operate as businesses with full-time paid staff selling to anyone with a recommendation. The demographics of California's "medical" buyers look more like those of recreational marijuana users than those of people receiving traditional healthcare. They are mostly young, healthy men with histories of marijuana use. For example, Thomas O'Connell and Ché Bou-Matar described 4,117 individuals who sought physicians' approval for marijuana use. The typical patient was a thirty-two-year-old male who started using marijuana as a teenager, and the rate of disability among the patients was actually below the overall national average.

Another study coauthored by one of us examined the medical charts of 1,655 applicants for recommendations. Most sought marijuana to relieve pain, improve sleep, or relax. Almost all were approved, since California allows medical-marijuana for any "illness for which marijuana provides relief," not just the diseases that motivated many voters to support compassionate use. Less than 5 percent were diagnosed with HIV/AIDS, cancer, or glaucoma.

California does not require patients to register, so it is hard to estimate the proportion of statewide consumption that is served by these nominally medical systems. However, the Montana experience shows that it is possible for a medical program to supply a large share of the market. Until 2011, when Senate Bill 423 revamped its Medical-marijuana Act, Montana combined a mandatory registry with lax criteria for determining who was eligible. In June 2011, Montana had 30,036 registered medical-marijuana users. That was almost half the state's past-month users as estimated by the 2008–2009 household surveys (66,000).

Within twelve months of the July 2011 tightening of Montana's medical-marijuana law, the number of medical-marijuana providers decreased from more than four thousand to less than four hundred, and the number of registered patients decreased from 30,000 to 8,700, although some of that decline may be due to a federal drug investigation targeting growers dealing in more than one hundred plants.

Couldn't users go to physicians for nonmedical-marijuana?

At first blush, this seems plausible, and Uruguay is giving pharmacies a prominent role in its legalization scheme. After all, doctors understand psychoactive chemicals better than the average person does, and the Hippocratic Oath binds them not to harm their patients. No doubt most would try to manage supply in such a way that patients do not escalate to abuse or dependence.

However, it would be an odd use of scarce and expensive medical resources, and it's not clear that medical education is the best preparation for acting as a rationing agent; after all, overdoses from nonmedical use of diverted prescription pharmaceuticals are an enormous problem, especially in the United States. Also, physicians in California who write large numbers of "recommendations" for people who want to purchase at marijuana dispensaries haven't displayed much interest in monitoring their patients for signs of drug abuse or dependency.

What if the government had a monopoly on the industry, or on retail sales specifically?

Government-monopoly supply would be full legalization, but it still constitutes a middle path—more favorable to public health—relative to legalization along the lines of US alcohol policy. In particular, a government monopoly would have a fighting chance of avoiding the drastic price decreases and aggressive marketing efforts that would likely result from commercial legalization.

After national legalization, production costs could fall so far below current prices that taxes could not easily make up the difference without inviting a black market in untaxed marijuana. Government control of production and distribution can be seen as a mechanism for capturing as revenue the difference between retail prices and production costs.

A government monopoly could also impose other conditions, such as requiring buyers to pass tests certifying their knowledge of the drug's dangers or limiting the amount sold to any given individual in a particular month. And there would be no incentive for anyone but the government to advertise and promote marijuana sales, which it could choose not to do.

In theory one could realize these benefits with a government monopoly only on retail distribution, with production outsourced to the private sector, but that would require stringent oversight to prevent diversion for illegal sale. Commercial production of branded products would also create strong incentives for marketing those brands; most alcohol and tobacco advertising is done by manufacturers, not retailers. However, the state-store system could require growers who want to sell their products through state stores to agree in return to refrain from advertising.

Legalizing private commercial production—or even home production with loose quantity limits—makes it harder to prevent price declines; taxes large enough to keep minimum prices high would invite illicit production, which is harder to police when it can hide alongside legal private production. On the other hand, a state monopoly on production would reduce the incentives for product innovation, including innovations that might make marijuana safer to use.

State lotteries already operate as government monopolies, so the model is not unknown. Nor are its limitations; many state lotteries advertise aggressively in ways that promote problem gambling ("Have you played your number today?").

Designing an ideal legalization regime is a popular academic exercise. The typical conclusion is that the author's design would be better than the status quo, and this is taken to prove that legalization is a good idea. The hidden assumption is that legalization would be carried out in the socially optimal manner. However, neither voter propositions nor laws passed by legislatures are written by civic-minded academics. Propositions are generally written by activists with the advice of pollsters; bills are often written by (or for) legislators under pressure from lobbyists. Once the laws are in place, private economic interests participate in an ongoing dance with officials that often tests the integrity of individuals and institutions. The outcome is too often what political scientists call "regulatory capture," in which the regulated industry gets control of the regulatory machinery for its own private ends.

What if the market were limited to nonprofits, "for-benefit" corporations, or other socially responsible organizations?

Legalization creates opportunities to impose regulations, generate tax revenues, and settle disputes through lawyers instead of violence. But at the end of the day, legal marijuana companies are as focused on profit as illicit drug dealers are. They may behave no better than the businesses that produce and distribute alcohol and tobacco, many of whom work hard to encourage heavy use and create brand loyalty among young consumers, while complying with regulations as little as they can get away with.

But prohibition, state monopoly, and unrestricted commercialization are not the only choices. The law could limit production and distribution to nonprofit organizations with board members chosen by—or at least including representatives of—public health or child-advocacy groups, and with charters defining their mission as filling current demand rather than expanding the market. "Nonprofit" is not the same as "no tax revenue": states could still collect marijuana taxes under this structure, and the employees of nonprofits pay income taxes just as employees of for-profit companies do (and employees of illegal operations may not).

Another option would be to limit the market to "for-benefit" corporations with charters that require them to focus on the "triple bottom line": people, planet, and profits. More than half the states— ranging from conservative Arizona to liberal Vermont—allow companies to incorporate as benefit corporations. While the governing laws vary across states, the Benefit Corporation Information Center highlights three central tenets: benefit corporations "1) have a corporate purpose to create a material positive impact on society and the environment; 2) are required to consider the impact of their decisions not only on shareholders but also on workers, community, and the environment; and 3) are required to make available to the public an annual benefit report that assesses their overall social and environmental performance against a third-party standard."

Another version of the same idea is provided by independent agencies that verify that for-profit enterprises are operating in the public interest. This is akin to the way products can be certified as being free-trade or organic. For example, the nonprofit B-Lab provides "B Corp" certification to applicants that "meet rigorous standards of social and environmental performance, accountability, and transparency," including such well-known firms as Patagonia and the New Belgian Brewing Company.

In February 2015, a bill to legalize marijuana was introduced in Vermont that would have permitted only "a nonprofit dispensary or a benefit corporation to register with the Marijuana Control Board as a marijuana cultivator, marijuana product manufacturer, marijuana testing laboratory, marijuana retailer, or marijuana lounge." The fact that such a bill was introduced illustrates that there are alternatives to the purely for-profit model adopted (with variations) in Alaska, Colorado, Oregon, and Washington.

What about limiting the quantity any user can buy?

People who use a modest amount of marijuana mostly don't have problems or cause problems, though a single incident of foolish intoxicated behavior can cause a lifetime of damage. By contrast, people who use two or three grams every day are often in the grip of diagnosable substance use disorder. So why not limit the quantity a user can purchase over the course of a month? Even in the context of a fully commercial system that otherwise resembled current alcohol distribution, a user quota might go a long way toward preventing big increases in problem use.

It's certainly feasible technically. Credit card companies already have the capacity to limit how much a cardholder spends, even though the cards are good at countless locations. It shouldn't be hard to put together a data system linking a finite number of sellers, and require that each purchase be subtracted from a monthly quota. Indeed, Uruguay plans to create such a system.

The problem is that those heavy users—the ones who would reach any externally imposed quota and then start looking for illicit supplies—use most of the marijuana. So forcing them back onto the illicit market would eliminate one big advantage of legalization.

But there is a middle-ground option available here: have a monthly quota, *but let the user him- or herself set it.* (Some states have this system, on a voluntary basis, for gambling.) Every user could be required to get a license, just as some states currently issue licenses for medical-marijuana buyers. Getting a license could require proof of age, and perhaps passing a short quiz—like a driver's license exam—designed to make sure buyers know the risks they face. When someone signs up for a license, he or she could be asked to specify a monthly quantity purchase limit, perhaps subject to some cap.

But why would anyone choose to set a limit, or choose less than the highest amount available? Because almost no one who starts using any drug intends to become dependent on it, and many are aware of the risks of picking up a habit that could spin out of control. Such a limit needn't be permanent; it just has to be fixed for a particular time period, and a little bit inconvenient to change. Just the need to do the paperwork to expand one's limit would serve as a warning sign. This is hardly a reliable way to prevent the development of addiction, but it is certainly better than nothing and probably worth the administrative effort. It could even be done in a way that fully protected privacy, simply by issuing quota cards with serial numbers but no names or other identifying information.

(And yes, a quota system could also work with alcohol; Sweden used to have mandatory quotas, apparently with good results, until the system fell victim to a political struggle with the Swedish Prohibition Party.)

Why have a middle path for marijuana but not for alcohol?

Some may balk at the asymmetry. "Isn't it unfair to require marijuana businesses but not alcohol companies to be socially responsible?" But the world is full of asymmetries. If allowing a for-profit industry to promote consumption of a dependence-inducing intoxicant was a mistake for alcohol, it hardly makes sense to insist on making that mistake again. Who knows? A successful test of some of these middle-ground ideas for marijuana might even pave the way for trying them out on the much harder problems posed by heavy drinking.

Additional Reading

Caulkins, Jonathan P. "Nonprofit Motive: How to Avoid a Likely and Dangerous Corporate Takeover of the Legal Marijuana Market."

Caulkins Jonathan P., et al. "Design Considerations for Legalizing Cannabis."

Fijnaut, Cyrille J. C. F., and Brice de Ruyver. *The Third Way: A Plea for a Balanced Cannabis Policy.*

Kilmer, Beau. "The 10 P's of Marijuana Legalization."

Laqueur, Hannah. "Uses and Abuses of Drug Decriminalization in Portugal."

MacCoun, Robert J., and Peter Reuter. "Assessing Drug Prohibition and Its Alternatives."

Rolles, Stephen, and George Murkin. *How to Regulate Cannabis: A Practical Guide.*

Rosmarin, Ari, and Niamh Eastwood. *A Quiet Revolution: Drug Decriminalisation Policies in Practice across the Globe.*

PART III
THE CRAZY QUILT OF
CONFLICTING POLICIES TODAY

12

WHERE ARE WE, AND HOW DID WE GET HERE?

How many states have legalized or decriminalized marijuana?

Many states have liberalized their marijuana laws; the exact count depends on the definitions one uses.

As of the fall of 2015, four states have legalized commercial for-profit industries to produce marijuana for general adult use, all via ballot propositions: Colorado and Washington in 2012 and Alaska and Oregon in 2014.

Initiative 71 in Washington, DC, made it legal for adults (21 and over) to possess up to two ounces, grow up to six plants (no more than three being mature), and give (but not sell) up to one ounce to another adult. That is a middle-ground option that does not allow for large-scale production or for any commercial enterprise.

All five of those jurisdictions, which encompass 5.6 percent of the US population, had already legalized medical-marijuana in some form. Legalization of marijuana generally (often called "adult," "retail," "commercial," or "recreational") has not eliminated the medical-marijuana industries, even in Colorado and Washington, where they have coexisted the longest. After a prolonged legislative battle, Washington is now moving to fold medical availability into the new, regulated, legal industry. Colorado intended all along to migrate the existing (already regulated) medical industry into the new system. However, Colorado residents continue to purchase most of their legal marijuana under the banner of the medical system in order to avoid the taxes levied on retail marijuana. At least as of 2014, the Colorado retail stores were selling as much to out-of-state tourists as to in-state residents.

Depending on definitions, about fifteen additional states—including such large states as California, New York, Ohio, and North Carolina—have decriminalized possession of small amounts for personal use. In those states possession is still illegal, but it is a civil offense, not a criminal one, and typically the only penalty is a fine. Those states include an additional 35 percent of the US population.

Twenty-three states and the District of Columbia allow some form of THC-bearing medical-marijuana (others allow only products that contain primarily the nonintoxicating CBD). That includes all states that legalized and most that decriminalized.

Medical-marijuana regimes run the gamut from well-controlled "tight" programs that make a serious effort to allow marijuana only to real patients suffering from a finite list of well-defined diseases to, at the other extreme, "loose" programs that effectively legalize marijuana for anyone who can fake an ache (see chapter 13). Tight medical-marijuana states haven't gone far in the direction of legalization; the number of people covered is a trivial share of all marijuana users. The loose states—including California—have virtually legalized, in ways that predate overt legalization in Colorado and Washington (both of them loose medical-marijuana states before they took the step of formal legalization). Loose medical-marijuana regimes usually also legalize commercial (albeit nominally non-profit) production to supply the retail "dispensaries" or "collective gardens."

Fifteen states, including Florida and Texas, have legalized medical use of material containing only trace amounts of THC but greater amounts of CBD, a cannabinoid that as far as anyone knows is not intoxicating and does not create dependence. If marijuana is understood as a dependence-inducing intoxicant rather than a plant, these states haven't actually legalized marijuana at all. Marijuana without THC is about as addictive as grape juice or, for that matter, industrial hemp.

If one were to view CBD laws as part of the legalization movement (which some advocates do, so they can boost their count of wins), then only a handful of states have not liberalized their marijuana laws to some degree, with Pennsylvania being the largest among that group. Since even non-THC-bearing marijuana for medical use is just as illegal under federal law as "skunk" sold for partying, that means that a clear majority of states now have laws permitting conduct that violates federal law.

How did we get to the current crazy quilt of conflicting policies?

Legal commerce was the original state. Prohibition came later—even later for marijuana than for the opiates or cocaine.

Before the late nineteenth century, there was little or no use of marijuana for intoxication in the United States or many other Western countries. Commerce pertained primarily to medicines and to the nondrug uses of the cannabis plant as a source of food, fuel, and fiber. So the absence of prohibition did not indicate a liberal stance toward recreational intoxication.

Marijuana as a prohibited substance is largely a twentieth-century phenomenon. Greece in 1890 became one of the first countries to ban the cultivation and use of marijuana, due to concerns about hashish use among the poor. Most other European countries did not outlaw marijuana until the 1920s. The United States followed later with the Marijuana Tax Act of 1937, which effectively prohibited marijuana nationally, but many individual states had already banned production and possession of marijuana. The history of that legal change, focused around the strange character of Harry J. Anslinger of the Treasury Department's Prohibition Bureau and around fears triggered by marijuana use among Mexican immigrants and African Americans, makes for fascinating reading.

Cannabis grown for fiber (industrial hemp) saw a brief resurgence during World War II when the United States was cut off from supplies of abacà (Manila hemp), but beyond such special circumstances hemp for fiber had already been supplanted by superior plants by the early part of the twentieth century, and later by synthetic fibers.

Prohibition was systematized globally in 1961 by the Single Convention on Narcotic Drugs, and by the end of the twentieth century most countries had made it a criminal offense to produce and distribute marijuana.

A notable exception is India. In 1985 India's central government passed a law prohibiting the production and consumption of cannabis resin (*charas*) and flowers (*ganja*), but made an exception for cannabis leaves and seeds (*bhang*), which have lower concentrations of THC and have been used in religious ceremonies for centuries. In some states there are government-authorized shops selling *bhang*-infused drinks and foods.

Through the early 1960s, strict prohibition in the United States was not given much thought, since so few people wanted to use marijuana. The FBI's publication *Crime in the United States* reports that in 1961 among 2,776 cities with populations over 2,500, there were just 25,080 people charged with drug law violations (for all drugs, not just marijuana), as against 126,477 for burglary: one drug arrest for every five burglary arrests. By 2013 that had reversed; there were six drug arrests for every burglary arrest.

The insignificance of drug laws and drug policy changed with the late-1960s explosion in the use of marijuana (and, with fewer users but greater consequences, heroin), which led to many users getting arrested and punished, sometimes severely. About a dozen states responded in the 1970s by sharply cutting back sanctions for possession of amounts suitable for personal use. (It is common to say these states all "decriminalized," although technically some merely reduced criminal penalties without eliminating them.)

There were a number of serious proposals to legalize marijuana at that time; none passed, but in 1975 Alaska's Supreme Court ruled that low-level marijuana activity was protected under the state constitution's privacy provisions.

The trend toward liberalization stalled in the late 1970s and 1980s, when first the Carter administration and then, more enthusiastically, the Reagan administration took a sharp turn toward more punitive drug policies. With respect to marijuana, this was a response in part to the growing parents' movement, responding to the downward drift in the age of first use of marijuana; in 1979, more than 10 percent of high-school seniors identified themselves as using marijuana every day or nearly every day. Members of the baby-boom generation (born 1946–1961) became notably less tolerant of drug use when they had children of their own. Later the crack epidemic produced a radical hardening of antidrug attitudes, and marijuana policies reflected those changes.

Energy for liberalization picked up again because of the confluence of at least four factors: (1) cancer and wasting disease associated with HIV/AIDS created a demand for drugs that stimulated the appetite and a compassionate urge to allow terminally ill patients access to anything they thought might help; (2) legalization advocates found deep-pocketed financial supporters and adopted medical-marijuana as a wedge issue; (3) sharp declines in crime and violence created space for discussing less punitive approaches to all sorts of offending, and (4) the steady decline in the share of the population that had come of age before marijuana use spread meant that a decreasing share of the electorate found marijuana strange and scary. Changing values, with tolerance growing and the demand for conformity fading, and increasing distrust of government may also have played a role.

How has support for legalization in the United States varied over time?

— policy legislation

Although there are myriad one-off surveys, just two—Gallup and the General Social Survey—have asked the same question consistently over time and so are the best indicators of trends. (Question wording can strongly influence response patterns.) As figure 12.1 shows, these surveys suggest that support among the American public for legalizing marijuana use grew from the mid-1960s to the late 1970s, fell sharply through 1990, and has risen steadily since, crossing the 50 percent mark in about 2013.

Across the two surveys, about 55 percent of Americans answer yes to legalizing use, about 40 percent say no, and about 5 percent are unsure or have no opinion.

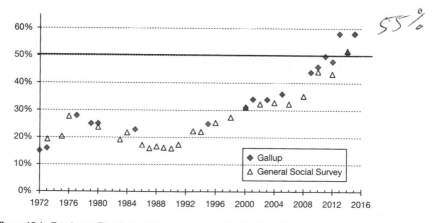

Figure 12.1 Trends over Time in Public Support for Legalizing Marijuana Use

Both surveys ask about whether the *use* of marijuana should be made legal; so neither bears directly on legalization of a commercial marijuana industry as in Alaska, Colorado, Oregon, or Washington. Simply legalizing use is closer to what is known as decriminalization than what we normally refer to as legalization. But other surveys that ask about both about legal use and about legal sales get similar answers to those two questions, suggesting that most voters don't make the same distinctions we do.

Who supports and who opposes legalization in the United States?

The demographic patterns mostly conform to stereotypes: there is greater support for legalization among men, liberals, those born after 1950, and those without children, with more education, and with weaker ties to organized religion (see figure 12.2). There is much stronger support in New England and the West than elsewhere. And marijuana users—particularly long-term users—are more likely to support legalization. But there are some twists.

While liberals are more likely to support legalization than conservatives, the association is stronger for political ideology than for

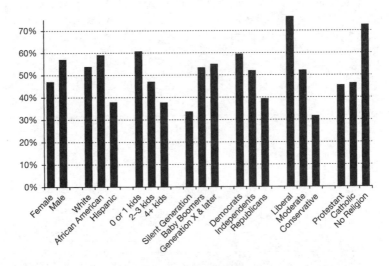

Figure 12.2 Support for Legalizing Marijuana Use among Respondents to the 2014 General Social Survey

party affiliation. Conservative Democrats are no more likely to support legalization than conservative Republicans.

Younger respondents are more favorable to marijuana than their elders. In the 1970s this showed up as a generation gap between baby boomers and both their parents and grandparents. But times changed. While the generation born before 1925 (the "greatest" or "GI" generation) remains staunchly opposed, support for legalization among the "silent generation" (those born between 1925 and 1945) has grown to one-third. Support among baby boomers fell sharply during the 1980s and then rebounded.

Parents with kids at home are substantially less likely to support legalization; thus the baby boomers' vacillation may stem from their becoming parents. Generally, the gap between parents and those without children is most pronounced in groups with higher rates of overall support for legalization (e.g., males and liberals). To simplify, conservatives oppose legalization regardless of whether they have kids; liberals tend to change their position depending on whether or not they are thinking about the issue from a parent's perspective.

In terms of religious affiliation, fundamentalist Christians are less likely to support legalization than liberal Christians. But the largest gap is between those who self-identify as having no religion (very likely to support legalization) and those who report some denominational affiliation.

Most demographic groups' support for legalization follows the V-shaped pattern over time shown in figure 12.1, but the recent growth in support has been particularly pronounced among African Americans. A decade ago non-Hispanic whites stood out from the rest of the population in their high rates of support; now Hispanics and Asian Americans stand out from both non-Hispanic whites and African Americans by having lower levels of support.

Arguably the most consequential variation is across states. While national polls reveal only a modest majority in support, there are individual states where the voters lean heavily toward legalization for nonmedical use.

Who votes for legalization?

Support for legalization does not always translate to yes votes on Election Day, for two reasons. First, the younger voters who are

most likely to support legalization have lower rates of voter participation, especially in off-year elections. That helps explain why
legalization advocates in California decided to wait until 2016 to try
their luck again, having failed at the ballot box in 2010 and been
unable to unite behind any one proposal in 2012. Conversely, liberal
candidates benefit from the get-out-the-vote effect of legalization
initiatives being on the ballot.

Second, someone can dislike particular provisions in a law.
Washington's 2012 proposition almost failed because some in the
medical-marijuana industry thought it didn't offer enough protections for users, and California's Proposition 19 might have passed if
it had been able to win the support of all those who favor legalization. In a postelection poll conducted by the Public Policy Institute
of California, 6 percent of respondents reported that they supported
legalization generally but nonetheless voted against Proposition
19. (The most common reason they gave was that the initiative was
poorly written.) Adding that 6 percent to those who actually voted
"yes" would have tipped the balance. In Ohio in 2015, a proposition
that would have legalized commercial marijuana production and
sale, but limited the right to grow to the ten companies whose owners had financed the ballot initiative, went down to crushing defeat,
despite polls showing majority support for legalization among
Ohioans.

On the other hand, ever since the 2008 global recession and
the ensuing state-level fiscal crises, legalization has been able to
draw support from those who are ambivalent about the drug but
excited about marijuana tax revenue. Potential tax revenue was the
single most common reason cited by those voting for California's
Proposition 19.

Who is funding the legalization movement?

Two billionaires, George Soros and the late Peter Lewis, bankrolled
the legalization movement for years, including giving over $3.5 mil-
lion in support of Washington's Initiative 502 (I-502) in 2012. The
cause attracts an eclectic mix of other wealthy donors, including
Richard Lee (the millionaire marijuana entrepreneur who founded
Oaksterdam University), Sean Parker and Dustin Moskovitz
(whose wealth came from Facebook), John Sperling (founder of the

University of Phoenix), and travel guru Rick Steves (who donated $450,000 to support of Washington's I-502). Nevertheless, Soros and Lewis have accounted for most of the spending; *Forbes* reports that Lewis contributed $40 million to support marijuana law reform (mostly through the National Organization for the Reform of Marijuana Laws, or NORML), and Soros has given about $200 million to fund drug policy reform generally and pledged $5 million per year to the Drug Policy Alliance from 2011 to 2021.

The antireform campaigns are poor by comparison. Mike Riggs reported in the *New Republic* that the opposition to I-502 raised just $15,995 versus a total of $6.2 million raised on the pro side, and similarly $5,950 versus $1,070,000 on a Massachusetts medical-marijuana initiative. In Ballotpedia's list of donors for and against California's Proposition 19, the largest donor on the no side (Julie Schauer, $50,000) was outspent by the smallest named donor on the yes side (PayPal cofounder and venture capitalist Peter Thiel, $70,000). The one exception to this pattern is Sheldon Adelson's contribution of over $5 million in opposition to Florida's 2014 proposition on medical-marijuana (which gained a solid majority of the vote but not enough to pass the 60 percent threshold required for a constitutional amendment).

Under the Clinton and George W. Bush administrations, federal officials openly campaigned against state-level efforts to liberalize marijuana policies; that practice has not continued under the Obama administration. But federal as well as state and local enforcement officials remain vocally opposed to legalization initiatives; their opposition, and the reluctance of state legislators to get on the wrong side of law enforcement officials, helps explain why, even in states with solid pro-legalization majorities among the voters, legalization advocates resort to ballot initiatives rather than the normal legislative process.

A more recent factor is the industry that has sprung up to exploit the opportunities in medical and commercial marijuana sales. Participants in that industry have not as yet put much effort into ballot campaigns (with the exception of Ohio in 2015), but their weight is likely to be felt increasingly in the future. Their interests and opinions may differ sharply from those of the previous generation of advocates. We are slowly seeing the replacement of the marijuana movement by the marijuana lobby.

Additional Reading

Caulkins, Jonathan P., et al. "Marijuana Legalization: Certainty, Impossibility, Both, or Neither?"

Courtwright, David T. *Forces of Habit.*

Musto, David F. *The American Disease.*

Room, Robin, et al. *Cannabis Policy.*

13

WHAT'S REALLY HAPPENING IN MEDICAL-MARIJUANA STATES?

When did medical-marijuana get started in the United States?

Marijuana has been used for therapeutic purposes for thousands of years (see chapter 5). However, in medicine as in other uses, marijuana had been largely replaced with newer substitutes even before it became prohibited.

Interest in potential medical applications in the United States returned alongside the spread of recreational use in the 1960s. Beginning in 1976, the federal government, under court order, distributed marijuana cigarettes to a handful of patients under a "compassionate use" program, but that program stopped accepting new patients in 1992. In the 1970s and 1980s a number of states passed legislation intended to enable marijuana therapeutic research, but few of the state programs became operational, and some of those laws were later repealed or allowed to expire.

There are many explanations for why medical-marijuana stalled. For one, mainstream pharmaceutical researchers had approximately zero interest in studying a traditional herbal preparation; their orientation was and is toward single molecular entities. Back then it was not possible to obtain FDA approval for "botanicals" of any kind, let alone one whose strongest contemporary association was with recreational and countercultural use. The fact that marijuana was usually administered by smoking constituted an additional barrier; the notion of the FDA approving a medication to be given amid clouds of toxic—even carcinogenic—gases appeared absurd. In retrospect, it seems obvious that vaporization or edibles could be substituted for smoking, but that flexibility is more apparent to people trying to get to yes than to those looking for reasons to say no.

Just doing research was difficult for some good reasons (with a plant, it is hard to define a "good manufacturing process" that ensures consistency from dose to dose) and others that amounted to bureaucratic obstructionism. The federal government had given a single laboratory the sole right to produce marijuana for research, and the product available from that laboratory was not always what researchers wanted to work with. Moreover, researchers couldn't simply purchase supplies, as they can for other controlled drugs; rather, they had to apply for a discretionary "grant" of the material, which could be (and sometimes was) refused for what seemed like arbitrary reasons. (This led many to suspect that the rejections were of studies that seemed likely to yield politically inconvenient results or that were sponsored by groups known to be legalization advocates.)

Support for medical-marijuana increased in the late 1980s and 1990s, partially in response to public empathy for patients battling cancer and AIDS, a trend that was skillfully (or, in an alternative view, shamelessly) exploited by legalization advocates. There was observational evidence that marijuana improved appetite while reducing nausea and pain for patients with AIDS, for whom loss of appetite was a life-threatening condition. Synthetic THC (Marinol) in pill form was approved for these purposes, but swallowing a pill is problematic if nausea and vomiting are the problem. Moreover, pure THC was poorly tolerated by many patients, who complained of anxiety and unpleasant overintoxication. There was irony in officials warning that illicit-market marijuana was getting more and more dangerous because it had higher and higher levels of THC and then turning around and offering sick people pure THC as a medicine, but probably the patients involved were too sick to appreciate the humor in the situation.

Few places were hit harder by AIDS than San Francisco, and in 1991 80 percent of voters there supported Proposition P, which recommended that "the State of California and the California Medical Association restore hemp medical preparations to the list of available medicines in California." The San Francisco Board of Supervisors responded by passing a resolution in 1992 advising the mayor to "urge the Police Commission and the District Attorney of the City and County of San Francisco to make . . . the arrest or prosecution of those involved in the possession or cultivation of hemp for medicinal purposes" the lowest priority. (Marijuana's popularity reached its modern nadir around 1992. That may explain why those crafting the proposition used the term "hemp," which is usually reserved for low-THC material used for fiber or other industrial purposes.)

It was in this political climate that the nation's first marijuana dispensary opened in the early 1990s. The San Francisco Cannabis Buyers Club was in clear violation of state and federal laws, but it was generally tolerated by county officials. However, in August 1996, state drug enforcement agents raided the club after a multi-year investigation, alleging that the Buyers Club was selling marijuana to nonpatients. One source reported that at the time of the raid there might have been another thirty cannabis clubs operating in the United States, but it would be another decade before medical-marijuana stores became common.

That November, California became the first state to exempt medical-marijuana patients from prohibition when Proposition 215 passed with 56 percent of the vote. Prop 215 established that "seriously ill Californians have the right to obtain and use marijuana for medical purposes where that medical use is deemed appropriate and has been recommended by a physician who has determined that the person's health would benefit from the use of marijuana in the treatment of cancer, anorexia, AIDS, chronic pain, spasticity, glaucoma, arthritis, migraine, or any other illness for which marijuana provides relief" (emphasis added). This last clause, combined with the lack of any regulatory control over providers, made it extremely easy to obtain a recommendation. This approach was copied by some other states, while others created far more restrictive medical-marijuana programs.

Where does medical-marijuana come from?

That depends on the state.

Originally, some medical-marijuana laws merely protected patients from arrest or prosecution for possession, but made no provision for legally obtaining the drug. In those states, patients without a green thumb or a convenient place to grow some plants had to obtain their marijuana from illicit sources. To help patients who were for whatever reason unable to grow marijuana themselves, provision was usually made for a "designated caregiver" to grow on the patient's behalf. This was defined originally in California as the person taking primary responsibility for the patient's well-being.

But some people suffer not only from grievous ailments but also from having spouses and siblings who can't even grow dandelions, so the notion of "designated caregiver" was stretched further and further, eventually including people the patient had never even met. Since some of these strangers were astoundingly magnanimous, they chose to grow not just for one patient but for several or even dozens of people they had never met. (One California dispensary claimed to be the "primary caregiver" for more than a thousand patients.)

Patients were allowed to pay caregivers in order to defray their costs of growing, which allowed money to change hands; the definition of "costs" proved elastic. Most states with medical-marijuana now allow retail stores—called dispensaries—to serve as intermediaries between the patients and the growers who supply them.

Of course, there are genuine caregivers rendering genuine services in these medical-marijuana states. But there are also a lot of people for whom it is just a business—a business whose product they believe in, but nonetheless a business with employees, advertising budgets, tax advisors, and all the other accoutrements.

States vary widely in how many dispensaries are allowed. Some states license only a limited number of dispensaries and intend them to serve only a modest number of patients; other states make no effort to limit the growth of this commercial sector. And within states, regulations that govern dispensaries can vary wildly by county.

In extreme cases, "dispensaries" function as wholesale dealers for illegal marijuana retailers; some outfits in California offer discounts for purchases of a quarter pound at a time (about two hundred joints' worth) and have posted signs asking their customers not to resell *on the street immediately in front of the dispensary.* In California, the medical-marijuana "system" seems to have replaced much of the purely illicit traffic as a source of high-potency marijuana for relatively prosperous people, though some poorer users still buy low-quality Mexican commercial grade from drug dealers not pretending to supply medicine. In Colorado, more than half the juvenile marijuana users coming in for treatment reported getting some of their pot from acquaintances with medical-marijuana cards. Some of this is diversion for profit; some (maybe most) is simply friends buying for friends.

How medical is medical-marijuana?

As our colleague Pat Oglesby notes, marijuana is strange medicine; healthy people don't want to use hospital services, antifungals, or prosthetic devices, but many like marijuana.

Leaving aside high-CBD strains (discussed below), "medical-marijuana" is not, for the most part, a distinct product from other domestically grown high-potency marijuana. Rather, it merely puts a different label on marijuana that could be used equally well for recreational purposes.

Some states' medical-marijuana laws are designed to ensure that people in genuine medical need are able to obtain a supply while discouraging abuse of the medical system by people who want to buy and sell for nonmedical purposes. Others—primarily in the West—basically make it available to any adult who wants it. Three percent of all adult Coloradans have medical-marijuana cards, while the comparable figure in Nevada is four-tenths of one percent; in Delaware it is four-*hundredths* of one percent. Perhaps many Delawareans are being deprived of essential medicine, or perhaps many medical-marijuana "patients" in Colorado suffer from nothing more than the aches and ills common to the human condition.

By the same token, California is thought to have more than two thousand dispensaries, about as many as it has Starbucks outlets. Oregon had even more, per capita. New York State will allow a maximum of twenty, and Minnesota no more than eight. California does not limit the number of growers; New York and Minnesota do (to four and two, respectively).

Ongoing work by RAND researchers divides these medical-marijuana laws into four eras: the ballot initiative era (1996–2000), early legislative era (2000–2009), late legislative era (2009–2014), and CBD era (2014–present). The first eight states to pass medical-marijuana did so via ballot initiatives, often written and funded by people interested in legalizing marijuana for nonmedical use as well. These laws tended to be liberal with respect to eligible medical conditions, requirements for doctors, and home cultivation. They did not originally authorize medical dispensaries.

The early legislative era saw state legislators grappling with the intricacies of medical-marijuana as well as trying to shape the markets within the constraints of propositions that had already passed; however, formal allowances for dispensaries were still rare, so the supply side of the industry still operated surreptitiously.

Then in 2003, the California legislature passed SB420—the bill number being a fairly open wink to nonmedical pot-smoking. SB420, among other things, "enhance[d] the access of patients and caregivers to medical-marijuana through collective, cooperative cultivation projects." This gave local governments a green light to permit and regulate dispensaries. For many years California stood alone in this regard, but New Mexico passed a bill in 2007 that created a legal framework for licensed marijuana producers, with its first legal dispensary opening in 2009.

The late legislative era includes states that implemented after the Obama administration signaled federal acquiescence to state-level medical-marijuana laws; the vast majority of these jurisdictions made provisions for dispensaries to operate. However, some are more restrictive on the recommendation side. For example, New York requires doctors to complete a training course and register with the Department of Health in order to recommend marijuana. In Minnesota, a doctor must certify that patients have one of nine specific medical conditions—that will be ten when intractable pain is added to the list in summer 2016—and patients must submit an online patient self-evaluation form before they can refill at a dispensary. The Illinois medical-marijuana law includes a sunset clause, which means that if the legislature does not take explicit action to continue the program by the end of 2017, the program will terminate.

So as a gross generalization, medical-marijuana regimes created by state legislatures east of the Mississippi generally appear to be good-faith efforts to provide compassionate access to people with well-defined medical conditions, while the regimes originally created by voter propositions farther west are extremely permissive and easy to manipulate.

The fourth wave of laws were enacted after 2013 and only permit high-CBD and (usually) low-THC marijuana products for intractable seizures and epilepsy. For the most part they are of a different ilk, since CBD is not an intoxicant and low-THC products have little value to anyone except real patients; however, a few of these states allow products to include up to 5 percent THC, which will produce intoxication.

Are CBD laws really about marijuana?

Yes, no, and yes.

In 2014, eleven states enacted laws allowing qualifying patients to access products containing non-intoxicating cannabidiol (CBD) but little or no intoxicating THC. CBD counteracts some of the adverse effects of THC (e.g., anxiety) and apparently can alleviate seizures in some patients. (Many other claims have been made for CBD, including analgesic and antipsychotic actions. Some of those claims may be true.)

So yes, these CBD laws are about marijuana, because they permit access to products derived from the cannabis plant, which makes it "marijuana" under federal law. But marijuana without THC has about the same potential for recreational use and dependence as carrots. So even if the high CBD/low-THC products come from the same species of plant as conventional marijuana, providing CBD-only products creates no meaningful risk of diversion or abuse. If there were another plant that contained CBD but not THC, that plant would never have been included in the Controlled Substances Act. So no, a CBD-only product is not the sort of marijuana involved in the past 50 years of cultural warfare.

But then again, yes, these CBD laws do play a role in the ongoing battle between advocates and opponents of legalizing THC-bearing products. To some advocates, CBD offers a convenient and nonthreatening door opener in conservative regions of the country that have so far resisted THC-based medical-marijuana. Those advocates intend approval of CBD to lead first to the legalization of THC-bearing cannabis products for medical use and then to open commerce without any medical pretext. Indeed, while most CBD laws limit THC content to 0.3 percent or 0.5 percent, what are called "CBD laws" in Georgia and Virginia already allow THC content of up to 5 percent. That is more than ten times the limit allowed in industrial hemp and higher than the average potency of all marijuana that was seized before 2000. Yet Americans for Safe Access—the primary medical-marijuana advocacy group—described this as "a slightly higher cap than [in] most CBD states."

On the other hand, many CBD laws target specific conditions and operate primarily as an affirmative defense against prosecution for possession, with no provision for production or sale. (The notion is that supplies can come from other states that have legalized marijuana products generally.) Some opponents of full legalization hope that CBD will be a stopping place rather than a steppingstone, and use their support for CBD availability to demonstrate their open-mindedness.

The absence of regulated in-state supply created an opportunity for out-of-state entrepreneurs to market mail-order products, some of which turned out not to contain CBD at all. This led the Food and Drug Administration to take a tough stance against companies making health-claims for nonpharmaceutical CBD products. This is somewhat ironic; the FDA has made no particular effort to rein in the extravagant claims made about the benefits of conventional, high-THC marijuana products.

Was there a "Sanjay Gupta" effect?

CNN's popular medical correspondent Dr. Sanjay Gupta was against medical-marijuana before he was for it. His change of heart is credited with triggering passage of CBD laws in many states.

In 2009, Gupta wrote an essay for *Time* magazine arguing against medical-marijuana. After noting that there were some medical benefits associated with THC, he quoted a statement of the director of the National Institute on Drug Abuse that "numerous deleterious health consequences are associated with [marijuana's] short- and long-term use." Gupta, who was highly regarded for his medical advice and talked about as a candidate for US surgeon general, concluded, "But I'm here to tell you, as a doctor, that despite all the talk about the medical benefits of marijuana, smoking the stuff is not going to do your health any good."

But in August 2013 he publicly apologized for the essay and explained why he changed his mind. He admitted, "I mistakenly believed the Drug Enforcement Agency listed marijuana as a schedule 1 substance because of sound scientific proof," and said he was too quick to lump legitimate patients together with those who only wanted medical-marijuana so they could get high.

About a week later, CNN aired Gupta's documentary about medical-marijuana, *Weed*, which received tremendous attention. The show interviewed medical doctors and highlighted the stories of patients who reportedly benefitted from medical-marijuana, including a 3-year-old with a rare and horrible condition called Dravet syndrome, who had experienced hundreds of seizures each week. The girl, Charlotte Figi, did not respond to traditional treatments, and her parents eventually sought a CBD oil produced by marijuana farmers in Colorado. The oil seemed to work wonders for the little girl, and her seizures decreased to about two or three a month. The oil, now sold as Charlotte's Web, comes from a strain of marijuana bred for very low levels of THC. Nonetheless, some activists argue that pure CBD will not deliver the promised antiseizure effect unless it is mixed with at least a small amount of THC.

After the first special aired, Gupta wrote, "Legislators from several states have reached out to me, eager to inform their own positions and asking to show the documentary to their fellow lawmakers." In 2014, eleven states—actively lobbied both by the parents of young seizure-disorder patients and by vendors of CBD products—enacted laws to make CBD oil available to qualifying patients.

The need for herbal CBD products may be transitory. GW Pharmaceuticals has developed a pharmaceutical CBD product (extracted from the cannabis plant) called Epidiolex. That product is now undergoing phase III clinical trials for treatment of both Dravet syndrome and Lennox-Gastaut syndrome. Another firm (Insys Therapeutics) has a synthetic CBD product that is expected to enter trials soon. Also, in 2014 the FDA gave Epidiolex a Fast Track designation and expanded access so children could obtain Epidiolex concurrent with the clinical trials, rather than waiting for the trials' final results and FDA approval. (By contrast, Sativex, another GW Pharma cannabis extract containing approximately equal amounts of THC and CBD, is still held up in the FDA approval process, years after receiving regulatory approval in other countries.)

Nevertheless, some families have moved to Colorado so they could get access to Charlotte's Web for their sick children. John Ingold of the *Denver Post* and his colleagues were selected as finalists for the Pulitzer Prize for their powerful series about some of these families and the science about CBD. They noted that the CBD migration to Colorado began after CNN aired Gupta's documentary, and the number of children registered as medical-marijuana patients increased from sixty in August 2013 to more than four hundred within a year.

The article also made it clear that CBD does not work for every patient and that some of the early claims were wildly overoptimistic. But anecdotes about CBD's potential are extremely powerful, especially for parents who have exhausted every other option to stop their children from suffering from frequent and violent seizures. Gupta's documentary and its two sequels have prompted discussions at dinner tables, doctors' offices, and state capitols across the country about medical-marijuana, including not just CBD but also THC-based products.

What is the federal government doing in states that allow medical-marijuana?

Producing, distributing, and possessing any form of marijuana— as opposed to FDA-approved pharmaceuticals containing cannabinoids—remains illegal under federal law, even where state law allows medical-marijuana. In the case of *Gonzales v. Raich* (2005) the US Supreme Court ruled 6–3 that Congress had the power to ban the medical use of marijuana. So federal agents could arrest, and US attorneys could prosecute, those who produce, distribute, or even use medical-marijuana. In practice, however, federal law enforcement officials have rarely gone after medical-marijuana patients or caregivers (unless they were growing or selling at a commercial scale or committing other crimes). For that matter, federal law enforcement ignores most marijuana users who *do not* have a medical recommendation; agents typically only pursue cases against people possessing hundreds of pounds or more, rather than just a few pounds, let alone a few ounces or joints.

There are storefronts across the country where those with a medical-marijuana recommendation from a physician can openly buy marijuana. It would have been—and still would be—legally straightforward for the Drug Enforcement Administration to raid these places and chain their doors, obtain injunctions against them, or, more simply, tell the landlords to evict those tenants or face confiscation of their property. That has happened occasionally, but often when the outlet was believed to be involved in other crimes.

Up until 2009, the producers were at somewhat greater risk, with sporadic prosecutions encouraging most to keep a low profile. Now, though, even large-scale distributors do business openly, their websites offering to make sales that count as felonies under federal law. The change came in 2009, when the Justice Department issued what became known as the "Ogden Memorandum." It was interpreted as indicating that agents and prosecutors would largely respect state medical-marijuana laws; the proliferation of dispensaries followed shortly.

In December 2014, Congress passed a budget amendment to block federal funds from being used to prevent states "from implementing their own State laws that authorize the use, distribution, possession, or cultivation of medical-marijuana." President Obama signed it into law, and many thought it would lead to important protections, especially for those currently involved in proceedings. But in April 2015 a spokesman for the US Department of Justice presented a different interpretation, arguing that the amendment only applies to the actions of states, not individuals or organizations involved with medical-marijuana. In October 2015, a US district judge issued a ruling that did not support the latter interpretation.

Who recommends medical-marijuana to patients?

Medical-marijuana patients are concentrated in those states—mostly in the West and Rocky Mountains—where the laws are very permissive. And within those states, recommendation-writing (not technically prescription-writing, because prescriptions apply only to FDA-approved medications) is concentrated among a relatively small number of clinicians, many of whom specialize in providing these recommendations rather than in any specific branch of medicine. In Colorado, for example, fewer than a dozen physicians accounted for more than half of the state's 100,000+ medical-marijuana registrations.

Some "kush docs" (also known as "420 docs") advertise, and pricing is competitive, with some charging as little as $35, reflecting the often-cursory nature of the "examination" provided. Some even give a money-back guarantee: they promise not to charge any patient who does not get a recommendation.

Although other providers are more diligent, the recommendation-writing practices of the extreme 420 docs would land them in severe professional or even criminal trouble if they were applied to any other controlled substance. Any physicians who openly advertised that patients should come to them for OxyContin prescriptions would be lucky to merely lose their medical licenses rather than face felony drug-distribution charges. But a clumsy attempt by the federal government to deter physicians from writing medical recommendations under California Proposition 215 led to a court order upholding physicians' right to do so as an exercise of their right to free speech. This leaves the kush docs free to do pretty much as they please.

In addition, as long as medical recommendations are the only way for genuinely sick people to access marijuana, there is a natural tendency not to inquire too closely into physicians' recommendation-writing behavior. One unanticipated effect of legalizing sales of marijuana for recreational use may be greater willingness to crack down on extreme recommendation-writing; the leading provider of such medical-marijuana recommendations in Colorado (more than eight thousand patients) is now facing criminal charges.

One factor that discourages most "regular" physicians from recommending medical-marijuana is the lack of laboratory-tested and standardized products. No physician, presented with a patient with an infection, would "recommend" that the patient "take some antibiotic." Instead, depending on the characteristics of the infection and the patient, the physician would write a specific prescription, naming the medicine, the dosage, and the frequency. There's no equivalent to that in the process of recommending medical-marijuana, both because the products aren't standardized and because the underlying research hasn't been done to specify how much of what sort of cannabis preparation will serve the needs of a patient with a given condition.

Another factor is the side effects. Medical-marijuana is usually used for chronic conditions, and a substantial proportion of those who use marijuana on a daily basis for an extended period become dependent. (Only a modest proportion of those who have ever tried marijuana become dependent, but historically only about one-third of those who tried marijuana went on to use it even 100 times. So rates of dependence among those who use on an ongoing basis are roughly triple the dependence rates that are typically quoted.)

For these and other reasons, most medical societies oppose medical-marijuana; that presumably signals to physicians that recommending it might carry risks to their professional reputations.

Was medical-marijuana invented as a wedge issue to open the gates for full legalization?

Some voters support medical-marijuana only for its therapeutic potential. That is clear from the fact that only a shade over half of Americans support legalizing (all) marijuana use, but the vast majority support legalizing medical-marijuana.

Yet some activists see medical-marijuana as the first stepping-stone on a path to full legalization. Kevin Sabet of the antilegalization group Project SAM often highlights a 1979 quote from NORML founder Keith Stroup: "We will use [medical-marijuana] as a red herring to give marijuana a good name." Dennis Peron, the coauthor and backer of California's 1996 medical-marijuana proposition, was shown on video at the election-night victory party lighting up a joint and announcing, "All marijuana use is medical now." And many of those who bankrolled the early medical-marijuana initiatives (e.g., George Soros and the late Peter Lewis) later supported the nonmedical legalization campaigns in Colorado, Oregon, Alaska, and Washington.

Medical-marijuana can serve as a steppingstone in two distinct ways, by softening the public's attitudes toward marijuana overall and by providing legal loopholes that allow entrepreneurs to produce for the recreational market under the guise of supplying to meet medical needs. Once partial legalization for all uses has emerged under the cover of medical-marijuana, the move to full formal legalization seems less threatening to voters: at least, that was the case in Washington State, Colorado, and Oregon, and may turn out to be true in California.

So clearly there are mixed motivations. For some, medical-marijuana is an end unto itself. For others it is merely a means to the ultimate end of full legalization. It is very hard to quantify the magnitude of these two complementary motivations, although it is noteworthy that very few advocates of medical-marijuana objected to the legal loopholes that allowed the medical system to create a quasi-legalization in several Western states.

On the other hand, medical-marijuana laws also create a set of commercial interests for which full-on legalization would be financially challenging. In Washington State, for example, a medical-marijuana vendor provided one of the major opposition voices to the legalization initiative.

Do medical-marijuana laws increase nonmedical-marijuana use?

Clearly, some of what is sold as medical-marijuana goes to nonmedical uses, either because people get medical-marijuana recommendations to supply their own needs or because registered patients (whether sick or not) resell to others. If the result is merely to replace purely illicit production and sale of completely unregulated products with quasi-legal production and sale of partially regulated products, it's hard to see what harm is done other than to respect for the law. But if making marijuana legally available (under state law) for medical use leads to more people using, or people who use it consuming more of it, medical-marijuana laws partly undo the purpose of marijuana prohibition.

Again, not everyone who uses marijuana has a problem with the drug; we should be especially concerned about the potential growth of the problem population (high-dose, high-frequency users reporting symptoms of substance use disorder) and of use among adolescents.

But medical-marijuana laws are a moving target; not only are the laws themselves changing, but the industries those laws create also grow over time, so the effects at the end of year one may not provide much insight into how things will look in year five or fifteen. Therefore all conclusions so far should be regarded as tentative. Moreover, while medical-marijuana laws—especially the very loose ones in the West—give us some insight into what commercial legalization might look like, it's only a hint.

There are now enough contradictory published findings that advocates on any side can weave whatever story they wish to tell. The quality of those studies varies. We place much greater weight on research that takes into account the differences among medical-marijuana laws and their implementation (e.g., whether they allow dispensaries and if so, how many). UCLA's Rosanna Smart and Georgia State University's Eric Sevigny are pushing the frontier in this field by focusing on how many patients there are per capita in various states. We find much less convincing the (many) studies that crudely divide the world into states with and without medical-marijuana, treating Colorado and Delaware alike as "medical-marijuana" states even though Colorado has more than a hundred times as many registered patients compared to its population.

In the first half of 2015 alone, four new peer-reviewed studies were published in very good journals. Each examined how medical-marijuana laws influenced marijuana use, but with different (high-quality) datasets. Two explored effects on adults and also looked beyond the typical binary measure. One found a positive correlation with past month use, but only for states that allowed medical dispensaries; merely passing a medical-marijuana law in and of itself was not associated with greater use. The other study came to a different conclusion: it found that passage of a medical-marijuana law was positively associated with past-month marijuana use and daily/near daily use, but there was no specific effect for states that allow dispensaries. In addition, this study also suggests that passage of medical-marijuana laws increased marijuana abuse and dependence, but the policy effect is delayed.

None of these four studies found evidence that implementing medical-marijuana laws increased the likelihood of youth admitting to using marijuana in the past month, but they each tell a different story. For example, one presents evidence suggesting that medical-marijuana may have *decreased* the proportion of eighth-graders using marijuana, while another finds strong evidence that the laws increase the probability of minors trying it for the first time. The others examined admissions to drug treatment for marijuana and generated different conclusions.

It would be desirable to look beyond prevalence and consider quantities consumed, products consumed, and detailed measures of problematic use. But generating those studies will take time.

What are the other population-level consequences of medical-marijuana laws?

Even if we knew how medical-marijuana laws affect marijuana use, the question about their effects on the use of other drugs would still be unresolved. If marijuana substitutes for other drugs, and especially for drugs that present greater dangers, a growth even in problem marijuana use might be accompanied by an offsetting, or even more-than-offsetting, decline in harm from those other drugs. On the other hand, the effect could go the other way: making marijuana more available might instead increase the problematic use of other drugs. The effects might have opposite signs for different drugs, or in different populations, and there's no assurance that short-run and long-run effects will be of the same magnitude or even in the same direction.

One study which unfortunately only distinguished crudely between states with and without medical-marijuana laws found that passage of such laws reduces alcohol consumption and alcohol-related traffic facilities. Another using the same simple binary approach but with a different dataset yielded a different conclusion: enactment of medical-marijuana laws increased the total number of binge drinking days for those over twenty-one as well as the number of events involving marijuana use along with binge drinking. The latter study also explored four aspects of these laws (allow medical-marijuana for non-specific pain, require patients registry, allow dispensaries, and allows home cultivation) and found that only the non-specific pain provision was positively associated with binge drinking.

There has also been interest in the relationship between medical-marijuana laws and the use of prescription opiates such as OxyContin. As noted in chapter 5, a handful of studies support the growing anecdotal evidence that some patients use marijuana instead of prescription pain killers. In a paper published in the *Journal of the American Medical Association*, researchers found that states with medical-marijuana laws had a 25 percent lower average annual opioid overdose mortality rate than other states. This paper spurred important discussions about how much we can learn from aggregate-level data, and there are also questions about how the results would look if the focus were on specific aspects of medical-marijuana laws instead of the binary "all or nothing" measure. (We've seen some excellent working papers which also suggest marijuana and prescription opioids can be substitutes. If they make it through peer-review we'll discuss them in the third edition.)

Oddly, little attention has been paid to the possibility that liberalizing policies toward smoking marijuana might affect rates of tobacco smoking. Given the enormous public health toll associated with cigarettes, it is not inconceivable that among the most important consequences of changing marijuana policy will be those accruing indirectly through effects on tobacco use.

A final note: extreme caution should be used by those seeking to make projections about legalization based on studies of medical-marijuana; much will depend on the type of legalization being considered. For example, with legalization based on for-profit commercial sales, we expect changes in price per unit of THC and marketing to be greater than we currently see even in states with liberal medical-marijuana regimes. In addition, the norms surrounding the simultaneous use of multiple substances could be quite different when marijuana products are less stigmatized and more likely to be used in public settings.

Additional Reading

Eisenstein, Michael. "Medical-marijuana: Showdown at the Cannabis Corral."
Ingold, John, Joe Amon, and Lindsay Pierce. "State of Hope."
National Conference of State Legislatures. *State Medical-marijuana Laws.*
Ogden, David W. *Memorandum for Selected United States Attorneys on Investigations and Prosecutions in States Authorizing the Medical Use of Marijuana.*

14

WHAT IS HAPPENING IN COLORADO AND WASHINGTON?

If Uruguay, Alaska, and Oregon have all legalized, why focus on Colorado and Washington?

As of this writing, five major jurisdictions have legalized large-scale production and retail sale for nonmedical purposes: Colorado and Washington State in 2012, Uruguay in 2013, and Alaska and Oregon in 2014. (The District of Columbia's legalization is limited to personal possession, use, and home-growing. Jamaica—on paper—is only allowing large-scale production for medical purposes; this is further discussed in chapter 15.) This chapter focuses on Colorado and Washington State because they are further along in the process.

While legalization of use or possession can take effect almost immediately, regulated systems of licensed production take time to implement. Commercial outlets in Colorado and Washington State have only been operating since January and July 2014, respectively, and to date they are not offering prices or services much different than what was already available from the medical systems in those states (although tourists can now purchase from the new stores). The real experiment won't start until commercial prices fall significantly below the prices that now obtain at medical dispensaries.

So far, the legal markets are all working, and the general absence of disasters is itself a noteworthy success (although the problems with edibles were worse than most predicted). However, the systems are too new to have generated many measurable outcomes; we can't really say for sure whether use by minors, or problem use, has increased or will later increase because of legalization. So beware of strong claims at this point from either side of the debate. As Zhou

Enlai is supposed to have replied when Henry Kissinger asked about the Chinese view of the results of the French Revolution, "In China, we think it's too early to tell."

What are the key provisions common to Colorado and Washington?

Colorado and Washington have both largely taken as their model their systems for alcohol—particularly liquor, as opposed to beer or wine. That places production and retailing in the hands of regulated, licensed for-profit companies. In theory marijuana can only be sold in stores that carry nothing else, though one company in Colorado has opened "Gas and Grass" operations that sell cannabis at filling stations, technically operating as two independent businesses sharing a location.

The regulating agencies (the Department of Revenue in Colorado and the Liquor and Cannabis Board in Washington) focus on "good government" (e.g., procedural fairness), revenue collection, and prevention of sales to minors more than they do on protecting public health by constraining problem use.

Both states have made vigorous, and apparently largely successful, efforts to prevent marijuana sales directly to minors from licensed stores. Both forbid driving under the influence and use in public. Neither limits potency; both forbid selling alcohol and tobacco where marijuana is sold. Taxation in both states includes an ad valorem (percentage-of-price) basis, although Colorado also imposes a tax based on weight. Taxes are substantial—somewhat higher in Washington than in Colorado—but not as high as the national average for cigarettes and not high enough to prevent a decline in retail prices once the production systems mature.

The regulatory limits on advertising in media that cater to youth have not yet been fully tested in the courts. It is not entirely clear why. It may be that the companies are still mostly too small to afford conventional media advertising and in some places there may be informal agreements within the industry to avoid this type advertising. Neither state has tried to ban off-premise marketing to adults 21 and older.

There are also differences between the states' rules. For example, Washington forbids discount coupons, which are common in Colorado. Washington also forbids growers from owning retail shops, while Colorado permits it (and initially required it). Colorado, unlike Washington, allows any resident to grow marijuana at home for personal use; Washington allows it only for people with medical recommendations. Colorado lets residents buy more per transaction (one ounce) than nonresidents (0.25 ounces), while Washington does not make this distinction.

Are revenues from taxes making a difference in state budgets?

A difference, but not a big difference.

By mid-2015, Colorado and Washington were each receiving about $11 million per month in marijuana taxes and license and fee income. Revenues are still rising as the commercial market takes sales from the illegal market and from the medical system, and that will continue; considerable production and distribution (perhaps as much as one-third in Washington) still occurs outside of the legal, taxed system. The total volume of marijuana consumed in those states is also likely to rise over time, though no one knows by how much. That, too, will boost revenues.

However, declining prices and competition from other states may limit or even reverse tax revenue growth. Since taxes in both states are taken as a percentage of sales prices, falling prices imply reduced revenues. (Wholesale prices have already fallen, and now, in 2015, retail prices are starting to also.) Not only could this put a hole in optimistic revenue forecasts; low prices could also constitute a public health risk with respect to use by minors and by problematic heavy users. But raising tax rates is rarely an easy proposition politically, and Colorado's Taxpayer Bill of Rights (TABOR) makes it procedurally very difficult by requiring a public referendum on each tax increase.

With respect to competition from other states, sales from stores in Washington State to Oregon consumers will likely shrivel when Oregon's lightly taxed commercial system ramps up. (Before Oregon legalized, the busiest commercial cannabis outlet in Washington State was the one nearest the border with Oregon.) Indeed, Washington State may lose additional revenue if Washington residents who live near the Oregon border decide to take their business south.

Colorado potentially has more to lose from state-level competition, since it has been getting significant revenue from sales to visitors.

However, Colorado's situation is more favorable than Washington's in the short term as it faces no imminent competitive threat on its borders, and there is potential to expand exports to states further east, especially if the federal government relaxes its stance.

Both states' propositions offered detailed prescriptions of how these tax revenues were to be distributed. However, the Washington legislature has already decided to divert some of the money that the initiative had earmarked for drug abuse prevention and treatment to the state's general fund.

Have black market sales disappeared in Colorado and Washington?

No, but they have changed, and (likely) shrunk.

Not all illegal transactions are alike. Supplying those under 21 remains entirely illegal, and about 20 percent of the marijuana consumed in the United States is consumed by people under the age of 21. In some technical sense that is all illicit supply, although when a 21-year-old purchases marijuana legally and then gives some to a 19-year-old friend, no criminal organization profits, and no one is likely to get shot, or even arrested.

The more interesting question is how many adult residents of Colorado and Washington continue to obtain marijuana from entirely illegal sources. Statistics on illegal activity aren't easy to gather, so it's impossible to say with any certainty. Some combination of the legalization of production for medical use and the subsequent legalization of sales to those without medical recommendations has put a dent in the revenues criminals derived from supplying users in Colorado and Washington. Right now, it's hard to say much more than that.

Are Colorado and Washington exporting marijuana to other states?

Yes, and this is nothing new.

Washington State (more than Colorado) has long exported marijuana from illegal outdoor grow operations and networks of "grow houses" run by criminal organizations; these have nothing to do with Washington's quasi-legal medical-marijuana system. There is no reason to think that Washington's I-502 has diminished that activity. The illicit market remains alive and well in the great bulk of the country that has not legalized, and for several reasons Washington State turns out to be a convenient place to locate illicit production.

What is new is the outflow of marijuana that is connected to the regulated system: from legal home-growing, from legal commercial growers diverting some of their product, or from "smurfing" (purchase from legal retail outlets for resale out of state). In addition, some visitors illegally take their purchases back home.

The Rocky Mountain High Intensity Drug Trafficking Area (HIDTA) Task Force reports that in 2014 there were 360 seizures of marijuana from Colorado that was bound for other states, mostly to the east. That was a substantial increase over the previous year. However, a bigger increase came with the opening of the medical stores back in 2009–2010 than with their conversion from medical dispensaries to adult-use or recreational stores. The US Postal Service also seized 320 parcels mailed from Colorado to another state that contained marijuana. The total weight seized, however, is only about two tons per year, whereas consumption by Colorado residents exceeds one hundred tons per year.

Why pay so much attention to edibles?

One of the biggest surprises for market watchers has been the popularity of "edibles"—cannabis-infused foods and beverages—compared to herbal marijuana and extracts designed for vaporization. That popularity may relate to the importance of tourist markets, the low cost of extraction done at large scale, and the fact that edibles get around rules against consumption in public and against smoking in common indoor areas.

One of the biggest surprises for users is what a potent punch some of those edibles pack; some of those surprises translate into emergency room visits. The situation was particularly bad in Colorado. A typical scenario involves someone eating an entire candy bar or cookie that contains multiple doses. There have also been instances of children eating sweet edibles, encouraged by their resemblance to conventional candy and pastries (e.g., cannabis-infused gummi bears). As discussed in chapter 3, the Centers for Disease Control and Prevention published a case study of a young man who jumped out of a building after overconsuming edibles. According to that study, "This was the first reported death in Colorado linked to marijuana consumption without evidence of polysubstance use since the state approved recreational use of marijuana in 2012."

Regulators rushed to implement a variety of rules intended to limit such accidents. These include defining a standard dose (10 milligrams of THC), requiring that bars containing more than one dose have score lines that clearly indicated how to break the bar up into individual doses, and disseminating clearer warnings about the possibility of ingesting too much.

A separate and less-publicized set of issues concerns general food safety. Some marijuana product manufacturers seem to have been conscientious about various marijuana-specific risks but not about meeting health and safety regulations for sanitary food preparation.

While edibles may always carry somewhat greater risks of unpleasant surprises from greater-than-desired doses, the spate of problems experienced in 2014 may in the long run look more like the growing pains of a new regulatory scheme than a major barrier to successful legalization.

What do Colorado and Washington tell us about the likely results of legalization elsewhere?

If we look at the first round of legalization as an experiment, then the experiment is biased toward finding only modest initial effects. Washington State and Colorado were two of the four states where the medical-supply system had penetrated most deeply. (California and Oregon were the others.) Both already had large numbers of dispensaries carrying a wide variety of cannabis products at relatively low prices, and, as chapter 13 explains, their rules about medical recommendations were so loose that virtually any adult could become a "patient." As a result, state-level legalization of marijuana production in those states effectively dates from 2009, when the Justice Department's Ogden Memorandum largely removed the threat of federal prosecution. The commercial legalization laws passed in 2012 didn't do much more at first than make the status quo official. In Colorado, for example, all of the original commercial outlets had already been supplying the medical market.

So the lack of any sharp change in marijuana use and problems in those states after full legalization isn't really surprising, and doesn't tell us much about what would happen if a state with no medical-marijuana system, or a tightly-regulated system, were to legalize cannabis for commercial distribution.

That said, 2015 is not the end of the experiment. The industry is still evolving technologically and organizationally to better exploit its new opportunities, and likely will continue to evolve for some years to come.

Nor does legalization in two fairly isolated states give us much insight into what would happen if marijuana stores opened somewhere on the Boston-Washington corridor. And since marijuana remains illegal federally, even legalization in, say, Vermont wouldn't provide a clear picture of the way the world would look if the federal law were changed. Production for, and selling to, a national market would be radically different.

Furthermore, data always lag years behind the actual events, and even when all of the data are available, there will still be unique challenges associated with evaluating legalization in Washington. Shortly before voters passed I-502, all of the state-run liquor stores were closed and the market was privatized (due to a ballot initiative passed in 2010). The effect of this change on consumption and the marketplace for intoxicants is the subject of ongoing research, and this will complicate efforts to understand how marijuana legalization influences the use of marijuana, alcohol, and other substances. In addition, legalization in Oregon may influence Washington's marijuana market, especially in the southern part of the state; that could limit the ability to make inferences about I-502.

Did legalization increase or decrease crime?

Comparing Denver crime data from the first six months of 2013 and those from the first six months of 2014, the *Huffington Post* noted that rates of property crime, as well as homicide, sexual assault, and robbery, were all down; only aggravated assault was up (by 2.2 percent). The author of that article wrote, "After just six months, it may be too early to identify any strong social trends. But evidence of a crime wave simply has not materialized—despite numerous dire warnings prior to legalization."

But those who consulted other data and looked beyond the FBI Part I crime categories came to a different conclusion; that the overall incident count increased, especially public drunkenness and drug arrests.

Three lessons can be learned: It matters which offenses are considered and which data sources are used; it is difficult to say anything definitive based on such a small amount of data; and it's not right to draw strong inferences about legalization using only data from places that have legalized. A more comprehensive analysis would incorporate crime-trend data from "control states" that did not legalize.

How did legalization affect use?

The National Survey on Drug Use and Health (NSDUH) provides state-specific estimates of the number of people who have used marijuana within the past year and month. But to improve the precision of the estimates, the data are reported for two-year periods rather than year-by-year. Focusing on self-reported past month use for those 12 years and older, the newly released 2013/2014 data indicated that Colorado had the highest rate in the country at 14.9 percent and Washington was number 3 at 12.8 percent (The national average was 8 percent). The other states in the top five were all in the northeast: Vermont (13.2 percent), Rhode Island (12.8 percent), and Maine (12.7 percent). Spots six through eight on the list went to three jurisdictions that voted for legalizing recreational marijuana in 2014 (the District of Columbia, Oregon, and Alaska). California did not even make it into the top ten.

While the Colorado and Washington voters passed these initiatives in November 2012, the retail stores did not open until 2014. Comparing the 2011/2012 NSDUH estimates with those from 2013/2014 shows that Colorado experienced a statistically significant 43 percent increase in self-reported past month use (from 10.4 percent to 14.9 percent). The increase for Washington was 25 percent.

Colorado's increase was the largest in absolute terms (4.5 percentage points), although three other states with lower base rates of use had larger proportionate increases. The other four states among the top five in terms of absolute increases in use were Maine, New Hampshire, Washington, and Maryland.

We expect that each year state-level prevalence data are released, similar tabulations will generate significant media attention. But simply analyzing these raw figures is not enough to make strong inferences about the effects of legalization. To be convincing, analyses will have to be careful in the choice of comparison states (preferably chosen before the data are released) and will attempt to account for other factors that could influence marijuana use. In addition, there will still be questions about the inferences, because they rely on self-reported data. For example, if legalization is linked to an increase in self-reported use, it is difficult to know how much of the increase represents real change and how much reflects respondents' increased honesty about their marijuana use.

The Rocky Mountain HIDTA—an organization strongly opposed to legalization—published data showing an increase in the number of THC-positive urinalyses conducted by probation officers in Colorado from 2013 to 2014 (most notably for those aged 26 and older: from 24,691 in 2013 to 33,303 in 2014); however, no information was presented about the total number tests conducted or the reasons for these tests.

What is the evidence concerning effects on youth?

At least until prices fall and marketing increases, one wouldn't expect legalization in Colorado or Washington to have effect on youth, since marijuana's legal status for minors did not change. In both states legalization applied only to adults—defined as those 21 and over. Furthermore, although legalizing purchase and growing by adults makes it easy for any adult to supply a minor, marijuana was already readily available to youth before legalization. Nationwide, 80 percent of high-school seniors report that marijuana is easy or relatively easy to obtain, and access was greater still in Colorado and Washington even before commercial legalization.

Some legalization advocates argued that legalization would diminish access to minors because licensed outlets are required to check the ages of their purchasers, whereas "dealers don't check IDs." But a moment's reflection ought to be enough to see through that bit of sophistry. Nothing about legalization prevents someone who has been selling illegally grown marijuana to minors from continuing to do so. (In theory, a state that legalized commercial sales could devote massive enforcement resources to suppressing illegal growing, but neither Colorado nor Washington has chosen to do so.) So minors who buy illicitly grown pot—mostly not from adult pushers but from age-mates or older peers—won't lose access when commercial stores open. In the case of alcohol, juveniles are lamentably well-supplied, even in localities where enforcement succeeds in blocking direct sales to underage buyers from licensed stores.

So in these states we would expect legalization for adults to have modest effects on youth use in the short run, and indeed that is mostly what the limited data available to date suggest.

On the one hand, Colorado's rates of use reported in the household surveys by 12–17 year-olds increased more than any other state between 2011/2012 and 2013/2014 both proportionately and in absolute terms (from 10.5 percent to 12.6 percent). That moved Colorado up from the fourth-highest rate of reported youth use to the highest. On the other hand, the changes were not statistically significant, perhaps because surveys of the general household population have small sample sizes for youth.

Also, the bigger increases in Colorado were associated with the proliferation of medical dispensaries between 2006 and 2009, not the subsequent legalization in 2012. The same is true for the increase in drug-related suspensions and expulsions from Colorado schools, which increased from 3,800 to 5,400 between the 2008/2009 and the 2010/2011 school years but have been fairly stable since. (There have been more recent upticks in drug violations as a percentage of suspensions and of referrals to law enforcement.)

Furthermore, examining the Youth Risk Behavior Survey data since 2005, researchers with the Colorado Department of Public Health and Environment noted that "the prevalence of marijuana use in Colorado has closely followed the national trends." Since Colorado has surveyed high-school students about marijuana use and other behaviors every other year since 1993, these would seem to be the perfect data for understanding how legalization affects youth use. However, the 2015 data have not yet been released, and the 2013 data were collected before the first stores opened. Furthermore, in 2013 the sampling methodology changed, so regrettably the 2013 data are not truly comparable to earlier data.

What happened to emergency department cases?

Emergency department (ED) episodes involving children are a particular concern, and counts of episodes from the Children's Hospital of Colorado have received considerable attention. That hospital's ED treated no cases of accidental ingestion from 2005 through 2009, but that changed after the arrival of dispensaries. They treated eight children (mostly under age of 3) in 2013 and fourteen in 2014, with almost half requiring intensive care.

Statewide total ED mentions (all ages) increased in Colorado from 14,148 in 2013 to 18,255 in 2014, although such mentions have also been increasing nationwide and for some time. (Data from 2011 and 2012 are noncomparable because of changes in reporting practices.)

The Associated Press reported that marijuana-related calls to the Rocky Mountain Poison and Drug Center poison centers show broadly similar trends, increasing from 61 in 2012 to 88 in 2013 and 151 in 2014. Calls to the Washington State Poison Center increased from 158 in 2013 to 246 in 2014. In both states calls involving children almost doubled.

What has happened to traffic safety?

Measuring impaired driving is complicated. As chapter 3 noted, the most common tests detect use, not impairment, and marijuana metabolites can stay in the body long after intoxication.

Also, simply examining trends in arrests for marijuana-involved driving offers an incomplete, and possibly misleading, basis for assessing the effects of legalization on traffic safety. Arrests depend on the energy invested in detection and enforcement as well as the prevalence of the underlying behavior.

Interactions with other substances also complicate interpretation. About two-thirds of operators in fatal crashes who tested positive for marijuana also tested positive for alcohol and/or other drugs. Furthermore, we are not so much interested in marijuana-impaired driving as in the total amount of impaired driving involving any substance, and marijuana legalization could affect (positively or negatively) the amount of driving done while impaired with alcohol or other drugs. Indeed, what we really care about is overall traffic crashes and fatalities, not impaired driving per se.

We know, for example, that in Washington State the proportion of drivers involved in fatal accidents who tested positive for marijuana generally, and also the proportion who tested positive specifically for THC as opposed to just its metabolites, rose in 2014 from that in preceding years. But that does not mean marijuana caused

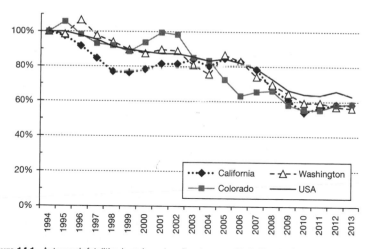

Figure 14.1   Auto crash fatalities have been trending downward in California, Colorado, Washington, and the United States overall since well before the marijuana-policy changes

(Fatalities per million miles traveled, normalized so 1994 = 100 percent)

those crashes. If consumption of green beans rose sharply, then the proportion of drivers in fatal crashes who had green beans in their stomachs would also probably go up.

On the other hand, people who point out that the total number of traffic crash fatalities has been stable over the last few years in Colorado should not conclude that marijuana liberalization is benign, because crash fatalities have been going down nationwide for many years as automobile technology (and emergency response and treatment technology) get better.

Figure 14.1 plots trends in traffic fatality rates per 100 million vehicle miles traveled from 1994 to 2013. Fatalities trended downward and at about the same rate in three states that liberalized marijuana laws and in the country as a whole. This chart by itself tells us nothing about the effect of legalization on traffic fatalities; that will require detailed analyses that control for a host of other factors that might influence traffic safety.

Do marijuana operations have to be cash-only businesses?

During this peculiar time when marijuana is state-legal but still prohibited by federal law, many marijuana businesses find it difficult to access banking services: not just loans but even checking accounts and credit-card processing. The problem seems to be more acute for retail stores than producers and processors, and it is not just the entrepreneurs who suffer. Large piles of cash tempt robbers, and the lack of banking records makes it harder for legitimate merchants to operate and easier for shady ones to evade the law, for example, by underpaying their taxes.

In the larger scheme, this is just a transitory hiccough. It is a quirk of marijuana's current semilegal status, not something inherent in the cannabis plant.

When financial firms shun marijuana businesses, they aren't acting on whim. Banks are bound by strict laws and regulations designed to prevent financial institutions from being conduits for illegal funds. Since marijuana is still prohibited by the Controlled Substances Act, all marijuana-related sales revenues are in that sense illegal funds.

While FinCen, the Treasury's central anti-money-laundering authority, has issued guidance designed to facilitate access to banking for the state-legal cannabis industry, not all of the regulatory agencies or banks are fully on board, and it appears that inspectors are continuing to nudge institutions to rid themselves of marijuana-related accounts. There have been proposals for special state-chartered financial institutions designed specifically to cater to the marijuana business, but so far federal regulators will not allow those institutions to function.

How do Colorado and Washington's medical-marijuana industries interact with the new legal systems?

At the moment, the medical industries are tax-evasion machines.

Before legalizing production for nonmedical use, both Colorado and Washington already had thriving medical-marijuana industries fueled by standards for writing recommendations that were so laughably loose that a mere dozen physicians in Colorado accounted for more than half of the state's 100,000+ medical-marijuana patients, including one doctor who had written more than eight thousand recommendations. Yet the absence of a legal alternative led law enforcement and the states' medical boards to turn a blind eye to physician practices that would never have been tolerated in writing prescriptions for narcotics or sedative-hypnotics. And some of their patients treated medical-marijuana dispensaries as wholesale suppliers for the patients' (purely illegal) retail marijuana dealing.

The two states' industries operated under very different circumstances. Colorado's industry was closely regulated; Washington's was merely tolerated and operated without any formal supervision. But in neither state was medical-marijuana subject to excise taxes, and therein lies the rub.

While some chemicals in marijuana have therapeutic uses and some (not all) dispensaries try to provide specific remedies for specific ailments, there's really not much difference between the "medical" and "commercial" products. Likewise, some of the advice confidently given out by budtenders about the effects of various strains may represent valuable folk wisdom, or they may be merely passing along "just-so" stories with no more validity than tales supporting traditional remedies for warts or male sexual dysfunction.

So there's not much special therapeutic reason for patients to seek supplies in medical rather than commercial outlets. But there is a strong financial reason for patients and people who use marijuana for other reasons alike to shop at dispensaries rather than retailers: the dispensaries do not have to charge excise tax. That makes it hard for the commercial sector to compete, which in turn limits how much revenue the state can collect.

Colorado sought to migrate both the producers and the customers of its existing medical industry over into its new recreational system. Indeed, for the first nine months, only businesses that had been operating as medical establishments were allowed to participate in the new market, protecting them from competition from new entrants. However, many individuals with medical recommendations preferred to stay in the medical market to avoid paying excise taxes. Indeed, this was one reason why Colorado's actual tax revenues have been so much lower than originally anticipated. At present many businesses in Colorado sell more or less exactly the same product as both medical-marijuana to residents with recommendations and as recreational ("retail") marijuana, mostly to tourists and others who do not have recommendations.

Washington State tried a different approach. Its regulators viewed the existing medical industry as having operated largely outside the law, and it wanted to start afresh with new companies that were not tainted by that past record. However, this led to both operational problems (the medical providers were the ones who knew how to produce and sell the product) and political ones (the medical industry was a potent political force). After considerable wrangling, a bill was signed in April 2015 intended to merge the medical and recreational markets by (1) explicitly forbidding unlicensed medical dispensaries, (2) prohibiting collective gardens, (3) limiting cooperatives to four individuals and requiring that they register with the state, and (4) extending the 37 percent excise tax to medical sales.

Other states with liberal medical-marijuana regimes will face similar challenges if they decide to legalize and tax marijuana for nonmedical purposes.

Additional Reading

Colorado Department of Public Health and Environment. *Monitoring Health Concerns Related to Marijuana in Colorado, 2014.*
Darnell, Adam. *I-502 Evaluation Plan and Preliminary Report on Implementation.*
Hancock-Allen, Jessica B., et al. "Death Following Ingestion of an Edible Marijuana Product—Colorado, March 2014."
Hudak, John. *Colorado's Rollout of Legal Marijuana Is Succeeding.*
MacCoun, Robert J., and Michelle M. Mello. "Half-Baked: The Retail Promotion of Marijuana Edibles."

15

WHAT IS HAPPENING IN ALASKA, OREGON, JAMAICA, AND URUGUAY?

As noted in Chapter 14, five major jurisdictions have legalized large-scale production for nonmedical purposes: Colorado and Washington State in 2012, Uruguay in 2013, and Alaska and Oregon in 2014. And there is Jamaica, whose 2015 law theoretically allows large-scale production only for medical consumption, but in actual practice is likely to be more liberal than that, as is described below. Chapter 14 discussed Colorado and Washington State. Here we consider what is happening in the other four jurisdictions.

What is happening in Uruguay?

In December 2013, Uruguay became the first country in the world to legalize production as well as retail sales. Unlike legalization efforts in the United States, this action was led by the president and other government officials, not the public. In fact, most Uruguayans remain opposed. Research conducted by Maria Fernanda Boidi, Rosario Queirolo, and José Miguel Cruz of the Latin American Marijuana Initiative found that in May 2014 only 33 percent of respondents agreed or strongly agreed with the new law.

Marijuana use and possession had already been legal since 1974. Hence, the prime motivation for legalization was not to reduce the number of user arrests, nor was it to raise significant tax revenue; rather, the goals were to reduce the illicit market and its associated violence (blamed by officials on imports from Paraguay) and to protect the health of users.

The law allows each adult (18 or older) to register with the government to obtain marijuana for nonmedical purposes in one (and only one) of three ways: growing at home, joining a cannabis club, or purchasing from a participating pharmacy. Uruguay prohibits marijuana marketing, and it bans sales to nonresidents in order to prevent drug tourism. Further, the law restricts total purchases by an individual to 40 grams per month, regardless of which source the consumer chooses.

As of fall 2015, only two prongs of the plan have been implemented. Approximately three thousand individual Uruguayans have registered to grow their own, and about twenty cannabis clubs (with a maximum of forty-five members each) have applied to obtain authorization from the government. That represents only a very modest proportion of Uruguay's estimated 160,000 users. Many consumers are fearful of the government registry, citing privacy concerns and their lack of trust in officials. In one recent survey, 40 percent of daily or near-daily users said they would refuse to register.

As this book is being written, there are still no pharmacies selling marijuana, but the Uruguayan press is reporting that two companies now have been selected to supply the pharmacies, with a guess that retail sales could begin in the middle of 2016, perhaps at the equivalent of $1.20 per gram (between one-sixth and one-tenth typical prices in Colorado and Washington stores).

What is happening in Jamaica?

In February 2015 Jamaica passed legislation legalizing medical-marijuana and industrial hemp and allowing personal use for sacramental, medical, or scientific purposes, although unauthorized public consumption is still subject to a modest $5 fine. Superficially, this might seem like a small step, but there is room for expansive interpretation. For example, any home cultivation of up to five plants will automatically be presumed to be for medicinal purposes and so be exempt from prosecution.

As of this writing, the new Cannabis Licensing Authority is still designing the regulatory structure under which the cannabis industry will operate. It remains to be seen how difficult it will be for Jamaicans to access medical-marijuana, as well as which types of medical professionals will be authorized to issue prescriptions or recommendations and whether the access provisions ultimately look more like the wide-open medical-marijuana markets in California or the tightly regulated medical-marijuana systems in Delaware or New York. Crucially, any tourist who asserts that he or she has a medical recommendation from a physician back home will be allowed to purchase marijuana on the island, on payment of a license fee.

As in any jurisdiction, a variety of motives come into play. However, to a greater extent than elsewhere, Jamaica sees legalization through the lens of economic development, as a way to address unemployment and develop an export industry. Decriminalizing minor possession and legalizing use by Rastafarians are also seen as ways to reverse decades of overly harsh sentences and abuse of those laws by police; similarly, officials hope that legal jobs in the marijuana industry will offer adequate legitimate livelihoods to small farmers accustomed to subsistence wages.

Jamaica hopes to derive revenue from at least five sources: (1) marijuana purchases by Jamaican residents, (2) marijuana purchases by tourists, (3) other spending by tourists attracted to Jamaica by the availability of marijuana, (4) spending on related services, such as festivals and tours of production areas, on the model of winery tours in France and California, and (5) exports of marijuana products.

The economic potential is considerable in a country of three million people that is visited annually by more than two million tourists plus another million day trippers (e.g., from tour ships). There is also interest in creating revenues from intellectual property such as branded products and strains to be sold abroad, although at this point it is not clear how exactly that would work. It may be expensive to market the Jamaican "brand" and difficult to defend its territory, particularly if it extends to broad aspects of Jamaican livelihood, including Rastafarian symbols and terminology. Privateer Holdings—a US-based marijuana-oriented private equity fund—formed a partnership with the estate of reggae legend Bob Marley to advance Marley Natural as the first global brand of cannabis products, but that is a private, not government, initiative, with production not planned for Jamaica and therefore no revenue going to the government of Jamaica. (Because the Marley Natural logo includes the Lion of Judah, a Rastafarian symbol protected under Jamaican law, it is not clear that Marley Natural could lawfully operate in Jamaica even if it wanted to.)

The new law is also intended to diminish religious discrimination against Rastafarians, for whom the drug has traditional and religious meaning, and to make Jamaican law accord with local rather than international culture. It allows Rastafarians to cultivate marijuana without a license, though there is no legal means for them to sell it commercially (except through the licensed medical sector); Rastafarian production and consumption will be entirely untaxed and not part of the formal economic development agenda.

The new law was passed against the background of large-scale illicit production of marijuana for export; drug control agencies in Central and North America often seize ton and multi-ton shipments that originated in Jamaica. Those illegal producers, which also serve the modest-sized local market (marijuana is not very popular in Jamaica outside the Rastafarian community), represent potential competition for licit producers, especially if taxes are high. A tiered market may prevail, with many locals continuing to buy from the black market, a few locals paying higher prices for more regulated medical products acquired at pharmacies, and tourists—especially those who never venture outside their resorts—paying even higher prices to vendors specializing in the medical tourist trade. Whether Jamaica will arrest tourists who try to buy the lower-priced untaxed product, to prevent loss of premium sales, is one of many still-unresolved implementation issues.

How do the laws in Alaska and Oregon compare to those in Colorado and Washington?

Alaska and Oregon's laws follow the broad outlines of those in Colorado and Washington, inasmuch as they establish both personal rights and also a licensed, regulated private industry. Like Colorado but unlike Washington, Alaska and Oregon allow all adults both to give marijuana away (up to one ounce) and to grow it at home (six plants in Alaska, four in Oregon). Like Washington but unlike Colorado, the industries in Alaska and Oregon will be overseen by the state liquor control agencies.

tax based of transaction or value

Excise taxes in the two new states were initially assessed per unit weight and at the producer level ($50 per ounce generally in Alaska; $35 per ounce on flowers in Oregon, with lower rates on trim and leaves), although Oregon has already converted to a 20 percent ad valorem tax, about half the Washington State level. The Oregon-Washington border, which has seen heavy southward-bound marijuana traffic, may see that flow reverse if lower taxes in Oregon lead to lower retail prices.

The Alaska and Oregon initiatives strike very different tones. Alaska's Measure 2 is spare, leaving many of the implementation matters to regulators, and it is cautious. For example, it explicitly defends employers' rights to bar employees' use. Oregon's Measure 91 is far more detailed, and is more pro-industry. For instance, it allows ordinary business expense deductions for the purpose of computing state taxes (unlike federal taxation under Section 280E), and while it technically allows local jurisdictions to opt out of allowing production and sale, it makes that option difficult to exercise. Early implementation decisions are consistent with that bias, such as allowing Oregon's existing medical dispensaries to start selling recreational marijuana by October 1, 2015, with the first three months of those sales being tax-free. It is also noteworthy that a substantial minority of the voting members of Oregon's regulatory advisory committees are industry representatives.

What exactly did Washington, DC, legalize?

In November 2014, voters in the District of Columbia approved Initiative 71. While it was passed at the same time as Alaska and Oregon's legalization initiatives, and is often referred to in the same breath, Initiative 71 is much more limited. Initiative 71 does not create a licensed marijuana industry. It merely legalizes personal possession, purchase, and transport of up to two ounces, plus the gifting of up to one ounce and growing of up to six plants per adult (with a maximum of twelve plants in a single residence). The law was written that way because the DC Home Rule charter allows the voters to change laws but not to create new administrative bodies. The advocates' plan was to have local elected officials follow up on the referendum with an ordinary law creating a system of commercial sales. But at least for now, threats from Congress have deterred the mayor and city council from following through.

The District of Columbia's elected officials have liberalized the law in other ways, however, decriminalizing possession by those under 21 (subject now only to a $25 fine) and expanding the medical-marijuana program in ways that mimic the liberal provisions of some Western states. Physicians can recommend medical-marijuana without reference to any specific condition or diagnosis, and the number of registered patients has grown steadily to nearly five thousand as of the end of 2015. The Medical-marijuana Supply Shortage Emergency Act Amendment of 2015 increased the number of plants allowed at each "growing center" to one thousand.

What states might vote on legalization in 2016?

Ever since Colorado and Washington's propositions passed in 2012, legalization advocates have been looking forward to 2016. Propositions, and for that matter legislation, can be passed in any year, but support for legalization is stronger among younger voters, and younger voters turn out in the greatest numbers in presidential election years.

The rules governing voter initiatives vary by state, but most must be submitted to the Secretary of State by early in the election year, and they only appear on the ballot if a requisite number of supporting signatures are obtained by a certain deadline (often between March and July of the election year). So as of this writing (fall 2015), predicting which states will vote in 2016 is a bit like filling out a March Madness bracket in January.

We are aware of plans for initiatives in the following states: Arizona, Arkansas, California, Maine, Massachusetts, Michigan, Mississippi, Missouri, Montana, Nevada, New Mexico, and Wyoming, and we expect serious legislative proposals to be considered in Rhode Island, Vermont, and perhaps some other states. Hawaii also makes it on some people's top-ten lists of places most likely to legalize next, and several other states (e.g., Florida, Idaho, and Nebraska) may well vote on medical-marijuana laws.

In short, there are many opportunities for increasing the number of states that have legalized. But mounting a campaign does not mean the campaign will succeed; most initiatives across all topics are voted down.

And money matters. In 2012, it was the two propositions that were backed generously by rich donors that passed (in Colorado and Washington). Even money, though, cannot promise victory: California's Proposition 19 failed despite proponents outspending the opposition by 10:1. Still, the cost of collecting signatures in a large state gives wealthy donors the effective power to decide which initiatives will go forward.

The need to raise money can distort the initiative process. This is what happened in Ohio in 2015 when 10 groups each invested $2 million dollars into a legalization measure in return for having their properties listed—in the state constitution!—as the only places where marijuana could be produced for the commercial market. (There was an option for the government to allow an eleventh site if demand was not being met.) Even some otherwise pro-legalization groups refused to endorse that proposition, and Ohio voters overwhelmingly rejected it.

While it is too early to make predictions for particular states in 2016, California bears special mention because it looms large in so many ways. If California legalizes large-scale commercial production, that could well effectively doom prohibition for the rest of the country, whether voters elsewhere want that or not.

Superficially, legalization in California might seem foreordained. Proposition 215 and subsequent legislative actions created the nation's first quasi-legalization, the near-passage of Proposition 19 in 2010 inspired the subsequent wave of state legalization efforts, and California voters tilt liberal generally, and especially so on marijuana.

However, there are complications. Legalizing large-scale commercial production—particularly if California's legalization then led to legalization nationally—might provide stiff competition for the smaller-scale production that now supports the economy in several northern California counties, including the "Emerald Triangle" of Humboldt, Mendocino, and Trinity counties. Much of what makes that area ideal for small plots growing a hundred to a thousand plants without attracting official scrutiny may not position it well to compete with the large-scale operations likely to arise after legalization. So current growers, and their workers, might be hurt by legalization. In 2010, all three Emerald Triangle counties voted against Proposition 19, and some of the leading figures in California's marijuana-reform movement have ties to those traditional growers.

Most states have some such special circumstances, so while at this point we expect some propositions to have a serious chance of passing in 2016, that list will likely be winnowed significantly by then.

Additional Reading

Boidi, María Fernanda, et al. *Marijuana Legalization in Uruguay and Beyond.*
Walsh, John, and Geoff Ramsey. *Uruguay's Drug Policy: Major Innovations, Major Challenges.*

16

WHAT HAPPENS WHEN MARIJUANA LAWS CLASH?

Can a state legalize something that the federal government prohibits?

The states retain a degree of sovereignty; the Constitution does not allow the federal government to order state governments to create any particular laws or to require state and local police to enforce federal laws.

It is not uncommon for state law to remain silent on actions that violate federal law. States generally do not have laws against counterfeiting or treason. Indeed, the country already had extensive experience with state-level legalization even before Colorado and Washington passed their propositions in 2012. That experience was called (alcohol) prohibition.

The Eighteenth Amendment, and the Volstead Act passed under its authority, banned the manufacture, transport, and sale of intoxicating liquor nationally. Most states passed their own legislation criminalizing violations of national prohibition. But Maryland never did, and in 1923 the state of New York—under Governor Al Smith—repealed its state ban on alcohol. For the following decade, selling alcohol in Maryland and New York was a violation of federal law but not state law. Local police had no authority to arrest alcohol sellers. By the time the Eighteenth Amendment was repealed in 1933, ten other states had already eliminated their state prohibitions.

So, ironically, the legal situation after we prohibited alcohol was similar to what we now have after four states have legalized marijuana. Indeed, in two respects state-legal marijuana in 2015 is still more prohibited than alcohol was in New York and Maryland during

Prohibition precedent

prohibition: the Controlled Substances Act (CSA), unlike the Volstead Act, criminalizes mere possession, and it contains language that preempts state laws that create a "positive conflict" with the CSA.

Enforcing the prohibition of alcohol was largely a federal project, even in states that passed their own bans. In this respect drug control is different; the bulk of drug law enforcement today takes place at the state and local level. Especially in big states, the federal government lacks the capacity to do the job now done by state and local marijuana enforcement effort; four thousand DEA agents cannot replace seven hundred thousand state and local police officers. That's emphatically true when it comes to punishing users for drug possession. Except in national parks and other federal lands, almost all possession arrests are made by state and local police.

Can there be local exceptions to state marijuana laws?

Just as there can be conflicts between federal and state law, there can also be disjunctions between state and local law. For example, a number of municipalities have decriminalized or legalized marijuana even if the rest of the state has not.

But if a state legalizes marijuana sales, can one of its towns or cities opt out, saying, in effect, "Not in our back yard"? The answer varies by state.

Alaska's Proposition 2 and Colorado's Amendment 64 explicitly allow local opt-out. As of this writing, 249 of Colorado's 321 local jurisdictions had banned nonmedical ("retail") licensees. Washington State's I-502 was silent on the matter, but its courts eventually ruled that opt-out was allowed for most purposes, as it is for alcohol. Oregon's Proposition 91, by contrast, bans local taxes and makes local opt-out difficult to exercise. Proposition 91 "shall be paramount and superior to and shall fully replace and supersede any ... local ordinances inconsistent with it"; subsequent opt-out can only occur through a referendum held after a successful petition drive.

Should local government be allowed to opt out of state legalization?

There's no clear way to resolve the conflict between local choice and uniformity. But when it comes to alcohol it is worth noting that

many states allow counties or towns to remain "dry." Residents
of areas that ban marijuana sales will obviously have to travel
longer distances to find the product than they otherwise would,
but marijuana is compact and nonperishable, and is typically
bought in fairly large quantities compared to a daily dose—more
like bags of rice than fresh bread—so the inconvenience won't be
overwhelming.

Allowing home delivery would provide access while sidestep-
ping the neighborhood issues associated with brick-and-mortar
facilities. Neither Colorado nor Washington allows home delivery, although some illegal services have sprung up, but Oregon
does, and home delivery also exists for medical-marijuana in
California.

Local opt-out would matter much more if a state allowed marijuana "bars": places where people can buy for on-premises consumption, perhaps with music or other entertainment. No state
allows this yet, though Colorado has some venues that do not sell
but allow on-premises consumption; their legal status remains in
question. Having to travel a long way to use marijuana would be a
bigger burden on consumers than having to travel a long way to buy
it, especially given the risks associated with stoned driving.

What could a town or county gain from banning retail outlets?
Residents of poor neighborhoods complain that the proliferation of
liquor stores both encourages heavy drinking and attracts disorderly conduct, and there is evidence backing both claims. It is possible that the same issues would arise around marijuana retailers;
some Dutch towns do have nuisance problems surrounding coffee
shops, particularly in towns near the border that attract drug tourists from abroad. The area surrounding a store is also a convenient
place for a minor to encounter an adult who might be willing to
make a proxy purchase.

Some of the opposition is based less on outcomes than on sym-
bolism. It's not unreasonable for opponents of marijuana legalization to find the open presence of a business activity that violates
still-valid federal law offensive. By the same token, some legalization proponents don't like the idea that a town could undo what
the state's voters have done. (There is, of course, some irony in
their insistence that the state should feel free to flout federal laws
but no town should be allowed to forbid what the state allows, but

immunity to irony is a characteristic of both sides in culture-war battles.)

In political terms, allowing local opt-out—and bans on use in public—might reduce the angst marijuana opponents feel after legalization, if it allows them to go about their daily lives without being confronted visually by the effects of legalization. So even a legalization advocate might favor local opt-out, gaining what might be a substantial softening of opposition while giving up only a little in terms of actual access.

Is marijuana actually legal in a state that legalizes?

No.

Pretty much everything related to marijuana, from growing and selling down to possessing small amounts of medical-marijuana, remains 100 percent illegal under federal law, and states cannot bar the application of federal laws within their borders. The Supreme Court underscored this when it concluded in the case of *Gonzales v. Raich* that the Commerce Clause allows the federal government to criminalize home production of marijuana even in states that permit its medical use.

Yet while the federal government clearly retains the right to enforce its drug prohibitions within any state, actually doing so is a different question. The federal government could easily shut down state-licensed operations; every application for a state marijuana license is a confession to a conspiracy to violate the Controlled Substances Act, and the federal courts could grant injunctions against acting on the permission given by those licenses. However, if the state simply stopped enforcing laws against purely illegal growing and dealing, the feds couldn't put enough boots on the ground to replace that effort.

The Obama administration has issued policy guidance assigning a low priority to enforcement against marijuana-related activity that is legal under state law unless it involves things the federal government is especially concerned with, such as sales to minors, violence and the use of weapons, other drug dealing, participation of organized crime, and interstate sales.

So "state-legal" marijuana activity is still illegal; it just does not carry much risk of arrest (at least under the current administration).

[handwritten annotation: TAXES — ok, unless intervene, Feds can't support them and court support]

Can a state regulate and tax a substance that the federal government prohibits?

While the constitutional issues are complex, the simple practical answer is yes, but only as long as the federal government decides not to thwart the effort—and such noninterference has been the policy under the Obama administration.

State and local jurisdictions in the United States currently collect taxes and fees from recreational and medical-marijuana. For example, in May 2015 the state of Colorado collected about $10 million in marijuana taxes and another $1 million in application and license fees. Arguably, the federal government could confiscate such revenues as the proceeds of illegal transactions, but as far as we know, the federal government has not touched a penny of the fees and tax revenues governments have received from marijuana sales, and it is not clear the courts would uphold any such attempt. *[handwritten: — role of courts]*

A distinct issue is whether state employees implementing state regulations could be in violation of federal laws, for instance, if state employees had to handle (possess) marijuana in the process of enforcing labeling or quality control regulations. Perhaps distinctions would be drawn between incidental possessions in the process of quality control monitoring and employees in state stores actually selling the marijuana, but that is just a guess. It is safer to predict that advocates and opponents will spar over this terrain in the future than to lay odds on which side would prevail.

As far as we know, at this time there is only one marijuana store in the United States that is operated by a governmental entity. That store, run by a public development authority in North Bonneville, Washington (population about 1,000), is so small that it may simply be flying under the radar of federal enforcement priorities. Or federal enforcement officials may have decided that a government-operated store might be preferable to stores operated for private profit.

What about the reverse: If the federal government legalized marijuana, could a state still prohibit it?

Legally, yes. Practically, only with difficulty. *[handwritten: — theme]*

The Constitution leaves each state free to make its own laws, within fairly wide boundaries. Early in the twentieth century, many states banned marijuana before the federal government did, just as some states remained dry after the repeal of prohibition. The Respect State Marijuana Laws Act of 2015, introduced by Representative Dana Rohrabacher, would effectively block federal enforcement of the Controlled Substances Act's prohibition on marijuana against persons who are complying with state laws but would still allow enforcement against those taking marijuana into any state that banned it.

But after federal legalization, any one state could become a potential source of illegal marijuana for every other state. The current multibillion-dollar market in smuggling cigarettes from low-tax states such as Virginia to high-tax states such as New York—a traffic also in violation of federal law—illustrates the readiness of entrepreneurs to take advantage of such opportunities. Residents of pot-prohibiting states bordering pot-allowing states wouldn't have to rely on illicit markets; they could just drive across the state border to buy, as Massachusetts residents drive to New Hampshire to buy low-taxed liquor.

So while states would be free to continue to prohibit marijuana, enforcing that prohibition would be a different matter. Prices would fall, and marijuana consumption would rise accordingly, undercutting the main reason for prohibition.

What could the federal government do in response to a state legalizing marijuana?

The Obama administration has chosen not to shut down state-regulated marijuana industries, and has even moved to change the banking regulations to allow state-licensed marijuana firms access to basic financial services. But it has left in place certain ancillary rules that would not make sense if the drug were truly legal. So the next administration could be tougher or still more accommodating of legalization, even apart from what actions Congress might take.

For example, Executive Order 12564 forbids federal employees from using illicit drugs on or off the job. That order continues to apply to marijuana and in all fifty states, including its provisions giving the federal government the authority to test any employee if there is "reasonable suspicion" of illegal drug use, as well as anyone in a "sensitive" position regardless of suspicion. An employee who

Fed employees cannot use pot.

IRS tax code prohibits deductions

tests positive can be fired for continuing to use or for refusing counseling and treatment.

Likewise, Internal Revenue Service Code Section 280E is quite strange if one views the marijuana industry as legitimate. Business taxes are typically based on total revenues minus allowable business expenses and other deductions. Section 280E forbids businesses from taking deductions if they traffic in Schedule I or II drugs, including marijuana. (The idea was to make tax-evasion prosecutions of drug dealers easier.) That applies to entities producing and selling marijuana in states where it has been legalized, greatly increasing the cost of supplying legal marijuana.

On the other hand, if the president wished, federal agencies could shut down at least the larger and more flagrant operations of the legal industry, perhaps at a fairly modest resource cost. (The political cost is harder to reckon.) Federal enforcement agencies would not need to arrest all of the thousands of people working in the legal industry. They could instead, for example, warn property owners that leasing to an illegal enterprise puts their property at risk of seizure and confiscation; this tactic has been employed successfully in the past against various medical-marijuana operations.

could confiscate property

The publication of the list of eight federal enforcement priorities as part of the decision to largely leave state-licensed marijuana markets free to function helped shape state regulatory decisions (for example, about maintaining exclusion zones around schools). That strategy could have been carried much further, in effect requiring the states to enact strict regulation as the price of federal acquiescence.

Or the federal government could create a system of effective regulation through selective enforcement, as the Dutch government has. For example, even some who support legalization view the selling of marijuana-infused candies that resemble conventional candies as a terrible idea; Colorado's experience demonstrates the potential for children to overdose on such candies. The federal government could enforce the CSA (only) against vendors selling such candies. Likewise, federal agencies could shut down marijuana-related businesses that advertised, did not maintain a minimum price, sold types of marijuana products deemed undesirable (e.g., dabs or very-high-THC flowers), and so on. The federal government could also shut down only for-profit enterprises, leaving government-operated stores alone so long as they behaved responsibly. That is, the federal

could enforce CSA against selected activity

government could use the threat of enforcement to impose minimum standards for industry conduct.

— economic risks

Could federal noninterference be formalized?

Yes.

The Obama administration implemented its lenient policy with a memo; the next administration could reverse that policy by issuing a different memo. Needless to say, that precarious situation is not desirable for the marijuana industry, its investors, or its employees. The hundreds of millions of dollars being invested in grow facilities could vanish, at the whim of the president, and the staff working nine to five in this new industry could, in principle, find themselves instead doing five to ten in prison; indeed, nothing would forbid prosecution under a new administration taking office in 2017 of activities taking place today. (In practice, it is likely only owners and perhaps investors who would be punished, not trimmers and budtenders.)

It does not have to be this way. Congress could create a statutory mechanism through which states with suitably responsible regulatory regimes could be formally exempted from the Controlled Substances Act's prohibition against marijuana. One option would model such a waiver on the program for waivers used in the domain of welfare reform during the 1990s. Under such a system, some federal official would have to certify that a given state's regulations were adequate to serve the purposes of public-health protection and prevention of interstate illegal trafficking in order for state-licensed activity in that state to qualify for exemption from federal law. How such a statute could be reconciled with the obligations of the United States under the international drug-control conventions remains an unresolved question.

Congress could act to protect states

Would marijuana legalization violate international law?

About a dozen international conventions—essentially multilateral treaties—concerning psychoactive substances have entered into force since 1919. The early conventions focused on regulating the licit opiate trade for medicinal purposes, but additional conventions encompassed more substances.

The multiplicity of those agreements—and their uncertain legal status after the demise of the League of Nations—stimulated proposals for a new comprehensive treaty to merge and update all of them. This led to the Single Convention on Narcotic Drugs in 1961, the cornerstone of modern-day international drug control. Currently 184 countries, including the United States, are parties to the 1972 version of the Single Convention.

If a signatory nation legalized marijuana possession and production for nonmedicinal purposes, that would violate the Single Convention. Parties to the Single Convention are required to make production, trade, and possession for nonscientific and nonmedical purposes a "punishable offense." The convention states that "serious offences shall be liable to adequate punishment, particularly imprisonment or other penalties of deprivation of liberty," although "abusers" may undergo treatment, education, rehabilitation, or social reintegration instead. It is up to each country to make its own decisions about what is serious and what the punishment will be. Another convention signed in 1988 states that possession of any prohibited substance for nonmedicinal or nonscientific use was "to be made not just a punishable offense, but specifically a criminal offence under domestic law."

With four of its fifty states having legalized large-scale production for nonmedical use, the United States' position vis-à-vis these conventions has changed dramatically. Traditionally, the United States was seen as the primary supporter of these treaties and their framing of the drug problem through a law-enforcement lens. That was always a bit of a simplification. Russia is aggressively conservative on this issue, and China perhaps equally so, albeit more quietly. Many African, Middle Eastern, and East Asian countries also hold conservative positions with respect to intoxicating drugs. So does Sweden. Nevertheless, the United States had clearly pursued drug policies that were much more conservative than those of its usual European allies and many of its Latin American neighbors.

Arguably, the United States remains in compliance with those treaties, because international treaties do not directly bind states within a federal union and the Controlled Substances Act remains on the books. However, the president of the International Narcotics Control Board (INCB), which has the authority to officially interpret the treaties, wrote a rebuke stating that "the United States has a treaty obligation to ensure the implementation of the treaties on the entirety of its territory."

The ambiguous position now occupied by the United States has changed its conduct in international forums. In October 2014 the top antinarcotics official at the US State Department, Ambassador William Brownfield, announced a new approach to addressing the international drug conventions. He then asked, "How could I, a representative of the Government of the United States of America, be intolerant of a government that permits any experimentation with legalization of marijuana if two of the 50 states of the United States of America have chosen to walk down that road?"

Does Dutch policy violate these international conventions?

The Dutch government says no.

As discussed in chapter 11, the Dutch have never legalized the production of marijuana for nonmedical use. Rather, they have a formal policy of not enforcing their laws against those possessing small amounts or against coffee shops selling small amounts.

Inaction against users does not conflict with treaty obligations. Although the 1988 convention pushed countries to make possession a criminal offense, the Netherlands ratified this clause with reservation so they would not have to comply with this provision.

Defending inaction against coffee shops requires lawyerly nuance. Technically, the Netherlands is in compliance with the Single Convention since it has a law on the books making trafficking a punishable offense. As noted by Dutch researcher Jos Silvis, the obligation to the Single Convention is met by the existence of the Dutch legislation, and "there are no clauses in the relevant UN conventions that concern the actual enforcement of the legislation." While this logic could just as easily be applied to the growers and middlemen who supply the coffee shops, the Dutch choose to actively enforce laws against production and wholesaling.

— none

What are the consequences of violating international conventions?

The consequences for an individual who violates a drug law are written into the law itself. In contrast, there is no formula specifying the consequences for a country violating the international drug control treaties; it is not as if the UN can lock up the offending country's president or prime minister.

The convention does state that if a dispute arises about the interpretation or application of the convention, it could be referred to the International Court of Justice (ICJ). The ICJ may render a decision, but it really does not have any enforcement power in these matters. Indeed, some countries made reservations so they would not have to accept the jurisdiction of the ICJ.

Countries that receive international aid may have something to fear; actions that displease donor countries could lead to reductions in aid. Countries that become centers of international trafficking may feel additional pressure, which might extend to trade sanctions.

In the view of many international lawyers—including some sympathetic to legalization—Uruguay violated the Single Convention when it legalized marijuana at the end of 2013; the Uruguayan government argues that its actions are in accord with the convention's announced goal of promoting "the health and welfare of mankind" and, moreover, that its other treaty obligations (e.g., regarding human rights) are inconsistent with a strict adherence to the letter of the drug treaties. However, to date it has only implemented the home-growing and cannabis clubs parts of its law, which do not allow anything that has not already been allowed in other countries. The more controversial portions pertaining to government supply of cannabis through pharmacies are as of yet not being implemented. So it is too soon to know what consequences, if any, are in store for Uruguay or any other country that legalizes large-scale production and sale.

Could these international treaties be changed?

Yes, with enormous difficulty.

The Single Convention can be amended, as it was in 1972 to include new substances. Any of the parties can propose an amendment, and it will enter into force if no party rejects the amendment within eighteen months. If a party does reject the amendment, there may be a conference for the parties to discuss the matter, or the UN General Assembly could take up the amendment. However, no international consensus on liberalizing policy toward marijuana is in sight; many countries in Africa and Asia, and some in Europe, remain staunchly opposed to legalization.

A number of amendments have been discussed by academics and advocacy organizations, including the removal of marijuana from the list of scheduled drugs. Australian sociologist Robin Room and his colleagues conducted an in-depth analysis of how to change policy in the context of the Single Convention.

One option is for a country simply to withdraw from the convention (a step known as denunciation). This is rare—less than 4 percent of ratifications involving multilateral treaties since 1945 have been denounced. But a country could also denounce the convention and then immediately re-ratify it with a reservation, essentially saying that the country agrees to abide by the rest of the convention but not that specific article. The reaccession takes effect if less than one-third of the signatories object to it within a year.

Bolivia has done this with respect to coca chewing. In July 2011, Bolivia announced it would withdraw from the Single Convention on January 1, 2012, and attempt to rejoin with a formal objection to the ban on coca chewing. As expected, the INCB and United States claimed that this action would weaken the integrity of the international drug conventions. However, only fifteen countries objected, well short of the sixty-one necessary to block it, so Bolivia's reaccession came into force on February 10, 2013. It remains to be seen whether Bolivia's actions set a precedent that will be followed by other countries with respect to marijuana.

Should there be international treaties on drugs at all?

Yes, because one nation's actions in this area can substantially affect the citizens of other nations.

The extent of the cross-border effects depends somewhat on geography, demographics, and international trade patterns. Germany's domestic policies affect its European neighbors; those of the island nation of Tuvalu (population 10,837) do not.

But broadly speaking, if a nation merely decriminalizes personal possession but retains sufficient sanctions (e.g., fines) to suppress flagrant use, that would have no meaningful effect on other nations, and, reasonably enough, the international treaties have been construed as not blocking nations from taking this step.

Going further to legalize personal possession and use outright might induce some drug tourism, particularly if gifting were also allowed. (That might let a bar legally "comp" foreign visitors some free marijuana.) The Dutch policy of de facto legalizing retail sale clearly has engendered drug tourism. So those actions do affect other countries. To date the effects have been mostly on neighbors sharing a land border, so the resulting issues might be addressable with bilateral negotiations rather than universal international treaties. However, Jamaica appears to be consciously pursuing an economic development strategy predicated on providing foreign tourists the chance to indulge in activities that are banned in their home countries.

With the further step of legalizing supply, the potential effects on other countries increase, but could depend on the specific policies adopted. Legalizing only small-scale production and/or production that is tightly controlled by a government monopoly (as Uruguay plans to do) might not affect others much, especially if there are rules against supplying non-nationals. On the other hand, if a small country surrounded by larger countries intentionally crafted its rules to facilitate large-scale production for diversion (akin to the way some nations facilitate large-scale smuggling of tobacco to evade excise taxes), that could undermine prohibition in other places and so be a matter of international concern.

So it does make sense to have international treaties governing the production and trade in consumer goods that (1) are highly compact and thus easy to smuggle and (2) can create considerable harm for their users and/or others.

That is not to say that the current international regime is ideal; there are many critics of the drug treaties. Brookings Institution scholar Vanda Felbab-Brown cautions, though, against attacking the treaties just because they are bad. There is enormous disagreement among nations today, with hardline states such as Russian and Saudi Arabia at one end and those in favor of liberalization on the other. That might make it impossible to agree on a new treaty if the current treaties broke down. Having no treaties at all governing the drug trade—including the licit trade in pharmaceuticals, especially the opiates—might be worse than having bad treaties.

Additional Reading

Cole, James. *Guidance Regarding Marijuana Enforcement.*

Jelsma, Martin. *UNGASS 2016: Prospects for Treaty Reform and UN System-Wide Coherence on Drug Policy.*

Kleiman, Mark A. R. "Cooperative Enforcement Agreements and Policy Waivers."

Mikos, Robert A. "Marijuana Localism."

Room, Robin, et al. *Cannabis Policy.*

Taylor, Stuart. *Marijuana Policy and Presidential Leadership.*

PART IV
THE FUTURE OF MARIJUANA
LEGALIZATION

17

WHAT MIGHT THE FUTURE HOLD?

As both Yogi Berra and Werner Heisenberg pointed out, it's tough to make predictions, especially about the future. Many of the forecasts below are likely to turn out to be wrong. But there can still be value in trying to think systematically about the likely dynamics of the changes now in progress.

Why isn't the status quo stable?

It is very hard to predict how marijuana legalization will play out in the coming years and decades; the only thing that seems clear is that the future will not look like the present.

It seems likely that more states will legalize production for non-medical use within the next four years. Public support has crossed the 50 percent threshold in most polls; there is an organized and well-financed advocacy community promoting legalization; and now there is a commercial sector with a business interest in expanding the legal market. By contrast, the opposition is poorly financed, politically fractured, and lacking both prominent leaders and a rallying event. (It is striking how little criticism the Obama administration's policy of acquiescence with state-level legalization has attracted from Republican politicians, including this year's crop of presidential candidates.)

The next wave of state legalizations may have greater impact than the four that have happened so far, because some of the likely candidates are very large (California) or have populous neighbors (Maryland, Massachusetts, and Vermont). While legalization to date has directly affected only about 18 million people—about 6 percent of the US population—the legalizations that may happen in 2016

⌐ more state level legalization that will affect larger populations.

political & practical costs of fed action are high.

could fundamentally change supply and availability for a significant proportion of Americans.

A reversal of the legalization trend cannot be ruled out. Marijuana remains banned by the federal Controlled Substances Act. If the next president so wished, he or she could shut down all of the overt aspects of the industry without excessive effort. At present that seems unlikely; the political costs would be high, and the practical challenge to federal enforcement grows as the number of states with legal recreational marijuana increases. However, legalization is still so new that it may yet stumble in the public-relations department, especially if there is evidence of increasing use among adolescents, making it attractive for politicians to be tough on marijuana.

What seems radically implausible is that the current situation, with just four states having legalized a commercial industry, will prove stable. The United States is one common market within which free movement is guaranteed. So in the long run, commercial legalization in a few states—unless those states take strong steps to keep prices high—will neuter prohibition in the other states, even if those states do not themselves repeal their bans.

Cf. Gambling & Fireworks

True, counties in Nevada have legalized prostitution, and that has not undermined prohibitions against commercial sex elsewhere. Likewise, for many years Nevada and New Jersey were the only states with casinos. But prostitution and gambling are services; customers had to physically travel to Nevada or New Jersey to evade their home states' prohibitions. Marijuana, like alcohol, is a product and therefore portable. Indeed, marijuana is much more portable than alcohol because it is much more compact; a year's supply for a heavy user weighs no more than a can of beer or two.

A state could unilaterally ban on-premise consumption at the marijuana equivalent of a bar, because on-premise consumption is a service for which the customer must be physically present. But products tend to leak across state lines; every Fourth of July sees backyard displays of fireworks in states where possession and sale of those fireworks are strictly banned.

There are state bans on various products, ranging from semiautomatic rifles to lead fishing tackle to foie gras. By and large, state bans reduce convenience but do not deter determined consumers.

Under the Obama administration's policy, legal marijuana is not supposed to cross state lines, but that is a bit of a fiction. Marijuana produced in Colorado is already being seized in other states, and the main reason that does not happen more often is that Colorado's industry is young and still expanding just to meet in-state demand; as a result the prices there aren't yet low enough to compete with illicit wholesale prices. But that is changing.

So legalization in just a few states is probably untenable, because marijuana will flow from (the marijuana equivalent of) wet to dry states, and excise tax revenues will flow in the opposite direction, from users in dry states back into wet states' coffers. Then, just as with the spread of lotteries and casino gambling, it will be natural for more states to legalize, if for no other reason than to keep some of those tax revenues. The logical endpoint of that process is legalization in more and more states, and eventually at the federal level as national prohibition becomes more and more unsustainable.

If all that happens, the results will be profound. It would be naive to imagine that either industry structure and conduct or patterns of use will remain the same after legalization, with the only change being fewer arrests. We should expect a continuation of what we are already seeing: a proliferation of products and increases in use.

Are high state taxes sustainable in the long run?

The ease with which marijuana can be moved across state lines will also make it difficult for one state to maintain taxes that are much higher than those in neighboring states. This is already an issue with cigarette taxes, and current marijuana taxes are much higher per unit weight or volume. For example, the $35-per-ounce tax that Oregon had planned on marijuana flowers—while much lower than the tax rate required to keep marijuana prices from plunging after legalization—is roughly equivalent, on a per-unit-weight basis, to a $25-per-pack cigarette tax. At $35 per ounce, considerable profits could be made from buying a trunk-load of marijuana (or even a duffel bag full) in a low-tax state and selling in a high-tax state.

The best prospects for keeping tax rates (and therefore prices) high—which is desirable in order to prevent an upsurge in heavy, chronic use and use by teenagers—may be to impose the tax at the federal level. States and localities could still tax marijuana-related services, such as marijuana served for on-site consumption, but they will find it difficult to collect high state-level taxes on marijuana products.

⌐ only a high federal tax could be sustainable

How much depends on 2016? Prediction

We will know more about the likely future of marijuana policy after this fall's election than we do today. If a number of states add momentum to the legalization movement by legalizing large-scale production—especially if that number includes California—then even a fairly determined anti-marijuana president might not dare to act aggressively to end the march of legalization.

Even if that didn't happen, if the next president is either pro-legalization or merely unwilling to act against legalization, then a critical mass of state-legal regimes might be created before the end of that president's term.

The primary recipe for a reversal would be the election of a staunchly anti-marijuana president in 2016 in conjunction with the failure of most of the legalization propositions that are on the ballot that year. At the time of this writing, that seems unlikely, unless the run-up to the 2016 election sees a rise in accidental overdoses involving children, deaths from explosions of extraction machines, famous people being killed by marijuana-impaired drivers, or a horrible crime committed by someone under the influence of marijuana. The much more likely slow-motion bad results in the form of increased substance use disorder are very unlikely to be detectable in the short run, even if they turn out to be real.

Another wild card is the possibility that antilegalization groups can find someone with deep pockets to fund their campaigns. Typically, pro-legalization groups wildly outspend their antilegalization counterparts. Florida's 2014 medical-marijuana campaign failed after casino magnate Sheldon Adelson pumped more than five million dollars into the opposition. Whether Adelson or other high-wealth individuals will try to fight legalization in California and other states remains to be seen.

The 2016 elections might also affect the nature of legalization, not just whether it proceeds. If state propositions that would legalize a commercial industry fail but (for example) the Vermont legislature enacts some middle-path strategy, then the legalization movement might conceivably get redirected away from the commercial model before industry lobbying interests became too powerful to overcome. (Canada, where the new Liberal government is committed to some form of legalization, is another possible venue for "middle-path" policies, which might provide an example for some US jurisdictions to follow.)

The president elected in 2016 could also shape the market by choosing to enforce the Controlled Substances Act against only those marketing certain products (e.g., THC-infused candies that appeal to kids) or against only businesses reaching a certain size. That might be politically feasible, and would retard the organizational and technological development of the industry, letting it remain closer to its current artisanal structure for a longer time.

Finally, if pressures rise to the point that federal laws get changed, then of course the particulars of those changes will be influenced by which parties and personalities emerge as dominant in the next Congress. Confusingly, Democrats, who have been somewhat more receptive to legalization in principle, might be more amenable to tight regulations for health and safety reasons than market-oriented Republicans.

Coded politics

Will alcohol-style commercial legalization beat out more moderate approaches?

alcohol-style may be regulation more convenient than sensible

The first four states to legalize large-scale production all opted for the commercial alcohol model not so much because that model prevailed in an exhaustive, balanced analysis but rather because it was the only option on the ballot. Other models are being discussed in Vermont, as well as in other countries. Indeed, one prominent guide to legalization by Steve Rolles and George Murkin of the UK organization Transform explicitly cautions against the commercial model. Tax scholar Pat Oglesby warns that the difficulty of taxing marijuana, without regard to other considerations, makes government-run supply a preferable alternative.

It is unclear whether those funding legalization initiatives in the United States really believe that regulating marijuana like alcohol is the best alternative. It could just be that it's easy to explain, and they do not want to risk losing votes by introducing complexity.

Yet, given the speed with which legalization is being adopted, widespread awareness that other options exist may not even develop until after the commercial model is a fait accompli. And once a commercial industry exists, it will presumably use its lobbying power to block any threat to its profits.

Arguably, the commercial alcohol model also better fits American culture, which often bristles at paternalistic government interventions such as taxes on sugary soda. There has been a long, slow erosion of direct government control of alcohol distribution; public trust in government generally is at or near historic lows. There are many intermediate options that do not involve direct government participation in the markets (see chapter 11), but those options are less well known and have no current organized political support.

How long will it take to see all the effects of legalization on the industry?

Marijuana legalization is a radical change which would render old business practices obsolete and trigger innovation, but it will take the new enterprises a long time to figure out fully what works best in the new (and still-changing) environment.

It is obvious but worth stating that different industries have different structures. Auto manufacturers are large corporations, while individual dairies and hair salons are not. Law firms traditionally operate as partnerships, but airlines are corporations. These variations are not random; they are adaptations to the characteristics of those different industries and their products.

Producing marijuana legally is not the same business as growing marijuana where it is prohibited. The plant is the same, but nearly everything else is different.

Prohibition shaped the structure and conduct of the traditional marijuana industry. For example, a primary consideration was avoiding detection, so many domestic operations focused on producing the most THC per unit area under artificial lights in small spaces such as basements. That creates many headaches: high electricity bills, stressed plants that are vulnerable to mites and disease, and awkward workspaces that hinder labor productivity. After national legalization, there is no reason why boutique flowering buds shouldn't be grown in greenhouses, or why cannabinoids such as THC for extracts couldn't be produced on large outdoor farms.

Yet companies in the state-legal systems are investing madly in warehouse-based indoor grow operations. That is in part because of regulatory barriers to other growing strategies, but also because it is a simple extension of familiar practices. The warehouses do

How prohibition has shaped the legal pot industry.

overcome the cramped conditions of basement grows, but their electricity costs alone exceed the total production costs one would expect professional farmers to achieve with greenhouse-based growing in states with a suitable climate. In the long run, firms will migrate to the most cost-effective models of production; if they don't, their competitors will, and will then undercut them on price. Likewise, national legalization would open up interstate commerce, and states with regulations that do not permit the most efficient modes of production will lose the economic benefits of hosting the industry when that industry "offshores" to states with a more hospitable regulatory climate.

Shifting from artificial to natural light is just one of many potential innovations. The extraction process is also ripe for change. The risk of seizure has traditionally precluded owning capital equipment such as hash oil extraction machines, so leaves and other parts of the plant with lower concentrations of THC were often discarded. State-legal production is already making extensive use of extraction, and the current extraction machines have yet to fully exploit potential scale economies.

One of the larger costs of traditional marijuana production is hand-trimming the buds, but hand-trimming may not be necessary with pre-rolled ("manufactured") as opposed to roll-your-own joints.

Selective breeding has already produced substantial advances in plant yield, but to date that breeding has mostly been conducted via traditional horticultural methods. There is no reason why land-grant universities couldn't bring their genetic engineering expertise to bear on the problem of developing improved strains and growing techniques after national legalization, the same way they now do for tomatoes, broccoli, and rice. Indeed, a 2015 Louisiana law gives the state's land-grant universities the first crack at growing all the medical-marijuana legalized there. As Michael O'Hare of UC Berkeley's Goldman School has pointed out, there's no reason why the transformation in wine production wrought by UC Davis—leading to high-quality wine at low prices—couldn't be duplicated for marijuana.

There are also opportunities for innovation in firm size and structure. As of 2015, most firms growing state-legal marijuana are relatively small, with gross revenues in the tens of millions of dollars per year or less. Such firms are far smaller than is ideal for managing a national brand and associated media campaigns. The tobacco, beer, wine, and liquor industries offer a range of models of typical firm sizes. It is not clear which the mature cannabis industry will most closely resemble, but all have firms that are considerably larger than the typical growing operation as of 2015.

All of these changes will take time to play out, almost certainly at least five to ten years after national legalization.

How long will it take to see all the effects of legalization on use and dependence?

At least a generation after the industry has matured.

Few people become a regular user of a dependence-inducing intoxicant if they have not already started using it by age 25. Some exceptions include when someone who is already dependent on one substance begins abusing another (i.e., addiction to one drug morphs into polydrug abuse), or someone becomes dependent on painkillers or sedative-hypnotics that were prescribed medically.

For that reason, a common rhetorical technique for reassuring people that legalization won't much increase use is not reassuring at all. Advocates of legalization will sometimes ask a room full of adults, "How many of you who are not already using marijuana would start using if it became legal?" Few hands go up. Presenters nod smugly. The more credulous in the audience think a clever point has been made.

The catch (besides people being shy of admitting such things publicly) is that the audience is answering on behalf of their adult selves, many of whom have too much common sense to walk into a bad habit now. The more relevant question is, "If marijuana had been legal, cheap, potent, and advertised with gorgeous models back when you were a foolish teenager with an immortality complex and an underdeveloped prefrontal cortex, how many of you might have used it more often than you actually used the expensive, low-potency, unlabeled black market weed that you had access to back then?" Again, the answer in lecture halls might well be "not much," but the people with childhoods privileged enough to allow them to pursue careers that land them in lecture halls debating public policy are not the primary consumers of marijuana; college graduates account for perhaps 15 percent of demand. So the proper hypothetical question would also ask the audience to imagine they were B– students with no exciting ambitions for life when contemplating the question of whether their hormone-intoxicated adolescent brains would have found cheap, potent, and heavily marketed marijuana appealing.

We won't really know how much legalization will affect consumption until we've watched the life cycle of a generation that reaches puberty after a legalized industry has matured in its business and marketing practices. If national legalization occurred in 2020 and the industry matured by 2030, we would only have a comprehensive understanding of the effects of legalization on use and dependence in 2070, when those who were 10 years old in 2030 turn 50. We would get some early projections in 2050, when that birth cohort turns 30, but it would be a bit dicey to presume that patterns of use from age 30 to 50 for that generation will mimic those of past generations.

As an imperfect analogy, the first practical machines for manufacturing modern pre-rolled cigarettes came into use in the 1880s. That innovation radically reduced production costs and transformed the industry, with giant international companies forming and driving out smaller regional companies over the next twenty years. Yet it wasn't until 1950 that the full effect on per capita smoking rates was felt, in part because it took time for the industry to develop the marketing strategies to normalize consumption in previously untapped markets (notably women).

Will other countries legalize?

Since Colorado and Washington's 2012 votes, Jamaica and Uruguay have legalized cannabis (the international term for marijuana), albeit under very different models. Neither has suffered much in the way of international retribution. So one might expect other countries also to legalize cannabis, now that the taboo has been broken. Many countries one might expect to be next in line are in Europe, but none seem poised to legalize shortly; perhaps Europe's geography, history, and its "European project" combine to make countries there more respectful of international treaty obligations than the United States, Jamaica, or Uruguay. Some countries might also be awaiting the outcome of the April 2016 UN General Assembly's Special Session (UNGASS) on the world drug problem; there has been optimism in the drug reform movement that UNGASS 2016 may lead to major treaty revisions. It seems quite possible that Canada will be next, given the Liberals' strong win in the October 2015 elections and Prime Minister Trudeau's promise to look into changing policies "right away." Commercial legalization there would have dramatic consequences for the United States, since it might well prove impossible to prevent not only drug tourism but also large-scale diversion to US markets; however, commercialization is neither Canada's nor anyone else's only option. Legalization by a Native American nation within US borders could also create such issues.

Arguably, a more important question is whether other countries will follow by legalizing cocaine or heroin, rather than only marijuana. Some in the United States and other final-market countries draw sharp distinctions between marijuana and the so-called hard drugs, because of differences in the risks they present to users. However, the main drug problem in source and transshipment countries like Colombia and Mexico is not use but violence and corruption related to drug trafficking. Someone killed by a marijuana trafficker is just as dead as someone killed by a cocaine trafficker, so the soft- versus hard-drug distinction resonates less in source and transit countries than it does in final-consumer countries. For many reasons, legalizing cocaine or heroin is both much riskier than legalizing marijuana, and also more likely to have substantial effects on neighbors. So the prospect of a country being the first to legalize a hard drug seems less likely than the prospect of a third or fourth legalizing marijuana. But it is important to recognize how differently source countries view the drug problem, and how the precedents set in Colorado and Washington may lead in unanticipated directions.

What is the chance all of our predictions will prove correct?

A snowball's chance in . . .

Colorado and Washington plunged us into a whole new world when their stores opened in 2014. No modern jurisdiction had ever legalized large-scale production for nonmedical use, so there is no roadmap. The only safe prediction is that, despite our sincere best efforts, the actual future will not match our imagined future, in small ways and large ones.

18

WHAT DO THE AUTHORS THINK OUGHT TO BE DONE ABOUT MARIJUANA?

We don't necessarily agree, and none of us is sure.

Mark thinks that marijuana prohibition is so broken that even a relatively badly managed legalization is likely to turn out better, especially in terms of arrests and the illicit market, as well as the gains to the majority of consumers for whom marijuana would be a harmless source of amusement and relaxation (perhaps even of enhanced aesthetic appreciation). But he's not certain of that; legalization could go very badly indeed, with such a big increase in heavy use and use by adolescents, leading to worse educational and developmental outcomes, that things could wind up, on balance, worse rather than better. Effects on the use of other drugs—alcohol, the opiates, and tobacco—remain unknown, and could overwhelm the direct effects of legalizing marijuana.

Jon thinks a badly managed legalization is the kind we're likely to get, and that will be worse than the current prohibition. He also thinks many of the objectionable aspects of current policies could be remedied by some feasible tweaking within a prohibition framework, such as limiting user sanctions to fines. He has great faith in the power of the free market, but less in consumers' wisdom. When businesses promote a dependence-inducing intoxicant—most of which gets consumed by the minority of people who use it multiple times every day—what is good for the business is not good for society. A temptation doesn't have to be deadly for it to be bad for you and your family. But Jon is not certain that legalization will turn out badly; perhaps the increase in problem use will be closer to 50 percent than 200 percent, in which case those losses would be trumped by eliminating the black market.

Beau is thrilled that a growing number of decision makers are taking the marijuana issue seriously, but worries that some jurisdictions are rushing into policy changes they may regret. For those considering alternatives to prohibiting marijuana supply, he believes it is reasonable to incorporate a sunset provision that makes the laws revert back to what they were before reform after a certain number of years unless the changes are extended by the voters or the legislature. As the sunset date approaches, the legislature or the voters could vote to sustain the reform if they thought it was a good policy, or they could try something different. This is especially important for policies that allow private companies to make money from the marijuana trade. The sunset provision could give pioneering jurisdictions an escape clause, a chance—by simply sitting still—to overcome the lobbying muscle of the new industry fighting hard to stay in business.

We all agree that if legalization leads to substantially increased tobacco smoking, that would be a terrible outcome. But we're not certain that will happen; vaping and e-cigarettes may alter the historical complementary relationship between marijuana and nicotine consumption. And if in the long run marijuana turns out to substitute for heavy drinking, then legalization could be a net win even if it scores badly on all marijuana-specific outcomes. Unfortunately we have not seen much evidence for substitution, and we have seen some evidence the other way.

None of us would be surprised to look up twenty years from now and find that legalization had turned out—again, on balance, weighing gains against losses—to be a very good idea. Or a very bad idea. Or (most likely) something in between.

So even three people who agree, more or less, about the facts and the causal relationships don't have to share the same ideas about what to do.

But we do agree on two things:

First, there are better and worse ways to implement legalization, where "better" mostly means a focus on protecting the minority of users who will lose control of their habits rather than maximizing convenience for the majority of less intense users for whom marijuana is a harmless pleasure.

Second, the approach to legalization now being adopted in US states—commercialization on the alcohol model—is one of the worse versions, most likely to yield big increases in problem use because compulsive users are the most profitable customers.

So, putting aside the question of *whether* to legalize, we're in broad agreement about *how* to legalize if we're going to, and what we agree on is very far from what the country is now doing.

Our ideal version of legalization would have the goal of making marijuana legally available to almost any adult, but not ubiquitous, while continuing—as much as possible—to protect people (especially youth) from their own lack of self-control.

That would mean:

- keeping prices close to current levels;
- minimizing the incentives of industry participants to encourage heavy use (which suggests something other than for-profit retailing);
- minimizing the power of industry participants to shape public policies;
- limiting marketing, by permitting sellers to inform potential buyers of the chemical composition of their products but not to try to make marijuana use seem appealing; and
- discouraging the use of marijuana in combination with nicotine or alcohol.

And each of us has his own favorite design element: personal quotas (Mark), limiting the business to co-ops and nonprofits (Jon), and introducing sunset provisions into legalization laws (Beau).

We don't know that these policies would be either necessary or sufficient to prevent big increases in marijuana abuse, dependency, and other negative outcomes. But we judge that the probability of reducing those risks is high enough to counterbalance the relatively minor losses in consumer convenience that would result from having stricter rather than looser policies.

ADDITIONAL READINGS

Belackova, Vendula, Alison Ritter, Marian Shanahan, et al. *Medicinal Cannabis in Australia—Framing the Regulatory Options.* National Drug and Alcohol Research Center, 2015.

Blue Ribbon Commission on Marijuana Policy. *Pathways Report: Policy Options for Regulating Marijuana in California.* 2015. Available online at https://www.safeandsmartpolicy.org/wp-content/uploads/2015/07/BRCPathwaysReport.pdf.

Boidi, Maria Fernanda, José Miguel Cruz, Rosario Queirolo, and Emily Bello-Pardo. *Marijuana Legalization in Uruguay and Beyond.* FIU Latin American and Caribbean Center, 2015.

Caulkins, Jonathan P. "Nonprofit Motive: How to Avoid a Likely and Dangerous Corporate Takeover of the Legal Marijuana Market." *Washington Monthly*, May 2014.

Caulkins, Jonathan P., Carolyn C. Coulson, Christina Farber, and Joseph V. Vesely. "Marijuana Legalization: Certainty, Impossibility, Both, or Neither?" *Journal of Drug Policy Analysis* 5 (2012): 1–27.

Caulkins, Jonathan P., Beau Kilmer, Mark A. R. Kleiman, et al. *Considering Marijuana Legalization: Insights for Vermont and Other Jurisdictions.* Santa Monica, CA: RAND, 2015.

Caulkins, Jonathan P., Beau Kilmer, Robert J. MacCoun, Rosalie Liccardo Pacula, and Peter H. Reuter. "Design Considerations for Legalizing Cannabis: Lessons Inspired by Analysis of California's Proposition 19." *Addiction* 107, no. 5 (2012): 865–871.

Center for Behavioral Health Statistics and Quality. *Behavioral Health Trends in the United States: Results from the 2014 National Survey on Drug Use and Health.* HHS Publication no. SMA 15-4927, NSDUH Series H-50. 2015. Available online at http://www.samhsa.gov/data/sites/default/files/NSDUH-FRR1-2014/NSDUH-FRR1-2014.pdf.

"Clinical Studies and Case Reports." International Association for Cannabinoid Medicine. Available online at http://www.cannabis-med.org/studies/study.php.

Cole, James. *Guidance Regarding Marijuana Enforcement.* US Department of Justice, August 29, 2013.

Cole, James. "Guidance Regarding the Ogden Memo in Jurisdictions Seeking to Authorize Marijuana for Medical Use." Memo to Paula Dox, Attorney General of the State of New Jersey, June 29, 2011. Available online at http://www.justice.gov/sites/default/files/oip/legacy/2014/07/23/dag-guidance-2011-for-medical-marijuana-use.pdf.

Colorado Department of Public Health and Environment. *Monitoring Health Concerns Related to Marijuana in Colorado, 2014: Changes in Marijuana Use Patterns, Systematic Literature Review, and Possible Marijuana-Related Health Effects.* Colorado Department of Public Health and Environment, 2014.

Compton, Richard, and Amy Berning. *Drug and Alcohol Crash Risk.* National Highway Traffic Safety Administration, 2015.

Cook, Philip J. *Paying the Tab: The Economics of Alcohol Policy.* Princeton, NJ: Princeton University Press, 2007.

Courtwright, David T. *Forces of Habit: Drugs and the Making of the Modern World.* Cambridge, MA: Harvard University Press, 2001.

Courtwright, David T. "Mr. ATOD's Wild Ride." *Social History of Alcohol and Drugs* 20, no. 1 (2005): 105–140.

Darnell, Adam. *I-502 Evaluation Plan and Preliminary Report on Implementation.* Washington State Institute for Public Policy, 2015.

Decorte, Tom, Gary Potter, and Marin Bouchard, eds. *World Wide Weed: Global Trends in Cannabis Cultivation and Its Control.* Farnham, UK: Ashgate, 2011.

D'Souza, Deepak Cyril, Richard Andrew Sewell, and Mohini Ranganathan. "Cannabis and Psychosis/Schizophrenia: Human Studies." *European Archives of Psychiatry and Clinical Neuroscience* 259, no. 7 (2009): 413–431.

DuPont, Robert, and Carl Selavka. "Testing to Identify Recent Drug Use." In *The American Psychiatric Publishing Textbook of Substance Abuse Treatment,* edited by Marc Galanter, Herbert D. Kleber, and Kathleen T. Brady, 5th ed. Washington, DC: APA Publishing, 2014.

Economic Research Service. *Industrial Hemp in the United States: Status and Market Potential.* Washington, DC: United States Department of Agriculture, 2000.

Eddy, Mark. *Medical-marijuana Review and Analysis of Federal and State Policies.* Washington, DC: Congressional Research Service, 2010.

Eisenstein, Michael. "Medical-marijuana: Showdown at the Cannabis Corral." *Nature* 525, no. 7570 (2015): S15–S17.

Erowid. "Cannabis Effects." Available online at http://www.erowid.org/plants/cannabis/cannabis_effects.shtml.

Federal Bureau of Investigation. *Crime in the United States, 2010.* Washington, DC: Federal Bureau of Investigation, Criminal Justice Information Services Division, 2010.

Fijnaut, Cyrille J. C. F., and Brice de Ruyver. *The Third Way: A Plea for a Balanced Cannabis Policy.* Leiden, the Netherlands: Brill, 2015.

Grinspoon, Lester. *Marihuana Reconsidered.* Cambridge, MA: Harvard University Press, 1971.

Hall, Wayne. "What Has Research Over the Past Two Decades Revealed about the Adverse Health Effects of Recreational Cannabis Use?" *Addiction* 110, no. 1 (2014): 19–35.

Hall, Wayne, and Michael Farrell. *Inquiry into Use of Cannabis for Medical Purposes.* National Drug and Alcohol Research Centre, University of New South Wales, 2013.

Hall, Wayne, and Rosalie Liccardo Pacula. *Cannabis Use and Dependence: Public Health and Public Policy.* Cambridge, UK: Cambridge University Press, 2003.

Hancock-Allen, Jessica B., Lisa Barker, Michael Vandyke, and Dawn B. Holmes. "Notes from the Field: Death Following Ingestion of an Edible Marijuana Product—Colorado, March 2014." *Morbidity and Mortality Weekly Report* 64, no. 28 (2015): 771–772. Available online at http://www.cdc.gov/mmwr/preview/mmwrhtml/mm6428a6.htm.

Hasin, Deborah S., Tulshi D. Saha, Bradley T. Kerridge, et al. "Prevalence of Marijuana Use Disorders in the United States between 2001–2002 and 2012–2013." *Journal of the American Medical Association Psychiatry* 72, no. 12 (2015): 1235–1242. doi:10.1001/jamapsychiatry.2015.1858.

Hedlund, James. "Drug-Impaired Driving: A Guide for What States Can Do." Governors Highway Safety Association, 2014.

Heyman, Gene M. *Addiction: A Disorder of Choice.* Cambridge, MA: Harvard University Press, 2009.

Huang, Y.-H. J., Z.-F. Zhang, D. P. Tashkin, B. Feng, K. Straif, and M. Hashibe. "An Epidemiologic Review of Marijuana and Cancer: An Update." *Cancer Epidemiology Biomarkers and Prevention* 15 (January 2015): 15–31.

Hudak, John. *Colorado's Rollout of Legal Marijuana Is Succeeding: A Report on the State's Implementation of Legalization.* Washington, DC: Brookings Institution, 2014.

Huestis, Marilyn A., Irene Mazzoni, and Olivier Rabin. "Cannabis in Sport." *Sports Medicine* 41, no. 11 (2011): 949–966.

Hughes, Caitlin Elizabeth, and Alex Stevens. "What Can We Learn from the Portuguese Decriminalization of Illicit Drugs?" *British Journal of Criminology* 50 (2010): 999–1022.

Humphreys, Keith. "Even as Marijuana Use Rises, Arrests Are Falling." *Wonkblog* (*Washington Post* blog), February 11, 2015, https://www.washingtonpost.com/news/wonk/wp/2015/02/11/even-as-marijuana-use-rises-arrests-are-falling/.

Ingold, John, Joe Amon, and Lindsay Pierce. "State of Hope." *Denver Post*, December 5, 2014.

Iversen, Leslie L. *The Science of Marijuana*. Oxford: Oxford University Press, 2000.

Jaques, Siobhan C., Ann Kingsbury, Philip Henshcke, et al. "Cannabis, the Pregnant Woman and Her Child: Weeding out the Myths." *Journal of Perinatology* 34 (2014): 417–424.

Jelsma, Martin. *UNGASS 2016: Prospects for Treaty Reform and UN System-Wide Coherence on Drug Policy*. Brookings Institution, 2015.

Johnson, Renee. "Hemp as an Agricultural Commodity." Washington, DC: US Congressional Research Service, Library of Congress, 2010.

Johnston, Lloyd, Patrick M. O'Malley, Jerald G. Bachman, and John E. Schulenberg. *Monitoring the Future: National Survey Results on Adolescent Drug Use*. Rockville, MD: National Institute on Drug Abuse, US Dept. of Health and Human Services, National Institutes of Health, 2014.

Joy, Janet E., Stanley J. Watson Jr., and John A. Benson Jr. *Marijuana and Medicine: Assessing the Science Base*. Washington, DC: National Academy Press, 1999.

Kaplan, John. *Marijuana: The New Prohibition*. New York: World Publishing, 1970.

Kilmer, Beau, Jonathan P. Caulkins, Robert J. MacCoun, Roslie Liccardo Pacula, and Peter H. Reuter. *Altered State? Assessing How Marijuana Legalization in California Could Influence Marijuana Consumption and Public Budgets*. Santa Monica, CA: RAND Drug Policy Research Center, 2010.

Kilmer, Beau. "The 10 P's of Marijuana Legalization." *Berkeley Review of Latin American Studies*, Spring 2014, 55–57.

Kilmer, Beau, Jonathan P. Caulkins, Brittany Bond, and Peter H. Reuter. *Reducing Drug Trafficking Revenues and Violence in Mexico: Would Legalizing Marijuana in California Help?* OP-325-RC. Santa Monica, CA: RAND, 2010.

Kilmer, Beau, Jonathan P. Caulkins, Rosalie Liccardo Pacula, and Peter H. Reuter. "Bringing Perspective to Illicit Markets: Estimating the Size of the U.S. Marijuana Market." *Drug and Alcohol Dependence* 119, nos. 1–2 (December 2011): 153–160.

Kilmer, Beau, Susan S. Everingham, Jonathan P. Caulkins, et al. *What America's Users Spend on Illegal Drugs, 2000–2010*. Santa Monica, CA: RAND, 2014.

Kleiman, Mark A. R. *Against Excess: Drug Policy for Results.* New York: Basic Books, 1992.

Kleiman, Mark A. R. "Cooperative Enforcement Agreements and Policy Waivers: New Options for Federal Accommodation to State-Level Cannabis Legalization." *Journal of Drug Policy Analysis* 6, no. 1 (2013). Available online at https://reason.com/assets/db/1377546588558.pdf.

Kleiman, Mark A. R. *Marijuana: Costs of Abuse, Costs of Control.* New York: Greenwood, 1989.

Kleiman, Mark A. R., Jonathan P. Caulkins, and Angela Hawken. *Drugs and Drug Policy: What Everyone Needs to Know.* New York: Oxford University Press, 2011.

Kleiman, Mark A. R., Celeste Miller, and Jeremy Ziskind. "Driving While Stoned: Issues and Policy Options." BOTEC Analysis Corporation. Available online at http://botecanalysis.com/wp-content/uploads/2015/12/Driving-While-Stoned 10-2014.pdf.

Laqueur, Hannah. "Uses and Abuses of Drug Decriminalization in Portugal." *Law and Social Inquiry* (2014): 746–781.

Leggett, Ted. "A Review of the World Cannabis Situation." *Bulletin on Narcotics* 58, nos. 1 and 2 (2006): 1–155.

Lincoln, Abraham. "Temperance Address (22 February 1842)." In *The Collected Works of Abraham Lincoln,* edited by Roy P. Basler, 1:271–279. New Brunswick, NJ: Rutgers University Press, 1953. Available online at http://www.abrahamlincolnonline.org/lincoln/speeches/temperance.htm.

MacCoun, Robert J., and Michelle M. Mello. "Half-Baked: The Retail Promotion of Marijuana Edibles." *New England Journal of Medicine* 372 (2015): 989–991.

MacCoun, Robert J., and Peter H. Reuter. "Assessing Drug Prohibition and Its Alternatives: A Guide for Agnostics." *Annual Review of Law and Social Science* 7 (2007): 61–78.

MacCoun, Robert J., and Peter H. Reuter. *Drug War Heresies: Learning from Other Vices, Times, and Places.* Cambridge, UK: Cambridge University Press, 2001.

MacCoun, Robert J., Peter H. Reuter, and Thomas C. Schelling. "Assessing Alternative Drug Control Regimes." *Journal of Policy Analysis and Management* 15, no. 3 (1996): 330–352.

Merriman, David. "The Micro-Geography of Tax Avoidance: Evidence from Littered Cigarette Packs in Chicago." *American Economic Journal: Economic Policy* 2, no. 2 (2010): 61–84.

Mikos, Robert A. "A Critical Appraisal of the Department of Justice's New Approach to Medical-marijuana." *Stanford Law and Policy Review* 22 (2011): 633–669.

Mikos, Robert A. "Marijuana Localism." *Case Western Reserve Law Review* 65 (2015): 719–767.

Musto, David F. *The American Disease: Origins of Narcotic Control.* New Haven, CT: Yale University Press, 1973.

National Commission on Marihuana and Drug Abuse. *Marihuana: A Signal of Misunderstanding.* New York: New American Library, 1972.

National Conference of State Legislatures. *State Medical-marijuana Laws.* 2015. Available online at http://www.ncsl.org/research/health/state-medical-marijuana-laws.aspx.

National Drug Intelligence Center. *Domestic Cannabis Cultivation Assessment.* Washington, DC: US Department of Justice, 2009. Available online at http://www.justice.gov/archive/ndic/pubs37/37035/37035p.pdf.

Netherlands Office of Medical Cannabis. *Medical Cannabis: Information for Patients.* Netherlands Office of Medical Cannabis.

Nguyen, Holly, and Peter H. Reuter. "How Risky Is Marijuana Possession? Considering the Role of Age, Race, and Gender." *Crime and Delinquency* 58, no. 6 (2012): 879–910.

Ogden, David W. *Memorandum for Selected United States Attorneys on Investigations and Prosecutions in States Authorizing the Medical Use of Marijuana.* Washington, DC: US Dept. of Justice, Office of the Deputy Attorney General, 2009.

Oglesby, Pat. "Marijuana Advertising: The Federal Tax Stalemate." *Huffington Post.* August 25, 2013. Available online at http://www.huffingtonpost.com/pat-oglesby/marijuana-advertising-the_b_3810341.html.

Office of National Drug Control Policy. *Arrestee Drug Abuse Monitoring Program II: 2010 Annual Report.* Washington, DC: Office of National Drug Control Policy, 2011. Available online at http://www.whitehouse.gov/sites/default/files/ondcp/policy-and-research/adam2010.pdf.

Pollan, Michael. *The Botany of Desire: A Plant's Eye View of the World.* New York: Random House, 2001.

Ramchand, Rajeev, Rosalie Liccardo Pacula, and Martin Y. Iguchi. "Racial Differences in Marijuana-Users' Risk of Arrest in the United States." *Drug and Alcohol Dependence* 84, no. 3 (2006): 264–272.

Reuter, Peter H. "The (Continued) Vitality of Mythical Numbers." *Public Interest* 75 (Spring 1984): 135–147.

Rolles, Stephen, and Craig McClure. *After the War on Drugs: Blueprint for Regulation.* Bristol, UK: Transform Drug Policy Foundation, 2009. Available online at http://www.tdpf.org.uk/resources/publications/after-war-drugs-blueprint-regulation.

Rolles, Stephen, and George Murkin. *How to Regulate Cannabis: A Practical Guide.* Bristol, UK: Transform Drug Policy Foundation, 2013. Available online at http://www.tdpf.org.uk/resources/publications/how-regulate-cannabis-practical-guide.

Room, Robin, Benedikt Fischer, Wayne Hall, Simon Lenton, and Peter H. Reuter. *Cannabis Policy: Moving Beyond Stalemate.* Oxford: Oxford University Press, 2010.

Rosenthal, Ed, and David Downs. *Beyond Buds: Marijuana Extracts—Hash, Vaping, Dabbing, Edibles and Medicines.* Piedmont, CA: Quick American Archives, 2014.

Rosmarin, Ari, and Niamh Eastwood. "A Quiet Revolution: Drug Decriminalisation Policies in Practice across the Globe." Release, 2013.

Schelling, Thomas C. "Ethics, Law, and the Exercise of Self-Command." In *Choice and Consequence,* 83–102. Cambridge, MA: Harvard University Press, 1984.

Schelling, Thomas C. "The Intimate Contest for Self-Command." In *Choice and Consequence,* 58–82. Cambridge, MA: Harvard University Press, 1984.

Sevigny, Eric L., and Jonathan P. Caulkins. "Kingpins or Mules: An Analysis of Drug Offenders Incarcerated in Federal and State Prisons." *Criminology and Public Policy* 3, no. 3 (2004): 401–434.

Sewell, R. Andrew, James Poling, and Mehmet Sofuoglu. "The Effect of Cannabis Compared with Alcohol on Driving." *American Journal on Addictions* 18, no. 3 (2009): 185–193.

Substance Abuse and Mental Health Services Administration. *State Estimates of Substance Use and Mental Disorders from 2008–2009 National Surveys on Drug Use and Health.* Rockville, MD: Substance Abuse and Mental Health Services Administration, United States Department of Health and Human Services, 2011. Available online at http://aos.samhsa.gov/data/sites/default/files/NSDUHStateEst2009-2010/FullReport/NSDUHsaeMainReport2010.htm.

Taylor, Stuart S. *Marijuana Policy and Presidential Leadership: How to Avoid a Federal-State Train Wreck.* Washington, DC: Brookings Institution, 2013.

Thurstone, Christian, Shane A. Lieberman, and Sarah J. Schmiege. "Medical-marijuana Diversion and Associated Problems in Adolescent Substance Treatment." *Drug and Alcohol Dependence* 118, nos. 2–3 (November 2011): 489–492.

United Nations Office on Drugs and Crime. *World Drug Report 2011.* New York: United Nations, 2011. Available online at http://www.unodc.org/documents/data-and-analysis/WDR2011/World_Drug_Report_2011_ebook.pdf.

Vantreese, Valerie L. *Industrial Hemp: Global Markets and Prices.* Lexington: Department of Agricultural Economics, University of Kentucky, 1997.

Volkow, Nora, Ruben D. Baler, Wilson M. Compton, and Susan R. B. Weiss. "Adverse Health Effects of Marijuana Use." *New England Journal of Medicine* 370 (2014): 2219–2227.

Walsh, John, and Geoff Ramsey. "Uruguay's Drug Policy: Major Innovations, Major Challenges." Brookings Institution/WOLA, 2015. Available online at http://www.wola.org/publications/uruguay_s_drug_policy_major_innovations_major_challenges.

Weil, Andrew. *The Natural Mind: A New Way of Looking at Drugs and the Higher Consciousness.* Boston: Houghton Mifflin, 1972.

Whiting, Penny F., Robert F. Wolff, Sohan Deshpande, et al. "Cannabinoids for Medical Use: A Systematic Review and Meta-Analysis." *Journal of the American Medical Association* 313, no. 24 (2015): 2456–2473.

Zimring, Franklin E., and Gordon Hawkins. *The Search for Rational Drug Control.* Cambridge, UK: Cambridge University Press, 1992.

INDEX

Page numbers in bold type indicate a chart or table on that page.